Baedeker
Copenhagen

Contents

The Principal Sights at a Glance

Preface

This pocket guide to **Copenhagen** is one of the new generation of Baedeker guides.

Baedeker pocket guides, illustrated throughout in colour, are designed to meet the needs of the modern traveller. They are quick and easy to consult, with the principal features of interest described in alphabetical order and practical details about location, opening times, etc., shown in the margin.

This city guide is divided into three parts. The first part gives a general account of Copenhagen, its citizens, the Danish Parliament, culture, transport, economy, Danish design, famous people and history. A brief selection of quotations leads into the second part where the principal places of interest are described. The third part contains a variety of practical information designed to help visitors to find their way about and to make the most of their stay. Both "Copenhagen from A to Z" and the Practical Information section are given in alphabetical order.

Baedeker pocket guides, which are regularly updated, are noted for their concentration on essentials and their convenience of use. They contain many coloured illustrations and specially drawn plans, and at the back of the book will be found a large plan of the city. Each main entry in the A to Z section gives the co-ordinates of the square on the plan in which the particular feature can be located. Users of this guide, therefore, should have no difficulty in finding what they want to see.

Facts and Figures

Arms of Copenhagen

General

Kingdom of Denmark

The Kingdom of Denmark lies between latitude 54° 34′ and 57° 45′ N and between longitude 8° 5′ and 12° 35′ E (island of Bornholm 15° 12′ E) and consists of the peninsula of Jutland and 474 islands, 100 of which are inhabited. It has a short land frontier of 68km/42 miles with Schleswig-Holstein, as opposed to a total coastline of some 7400km/4600 miles. A large part of Denmark falls within the Baltic area and the North Sea forms the country's western frontier. The adjoining seas, known as the Kattegat and the Skagerrak, mark the transition between the Baltic and the North Sea. Nowhere in Denmark is further than 52km/32 miles away from the coast. Because of its situation the country forms a bridge between Central Europe and the countries of the Scandinavian peninsula (bird migration line).
The Faroe Islands and Greenland are overseas territories belonging to Denmark.

Capital

Copenhagen is the capital of Denmark, the seat of Parliament (Folketing) and the country's government; in addition, the residence of the Danish royal family is to be found here (the Amalienborg Palace).

Name

København, in English Copenhagen, was first mentioned in 1043 under the name "Havn". In 1167 Bishop Absalon had a fortress built near the fisherman's harbour and nearby a lively trading centre quickly developed known as "Købmændes Havn" (Merchant's Harbour).

Geographical situation

Copenhagen lies between longitude 12° and 13° E and in latitude 55°45′ N, partly on the eastern shore of Zealand (Sjælland), the largest Danish island (area 7525sq.km/2905sq.miles), and partly on the island of Amager in the Øresund.

Area and population

The actual area of the city of Copenhagen comprises the community of Copenhagen with 88sq.km/34sq.miles and the community of Frederiksberg with 9sq.km/3.5sq.miles. The population is approximately 570,000. In addition, there is the "department" of Copenhagen in which eighteen communities are merged. This enlarged district has a total area of 571sq.km/220sq.miles and a population of 623,000. Greater Copenhagen, called in Danish "hovedstadsområdet" (capital and surroundings), is therefore made up of the two communities of Copenhagen and Frederiksberg together with 26 other communities. The area of the capital is thus 668sq.km/258sq.miles and the total population 1.4 million. Copenhagen is therefore the largest town in Denmark – more than 24% of the country's population live in Copenhagen and its surroundings.

◀ *Nyhavn, an open-air museum and a popular meeting place*

Administration

The unusual thing about Copenhagen is that within the city area lies the community of Frederiksberg, an independent authority with its own mayor, town council, town hall and administration, and yet otherwise integrated into the economic structure and transport system of Copenhagen. The following communities with their own administration belong to the department of Copenhagen: Albertslund, Ballerup, Brøndby, Dragør, Gentofte, Gladsaxe, Glostrup, Herlev, Hvidovre, Høje-Tåstrup, Ishøj, Ledøje-Smørum, Lyngby-Tårbæk, Rødovre, Søllerød, Tårnby, Vallensbæk and Værlose.
Copenhagen in the narrower sense is governed by a council of 55 elected members. These appoint from among their number a Chief Burgomaster (Mayor) and six assistant burgomasters who, as full-time local government officials, form the city executive. These elected representatives have the same voting rights as all other council members.
Since the individual communities of Copenhagen enact their own independent legislation (particularly in the fiscal area), some are "richer" and some "poorer". As a result people tend to move into communities with more favourable tax laws.

Population and Religion

Population development

Copenhagen's development into a city of more than a million inhabitants is not primarily due to population growth. It resulted principally from the expansion of the city area and the incorporation of adjoining communities. Indeed, at present the city is losing about 15,000 inhabitants a year.
Compared with the exemplary housing standards in Denmark, living conditions in parts of the old town are less ideal: one-fifth of the houses date from before 1900, more than half from before 1930.
In view of the relative smallness of Denmark, there is a very intensive movement and exchange between the third of the population living in Copenhagen and the two-thirds living elsewhere – particularly in the towns of Roskilde, Helsingør and Køge, which are all less than one hour's drive away from the capital. The nearness of Copenhagen to the country areas of Denmark also prevents the capital from becoming an isolated, alien metropolis.

Religion

The Danish national church (folkekirken), of which the queen is nominal head, is Protestant (Lutheran). The country has ten dioceses ("stifter") with 107 deaneries and 1349 pastoral charges. Copenhagen is a bishopric.
For the people of Copenhagen, as for all other Danes, the church is a firmly established institution. About 94% of the population belong to the national church, though services are nowadays not well attended. Nevertheless about 87% of all children are baptised. Almost 18% of the pastors are women. Roman Catholics and Jews represent religious minorities.

The Danish Parliament

Constitution

Under the 1953 Constitution Denmark is a democratic parliamentary monarchy. The throne is hereditary, and under the 1953 Act of Succession the right of succession for females was restored.

Monarch
The political function of the monarch is regulated by the constitution. He has "supreme authority in all the affairs of the kingdom and exercises this through his ministers". This means in practice that sole responsibility rests with the ministers concerned. The monarch's most important political tasks are: to represent the kingdom of Denmark abroad; to initiate and pass laws; to frame laws temporarily whenever Parliament (the Folketing) cannot assemble, so long as such laws conform to the constitution; to call a

The Folketing, the Danish Parliament

general election (though only at the instigation of the Prime Minister), and to appoint the Prime Minister and the Cabinet. Since 1972 the monarch has been Queen Margarete II (of the House of Glücksburg, Schleswig-Holstein-Sonderburg-Glücksburg line).

Council of State
In the Council of State (consisting of monarch and ministers) all laws and important government measures are dealt with.

Council of Ministers
The Cabinet is known as the Council of Ministers. Each individual minister, as head of a department, is responsible to Parliament and can be forced out of office by a no-confidence vote. Furthermore, any minister can, in the State Court and at the instigation of the monarch or of Parliament, be charged with maladministration.

Prime Minister
The Prime Minister is appointed not by Parliament but by the queen, after consultation with party representatives. If he risks being voted out on a no-confidence motion, he can counter by calling for a general election. These two provisions allow minority governments in Denmark to continue in office for prolonged periods. The present Prime Minister is Poul Schlüter.

Folketing

Since the abolition of the first chamber (in 1953), the Folketing has been the sole representative body. Its 179 members – including two each from the Faroes and Greenland – are elected for a four-year term on the basis of universal suffrage (women having been given the vote in 1915), by direct and secret ballot.

The voting age is eighteen. The dissolution of Parliament is mandatory whenever any change in the constitution is made.

Culture

General

Copenhagen is not only the political and economic centre of Denmark but also its cultural centre. Here can be found Danish radio and television, a university, theatres, galleries, the country's principal museums and the largest library in Scandinavia (Det Kongelige Bibliotek). No other city in Denmark offers comparable access to Danish cultural life.

University

Copenhagen University, founded in 1479, has some 27,000 students. The main building on the university site was laid out on the ruins of a medieval bishop's palace in the former Latin quarter. In addition to the university, there is also the Polytechnic, with its Engineering Academy, as well as veterinary, agricultural, dental, pharmaceutical and commercial colleges, an academy of art (to which the architectural school is attached), a music conservatory and colleges of librarianship, education and sport.

The growing demand for space for an ever-increasing student population has resulted in many of the institutes no longer being situated in the old town but in Frederiksberg, in the university complex on the island of Amager (including branches of the University Library), as well as in Lundtofte.

Cultural scene

Copenhagen's theatrical life is diverse. In addition to the Royal Theatre (Det Kongelige Teater) the Kongens Nytorv, there are twelve other theatres which are amalgamated in "Den storkøbenhavnske Landsdelsscene", as well as children's and other theatres and fringe groups.

The Royal Theatre, with its performances of drama, opera and especially ballet, is world famous. After renovation lasting many years, the "Gamle Scene" (the "Old Stage") was reopened for ballet performances in 1985. For tourists who have no command of the Danish language, a prime recommendation would be a visit to the ballet performances or the English

University Buildings in the former Latin Quarter

The "Blue in Green" group at the Copenhagen Jazz Festival

plays in the Mermaid Theatre. In addition, numerous small companies offer an extensive repertoire of modern dance theatre – principal among these is the "Huset". Furthermore, a typical form of Danish entertainment are the "Revyen" – a blend of music, dance, cabaret and satire, and these are performed, for example, in the amusement parks of Bakken and Tivoli. Internationally acclaimed are the annual Copenhagen Summer Festival, as well as the Jazz and Blues Festival. Finally, the capital's cultural scene must also include the numerous street musicians, the "Vise-sangere" and live musical events in the bars and variety theatres of the old town, as well as the wide range on offer for cinemagoers, particularly in the new cinema complex on the Axeltorv.

Press, Radio, Television

In Copenhagen there are nine daily newspapers, the best known of which are the "Politiken" and the "Berlingske Tidende".
Danish radio and television are run by Danmarks Radio, a public corporation, which is financed exclusively by the licence fees it levies, with no advertising.

Transport

Port

The freight and passenger traffic using the port of Copenhagen (area approximately 450 hectares/1110 acres), which for centuries has made the Danish capital one of the leading industrial centres in the Baltic area has, since the Second World War, been in sharp decline. When, in the post-war period, ocean-going vessels were no longer able to put into harbour because of its shallow depth (10m/33ft), the importance of Copenhagen diminished in favour of other ports such as Rotterdam, Gothenburg and Hamburg – Rotterdam harbour has, by comparison, a depth of 22m/72ft. Furthermore, the volume of goods traffic within the country shifted more and more towards other means of transport (lorry, train, plane). The last

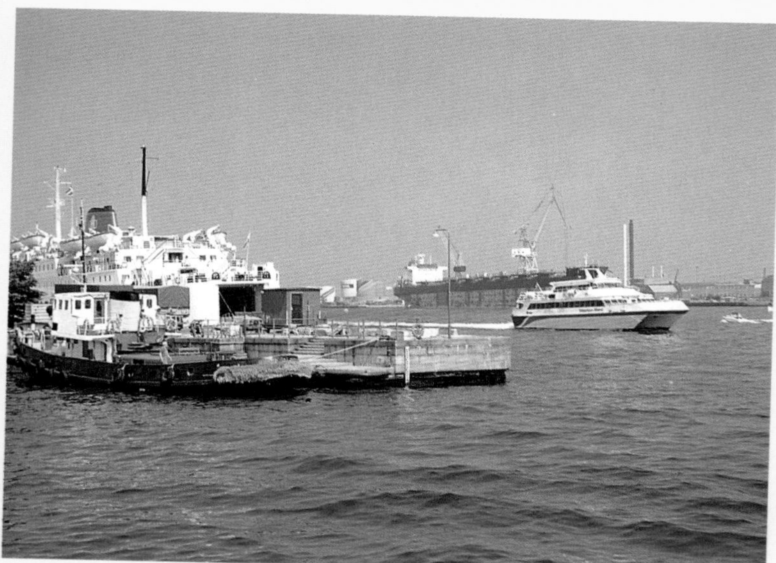

The Inderhavnen

inland route had to be closed in 1971. As a result, the significance of the port is nowadays confined essentially to the Copenhagen area.
Increasing containerisation has led to the closure of countless warehouses. Some of these have been converted and are now being put to other uses; others are being demolished. As a result of the introduction of modern equipment for the unloading of cargo, the previous 44km/27 miles of quayside have been considerably reduced. In recent years, however, increasingly frequent efforts have been made to revive the harbour area, and these efforts have already produced the first signs of an increase in the volume of parcel freight.
The port is divided into three different areas according to use:
Yderhavnen and Nordhavnen: container ports for freight transport, shipyards.
Frihavn: principally warehouses.
Inderhavnen: passenger port with Customs office, administration blocks and converted former harbour buildings, now housing hotel accommodation, service industries and flats.
Sydhavnen: industrial port with industrial firms, office blocks, owner-occupied flats and hotels.
The most recent planning idea is to identify Yderhavnen and Nordhavnen as the true harbour district. The intention is that they will also pick up the ferry traffic, while Inderhavnen, with the help of existing building assets, is to be built up into a cultural centre ("Folket Hus Center") with hotels, restaurants, function centres and conference rooms. Sydhavnen will continue to function as an industrial port and around Gasværkshavnen in Vesterbro there are plans for a local holiday area with sport and leisure facilities.

Passenger shipping services

A regular ferry service operates from Copenhagen to Sweden (Tuborg Havn-Landskrona; Dragør/Amager-Limhamn), to Norway (Dragør/Amager-Oslo) and within Denmark to Bornholm (Dragør/Amager-Rønne).

Denmark's capital can be reached by boat via the car ferry link from Sweden (Landskrona, Limhamn) and Norway (Oslo). Passenger ships go from Copenhagen to Helsingør; hydrofoils provide an additional connection between Copenhagen and Sweden (Malmö, Hven).

Airport

Copenhagen's Kastrup airport is today among the busiest in Europe. It lies on the island of Amager, some 10km/6 miles south of the city centre. Kastrup is served by over 40 airlines and with approximately ten million passengers a year it is the sixth largest airport in Europe. By the year 2000, however, its passenger capacity is due to rise to fifteen or sixteen million, by virtue of a multi-phase rebuilding programme (begun in the mid-1980s). The terminals and waiting-rooms have already been enlarged, but the principal attraction is the modern departure lounge in the main building, with a shopping centre in the style of Copenhagen's pedestrian precinct ("Strøget"), which offers space to more than twenty shops. The airport's duty-free arcade, in contrast to normal price levels in Denmark, offers some of the most reasonable prices to be found in the whole of Europe.

Rail and road network. Future transport plans

Rail traffic has hitherto been influenced by the fact that trains to other parts of Denmark and abroad have to be carried on rail ferries. However, by 1993 an 8km/5 miles long rail tunnel is due to be completed. This will be a twin-tunnel crossing running beneath the east channel of the Great Belt between Korsør and the small island of Sprogø, and will make it possible for passenger and freight trains to reduce by one hour the current ferry time between Fünen (Fyn) and Seeland (Zealand).

By 1996 motorists will also be able to cross the Great Belt without a ferry in fifteen minutes rather than 90 minutes when a 6.8km/4 miles long four-lane suspension bridge is built beside the rail tunnel, linking Halskov on the island of Zealand to the island of Sprogø (the latter becoming an intermediate landing-place). From here it is planned that a 6.6km/4 miles long low

The new shopping arcade at the Airport

The Main Station

bridge will carry both cars and trains to Knudshoved near Nyborg (Fyn) – toll charge payable.

Environmental problems connected with this giant project (expected costs five billion marks) are coming to light because of the planned expansion of the island of Sprogø (by sand deposition) to almost four times its original area, and also because of the bridge piers (weighing up to 6000 tonnes), which are to be sunk into the seabed and which will bring about changes in the currents of the Great Belt. Even the oxygen supply of the already badly affected Baltic Sea is being impaired, but a deepening of the Belt should counteract this development. Conservationists are also expressing considerable misgivings about the massive extension of public transport. In connection with the motorway bridge, some 350km/217 miles of roads are to be extended in Jutland and on Zealand alone.

After the linking of the different areas of the country, Denmark is planning further connections with its neighbours Germany and Sweden. By the mid-nineties the two islands of Fehmarn and Lolland are to be linked by a twin-tunnel crossing, which should considerably speed up future rail travel.

In 1991 Denmark contractually agreed with Sweden to construct a 17km/10 miles long bridge and tunnel combination for car and rail traffic across the Øresund. This is due for completion by 1999. Environmentalists make the criticism that the projected bridge passes through a bird sanctuary. In addition they are concerned about what effect such bridgebuilding may have on the freshwater inflow and fish stocks of the considerably polluted Baltic. The Danish Conservation Agency lodged a complaint with the European Commission. Supporters of the project hope, however, that this new arterial system will stimulate a revival of the entire Øresund region together with the cities of Copenhagen and Malmö (Sweden).

Motorways and trunk roads

Some motorways reach the outskirts, others even extend right into the city itself.

Main routes from and to Germany:
The E47 to Køge and Rødbyhavn, thence by ferry to Puttgarden in Germany;
The E20 to and from Korsør, with ferry to Nyborg on the island of Fünen (Fyn), thence across the bridge to Jutland and then south to the Danish/German border at Flensburg;
The E47 also runs north to Helsingør.
Copenhagen is surrounded by ringroads, which help to avoid city centre routes. Coming from Puttgarden, motorists take Ringroad II or, on the way from Puttgarden or Korsør, avoid the city centre on Ringroad III or IV.
With the exception of the E47 to Helsingør, Danish motorways are still unfinished – as, for example, the route between Copenhagen and Rødbyhavn – and some stretches have to be completed on ordinary roads. As part of the planned future transport projects (see above), such stretches are to be built up to motorway standard.
One trunk road which is important to domestic Danish transport is the expressway (21/23) which runs from Copenhagen and Roskilde westwards to Kalundborg (from where there is a ferry to Jutland).

Suburban train and bus services

A well-developed suburban rail system connects Copenhagen city centre with the suburbs, supplemented by an extensive bus network.

Commerce and Industry

Commercial centre

Copenhagen is the centre of Danish commerce and industry (which are entirely in private hands) and the headquarters of numerous banks and industrial firms. Around 73% of Danish industrial products are exported in order to finance necessary imports. Half of the exports go to EC countries. By national standards, however, Copenhagen's contribution to the Danish economy is in decline.

Branches of industry

Amongst Copenhagen's leading industries are the two breweries Tuborg and Carlsberg (now amalgamated), much of the output of which is exported.
Other important branches of industry are iron and metal industries (including shipyards, engine manufacture and the largest cableworks in Denmark), textiles and clothing, chemicals, foodstuffs, as well as graphic products, glass, silver and porcelain.
Apart from agriculture, Denmark possesses few natural resources. It is, however, rich in ideas with a feeling for colour and design and a practical good sense. The desire to enjoy a good living standard has brought Danish design a worldwide reputation.
As well as the commercial goods already mentioned, the following are also made and sold: furs, furniture, knitwear, tobacco pipes, toys and – as commercial objects – antiques of all kinds.

Exhibition and convention centre

On the island of Amager is the Bella Centre – a modern exhibition and convention centre. With a covered area of some 85,000sq.m/914,940sq.ft, it is Scandinavia's largest, and every year up to 30 international and national conferences take place here.

Danish Design

General

Danish design, that is items of furniture conceived and produced by Danes, has a long tradition. Key historical dates have, since 1775, shaped the foundation of the capital's Royal Porcelain Manufactory, the Bing & Grøndahl porcelain factory, the Georg Jensen silverworks and the Holmegaard glassworks at Næstved (southern Zealand), as well as the setting up of various furniture workshops. The hallmarks of Danish design were, and

still are, its outstanding craftsmanship and later the industrial quality of its products, the artistic design (numerous designers were formerly eminent artists of their time) and the value of "functionality" (demonstrated by Kaare Klint), following the principle that "the form of an object follows its function".
An overall view can be gained from the exhibition entitled "Danish Design" to be found in the Museum of Art in Industry (see A to Z, Kunstindustriemuseet) in the Bredgade.

Royal Copenhagen

One of the most important amalgamations in the evolution of Copenhagen design took place in 1985, when the Royal Porcelain Manufactory merged with Georg Jensen's silverworks and the Holmegaard glassworks to form "Royal Copenhagen". The famous porcelain, silver and glass products can nowadays be bought in and around the pedestrianised street known as "Strøget" (see A to Z, Strøget; Practical Information, Shopping).

Ceramics

The history of Danish ceramics is closely connected with the two famous Copenhagen porcelain factories, the Royal Porcelain Manufactory and the Bing & Grøndahl porcelain factory, which produce objects both for practical and decorative purposes.

Royal Porcelain Manufactory

The Royal Porcelain Manufactory, founded on May 1st 1775 at the instigation of the dowager queen Juliane Marie, was for a long time partly or wholly in the possession of the royal family. The firm chose as its porcelain mark three wavy lines, symbolising the three Danish sea channels: the Øresund, the Great Belt and the Little Belt.
The Royal Porcelain Manufactory achieved its renown above all through its superb tableware and its artistic underglaze decoration. The oldest service,

Household articles of Danish design in Illums Bolighus

A high-class Royal Copenhagen dinner service

the so-called "Blue Painted" (with decoration based on Meissen models) has, apart from a few modifications, been produced ever since the year of foundation. The famous "Flora Danica" service, designed in 1789, had originally been commissioned by the Danish king as a gift for the Russian tsarina, Katharina II, but she died before its completion. The tableware was then named after the distinguished botanical reference work of the same title, which deals with the flora of Denmark.

The decorative technique of underglaze painting, in which, before the application of the feldspar glaze, a design is put on using paint akin to watercolours, for technical reasons allows the use of only a few colours. Hence the derivation of the name "Blue Copenhagen Porcelain".

The Royal Porcelain Manufactory enjoyed its heyday under the management of Arnold Krog towards the end of the 19th c. Characteristic of this period are the many Danish landscape motifs. The fairly recent development of the Functional and the Discrete was given significant impetus by the ceramicist Gertrud Vasegaard with her "Gemma" and "Gemina" tableware (designed in 1960), as well as by the architect Grethe Meyer with her faïence ware "Blue Border" (1962) and "Red Pot" (1981). Less functionality is to be seen in the works of the goldsmith Arje Griegst who, amongst other things, introduced in 1978 his "Konkylie" service.

Bing & Grøndahl porcelain factory

In the porcelain factory of Bing & Grøndahl (established 1853) the painter Pietro Krohn introduced the technique of underglazing. His "Heron" service, designed in 1888, was developed with the collaboration of Effie Hergermann-Lindencrone and of Fanny Garde, who in 1901 created the famous "Seagull" service. The factory's "Blue Painted" service, the design of which, unlike that of the Royal Porcelain Manufactory is three-part, not four-part, was designed by the painter F. A. Hallin (who in 1895 also created the first "Christmas Plate", called "Behind the frosty window-pane").

"Blue-ware" in a fine setting

Impression of "Spring" designer group

Representatives of modern Functionalism in the 1930's were the silversmith Kay Bojsen and the artist Ebbe Sadolin with her white tableware, who managed her designs without coloured decoration. The sculptor Henning Koppel initially also produced pure white services, but later worked in addition with coloured compositions (e.g. "Comet", 1978). Even more practically orientated work was introduced by the ceramicist Erik Magnussen, whose everyday tableware "Hank" (1972) is used by, amongst others, the Danish National Railway.

Silver

Georg Jensen's silverworks

In the early years of the silverworks established by Georg Jensen in 1904, Jensen himself, together with the painter Johan Rohde, created the designs that were to point the way ahead. From the outset the firm produced cutlery, dishes, bowls and jewellery. The skilled goldsmith and sculptor Georg Jensen, who can be regarded as among the leading silver designers of his time, created *inter alia* the highly praised silver cutlery "Antiquity" (1906). Other established figures in the field were Harald Nielsen, Sigvard Bernadotte, Magnus Stephensen, Søren Georg Jensen and the sculptor Henning Koppel, renowned for his ceramic designs and his bowls and dishes. Jensen, in producing countless functional objects, transformed the silver into new forms of expression (e.g. "Fish Platter", 1954). As silver prices rose, the craftsmen reorientated their work in part towards new materials (including steel). The firm's leading jewellery designers include figures such as Nanna Ditzel, Torun Bülow-Hübe, Arje Griegst, Anette Kræn and Ole Bent-Petersen. Numerous Danish cutlery designers used as a model Kay Bojsen's silver service "Grand Prix" (1938) – which was also produced in steel in 1951. Flowing shapes were evident in, among others, Arne Jacobsen's "A J-Cutlery" (1960). Kay Bojsen's reputation was enhanced by his wooden toy designs.

Glass

Holmegard glassworks

After a gap of almost 200 years, in which no more glassware was produced in the whole of Denmark, there was a renaissance in the craft of Danish glassmaking, initiated by Count Christian Danneskiold-Samsoe in the town of Holmegard, 7km/4 miles north of Næstved (southern Zealand). Peat from the moors provided an important fuel, the glassmakers which Denmark itself lacked were recruited in Norway, and eventually the first glass kiln began operating in 1825. At first only green bottles ("bouteilles") were produced, followed in 1835 by plate glass, manufactured by master craftsmen also brought in from south Germany and Bohemia. It is thus no surprise that some terms associated with glass production are of German origin. Later various refinement processes were added, together with grinding, etching and decoration. With the advent of mechanisation and the use of stencils, mass produced industrial glass became as important as the hand-produced variety. The principal product is still plate glass. In recent years the manufacture of semi-crystal glass has also been established.

The present-day craft of glassmaking in Denmark is characterised by two different, though not always distinguishable lines of development. On the one hand shapes evolve virtually by themselves, appropriate to the material and bound by tradition; on the other hand, the glass-blowers get their inspiration for creative design from the artistic directions currently followed by painting, graphic design and sculpture.

Furniture and Lighting

Furniture design

The art of Danish furniture design emerged at international level in the course of the fifties. The way for its success was paved by the architect Kaare Klint, who was a teacher of furniture design in Copenhagen's School of Architecture. With his study of human proportions Klint initiated a new working method which made the comfort and functionality of furniture a priority. On this basis he made use of pre-existing suitable types of furniture, which he then developed further (amongst others, he simplified English Chippendale). In so doing, he created a new appreciation of furniture design. Since then many Danish artists have derived their inspiration from the furniture of other countries, which they have then so greatly improved that the end-product appears quintessentially Danish. Among the best known representatives of the younger generation are Klint's pupil Børge Mogensen, the chair designers Erik Krogh and Hans J. Wegner, whose model, entitled "The Chair" (designed 1949), became a byword, Carsten Nikolaj Becker, Brigitte Borup, Jørgen Gammelgaard, who also works as a lighting designer, Karin Gammelgaard, Grete Jalk, Krestine Kjærholm, Jørgen Larsen, Jørgen Rasmussen, Leif Erik Rasmussen, Johnny Sørensen, Rud Thygesen, the "Design 134" group of Erling Christoffersen, Flemming Steen Jensen, Bjørli Lundin and Annette Juel, as well as the "Spring" designer group comprising both the three textile designers Mette Dammand Jensen, Mette Mikkelsen and Inger Mosholt Nielsen and the product and furniture designer Hans Sandgren Jakobsen.

Lighting design

The best known designer of Danish lighting appliances is Poul Henningsen, whose technical work in the field began in 1925, when he won a competition for the lighting of the Danish stand at the Paris World Fair. Poul Henningsen, however – whom the Danes call PH for short – not only designed lamps but also supplied the theoretical basis which serves so many lighting designers today. His principles can be summarised in four ways: 1. the light must not dazzle, 2. there should be a smooth transition between directly and indirectly lit surfaces, 3. the lamp must produce a good shadow outline, 4. the lighting must correct the predominance of the light towards yellow and green.

PH's lighting installations characteristically have several shades, which help to correct the colour of the light.

Danish furniture by J. Gammelgaard, G. Jalk and C. N. Becker

Chairs, by E. Krogh and the "134" designers

Henningsen's "PH-5" lamp, introduced in 1958, can nowadays be found in countless Danish households, as can the "PH-Plate", originally designed for the Copenhagen restaurant "Langelinie Pavillionen". As far back as 1962 his "PH-Contrast" made it possible for the user to correct the light colour.

Architectural Design

In the field of Danish design many outstanding results have been achieved by completing functional tasks in connection with the construction of new buildings. So, for example, the architect Arne Jacobsen designed in 1960 not only the building for the SAS Royal Hotel in Copenhagen, but also applied himself to the furniture design and even to the restaurant glass and cutlery.

Industrial Design

The task of modern industrial designers is less the use of a particular material than the design of products which have the power to communicate. One example of a firm with a conscious design policy is that of Bang & Olufsen, which has received several awards for its products (T.V. and Hi-Fi equipment). This firm is increasingly trying to make technically complicated equipment look less forbidding and more elegant. In pursuit of this goal, they adhere to the maxim "Form follows function" and, by dint of simple design, try to make it absolutely clear for what purpose and in what way each piece of equipment should be used.

Famous People

The following alphabetical list consists of a series of well-known figures who, because they either were born, lived, worked or died there, are connected with Copenhagen, but have achieved national or international fame.

Absalon
(*c.* 1128–21.3.1201)

The Danish statesman Absalon may be regarded as the founder of the city of Copenhagen. In 1901, the 700th anniversay of his death, the town erected a memorial to him on the Højbro Plads. The grandson of the powerful Skjalm Hvide, who had ruled over Zealand during the reign of Sven Estridsen, was born in the family seat of Fjenneslev near Sorø. After he had supported the men of King Waldemar I in the struggle for the throne in 1157, Absalon was appointed Bishop of Roskilde in the following year. As a further reward from the king, he was granted rights to the district of "Havn" where, some ten years later, on the island of Strandholm (now called Slotsholm), he had a fortress built as a protection against Wendish pirates. The rapidly expanding settlement around the castle acquired the name "Købmændenes Havn" (Merchant's Port).
In 1177 the office of Archbishop of Lund was conferred on him. Furthermore, he became one of the most influential advisers of Waldemar I and Knut VI; he strengthened the position of the Danish church and extended its sphere of influence as far as Rügen and Pomerania. In the spring of 1201 Absalon died in Sorø, where he was buried in the monastery church.

Hans Christian Andersen
(2.4.1805–4.8.1875)

Hans Christian Andersen, born the son of a shoemaker in Odense on the island of Funen (Fyn), lived from 1819 onwards in Copenhagen. There he trained for the theatre and worked as chorus member and supernumerary until his voice broke.
Andersen was blessed with an immense and natural literary talent. As a result of his early publications – including "The Improviser" (1835), a novel showing the development of a character – he received from 1838 onwards an allowance from the King. Between 1831 and 1871 the writer made numerous trips abroad, in particular to Germany, where his autobiography "The Fairy Tale of My Life" was also published in 1845/46 (in Danish in 1855). But Andersen achieved world fame with his fairy tale collection called the "Eventyr" (1835-1872). Among the best known are "The Emperor's New Clothes", "The Princess on the Pea", "The Ugly Duckling", "The Swineherd", "The Steadfast Tin Soldier" and "The Mermaid". In these stories, using an apparently naïve style, he creates a world which bears touches of humour, irony and resignation. Since these tales often have a deeper meaning, they are also directed at adults ("The mermaid has no immortal soul, nor ever can possess one, unless she wins the love of a human being!"). Andersen had the ability to derive unexpected perspectives from even the smallest of things.
With his less well-known novels Andersen laid the foundations of modern realistic prose writing in Denmark. His work also includes poetry, diaries and letters.
He died in Copenhagen in 1875, where he is buried in the Assistens Kirkegård – the city's largest cemetery.

Martin Andersen Nexø
(25.6.1869–1.6.1954)

Martin Andersen Nexø, who came from Copenhagen, spent most of his youth as shepherd-boy and cobbler's apprentice on the island of Bornholm. After attending various evening classes, he worked as a teacher, then writer. Having embraced Communism after the First World War, he lived in Dresden from 1951 up until his death in 1954.
The main themes of his artistic works are, on the one hand, social criticism and on the other, sympathy for the poor and the outcast. In his novel "Pelle

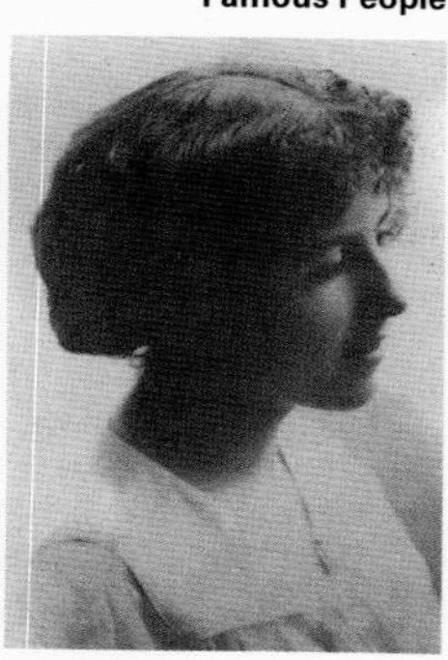

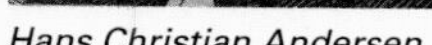

Hans Christian Andersen *Martin Andersen Nexø* *Karen Blixen*

The Conqueror" (1906–1910; four vols.), which has autobiographical traits, he describes the life of farmers, fishermen and labourers. Over and above that, he describes the aims of the Workers' Movement around 1900. His second novel cycle, "Ditte. Daughter of Man" (1917–1921; 5 vols.), written in a more pessimistic tone, has as its subject the life of a woman from the lower classes, who fails to break out of her unsatisfactory environment. Andersen Nexø has also emerged as an author of novellas, travel books and memoirs.

Karen Blixen (17.4.1885–7.9.1962)

The Danish writer Karen Blixen was born in Rungstedlund near Copenhagen, the daughter of the captain and author W. Dinesen. Her study of painting at the Danish Academy of Art was followed by trips to England, France and Italy. At the age of 28 she married the Swedish baron Bror von Blixen-Finecke, with whom she went to Kenya, where she managed a coffee plantation till 1931. During this time she met Denys Finch Hatton – the real love of her life – who died when his plane crashed in 1931. As a result of the economic crisis of the same year, she had to return to Denmark and then lived as a freelance writer on her father's estate in Rungstedlund where, in 1991, the manor house was turned into a museum. Karen Blixen, whose full name was actually Baroness Karen Christence Blixen-Finecke, published her works (written in Danish and English) under the pseudonyms Tanja Blixen, Isak Dinesen, Tania Blixen and Pierre Andrézel. Her highly imaginative stories and novellas, frequently characterised by the theme of fate, were developed outside of contemporary literary trends. Distinctive features of her writing are her rich storytelling skill, her frivolously ironic sense of humour, her sensitivity and the cryptic nature of her subject matter. With great empathy she portrayed in her books about Kenya the natural life of East Africa and the life of the natives. Among her best known works are: "Africa, Dark Alluring World", which in 1985 was made into an Oscar-winning film starring Meryl Streep and Robert Redford, entitled "Out of Africa"; "Winter's Tales", 1942; "Shadows on the Grass" ("Skygger på græsset", 1960) and the story "Babette's Feast" (first published 1950) from "Anecdotes of Destiny", 1960, the 1988 film version of which by Gabriel Axel won the Oscar for Best Foreign Film.

Niels Bohr (7.10.1885–18.11.1962)

Denmark's greatest physicist, Niels Bohr, was born in Copenhagen and became Professor of Theoretical Physics there in 1916. He definitively redeveloped Ernest Rutherford's atomic model into the Bohr atomic model (1913) and discovered the principle of correspondence between classical physics and quantum physics. In recognition of his research work, he was awarded the 1922 Nobel Prize for Physics. At the beginning of 1943, during the German occupation of Denmark, Bohr was smuggled out of the country, disguised as a fisherman. From here he found his way via Sweden and

Niels Bohr

Tycho Brahe

Christian IV

England to the U.S.A., where he collaborated on the development of the atomic bomb, despite fearing its repercussions. After the war he returned to Copenhagen and continued his work at his institute of theoretical physics (directed since his death by his son). In 1947 he received Denmark's highest honour, the Order of the Elephant.

Tycho Brahe (14.12.1546–24.10.1601)

Tycho Brahe, born in 1546 in Knudstrup (southern Sweden), initially studied law and then turned to astronomy. In 1572 he discovered in Cassiopeia (a northern constellation) a new star, the Nova Cassiopeia. After a trip to Europe, Brahe gave lectures in Copenhagen and, on the island of Ven in the Sund (lent to him in 1576 by the Danish king Friedrich II), he built the Uranienborg observatory, where he carried out his research. After the death of Friedrich II in 1588, he found increasingly less support and, at the beginning of 1597, he left Denmark and two years later went to Prague, where he took up the post of Imperial Astronomer in the service of Rudolf II. He died there in October 1601. His memorial tablet in the Teyn church (fourth pillar from the right) is always adorned with the Danebrog.

Brahe was the leading observational astronomer before the invention of the telescope. Through his observations of planetary bodies, in particular of Mars, he prepared the way for Kepler's work on planetary orbits. Brahe developed the so-called "Tychonic System", named after him. According to this, sun and moon circle the earth which is situated at the centre of the world, while the remaining planets circle the sun. In addition, he proved that the comets cannot simply be phenomena in the earth's atmosphere, as Aristotle had assumed. In memory of the great astronomer, Copenhagen's planetarium, opened in 1989, was named after him.

King Christian IV (12.4.1577–28.2.1648)

Christian IV, Denmark's most popular king, was responsible for some of the finest buildings in Copenhagen. He brought the Renaissance style to Denmark – a style evident in such buildings as the Copenhagen Stock Exchange, the Rosenborg Palace, the Round Tower and Frederiksborg Castle. This royal building commissioner, however, did not confine his activities to magnificent palaces and public buildings. For his seamen he built housing in the Nybodn district, and the district of Christianshavn was also developed on his initiative. In addition, he left his mark on towns in Sweden (Christiansstad), Germany (Glückstadt) and Norway (Oslo, Kongsberg).

In the field of politics Christian, who was crowned in 1596, had little success. He was unable to compel Sweden to join a league of northern states under Danish leadership, and moreover, in the Thirty Years' War, he was forced to accept heavy defeats. The king, who was popular with his subjects principally for his informality, finally died in 1648 in Copenhagen, an unhappy and disappointed man.

Carl Th. Dreyer (3.2.1889–20.3.1968)

Carl Th. Dreyer, who was born in Copenhagen, is Denmark's most celebrated film director (especially in the realm of silent films). He made a crucial contribution to the development of film as an art form. His films "Joan of Arc" (1926–7), which made consistent use of close-ups, and "Vampire" (1928–9), achieved worldwide success, but his later films failed to make a similar impression.

Nikolai Frederik Severin Grundtvig (8.9.1783–2.9.1872)

Grundtvig, after whom one of the most unusual modern churches in Europe (the Grundtvig Church in Copenhagen) is named, was the founder of the adult education movement and is the spiritual father of its systematic development. In 1844 he established the first such centre in Europe at Rødding (Jutland). After the incorporation of northern Schleswig in Prussia in 1864, the school had to be moved to Askov (also in Jutland).
Grundtvig, who was a pastor in Copenhagen from 1839 and who became bishop in 1861, also translated old Norse sagas and wrote over 400 hymns.

Max Hansen (22.2.1897–12.11.1961)

The singer Max Hansen, born in Mannheim (Germany), achieved his first successes in Copenhagen's Apollo Theatre in 1919. He became an international star in the 1920's in the Metropol Theatre in Berlin, where he appeared in numerous operettas and revues – one of his most notable roles was that of the waiter Leopold in "White Horse Inn". After performing as a guest star in Copenhagen, he became manager of the Tivoli Theatre in 1956, retaining the post until his death.

Ludvig Holberg (3.12.1684–28.1.1754)

Ludvig Baron von Holberg, born in Bergen (Norway), was the creator of the modern Danish theatre. He studied theology in Copenhagen and then worked as a domestic tutor in Holland, Germany, England, France and Italy, before becoming, at Copenhagen, professor of Metaphysics in 1718 and later of Rhetoric and History in 1720. In addition to his work as professor, historian and university treasurer, Holberg wrote comedies of social criticism and letters on the most varied subjects. After the foundation of the Copenhagen theatre in 1722 he wrote more than 33 comedies (including "The Alehouse Politician", 1723; "Jean de France", 1723; "Ulysses of Ithaca" and "Erasmus Montanus", 1731), in which he combines earthy realism with the ideas of the Enlightenment. His work at the university led him also to write historical and moral works in the spirit of the Enlightenment. He lived in Copenhagen from 1708 to 1740, and died there in 1754. This great dramatist is commemorated today by a statue outside the Royal Theatre.

Johannes Vilhelm Jensen (20.1.1873–25.11.1950)

Jensen, born in Farsø on Jutland, is one of Denmark's leading writers. He initially studied medicine, but then moved to the United States in 1896, where he lived for some time. Later he made several trips to France, Spain and East Asia as newspaper correspondent. For his masterly novels and stories he was, in 1944, awarded the Nobel Prize for Literature. He spent his last years in Copenhagen, where he died in 1950.
Jensen's work reflects his attachment to his native land and a strong love of Danish tradition. One of his prime works, the six-part novel cycle "Den lange rejse" ("The Long Journey") depicts the history of Nordic man from the beginnings up to the discovery of America by Columbus. The same devotion to homeland is evident in his "Himmerlandhistorier" ("Stories of the Homeland"), 1898–1910, a volume of fairy tales, sagas and stories.

Søren Kierkegaard (5.5.1813–11.11.1855)

The Danish philosopher Søren Kierkegaard was born the seventh child of a prosperous wool dealer in Copenhagen and studied theology and philosophy from 1830 to 1841 at Copenhagen university. In September 1840 he became engaged to the seventeen-year old Regine Olsen, but broke up with her a year later. Thereafter he lived on his inheritance, working as a freelance writer.

Søren Kierkegaard *Friedrich Gottlieb Klopstock* *Bertel Thorvaldsen*

Most of his books were published under pseudonyms. Following the practice of Socrates, his chosen form of writing was frequently dialogue. In his writings the concepts of "angst" and "existence" occupy a central position, together with the related notions of "freedom" and "decision". His thinking leads to the realisation that the conquest of angst and despair is possible only through God's grace. Since Kiergkegaard, as a religious thinker, adopted an emphatically subjective stance, he came into conflict with the Danish Lutheran Church of his time (a church which professed to possess a unified system of objective truth) – and finally rejected it completely. His works on the philosophy of religion have greatly influenced many 20th c. thinkers: the ideas expressed in these works to a great extent form the basis of dialectical theology and existential philosophy.
Among his important works are "Either-Or" (1843), "Fear and Trembling" (1843), "The Concept of Dread" (1844), "The Sickness unto Death" (1849) and "Training in Christianity" (1850).
Kierkegaard died in Copenhagen in 1855, where he was buried in the Assistens Kirkegård cemetery.

Friedrich Gottlieb Klopstock (2.7.1724–14.3.1803)

Born in Quedlinburg (Germany), Klopstock studied theology at Jena and while there began his three-part biblical verse cycle "The Messiah" (1748–73), the first twenty cantos of which were enthusiastically received. This brought him an invitation to Copenhagen from the Danish minister Bernstorff in 1751, together with the offer of a good salary. Freed from material want, he lived in Copenhagen as a poet till 1754, then returned to Germany for ten years before coming back again to Copenhagen in 1763. After Bernstorff's overthrow and replacement by Struensee, he left Copenhagen in 1770 as Danish counsellor of legation (and with the right to a pension), and thereafter lived mainly in Hamburg.
Among Klopstock's principal works, apart from "The Messiah", are the odes (published individually in 1748 and in one volume in 1771). These poems, influenced by the bible and the verse of Horace, Pindar, J. Milton and E. Young, deal with lofty themes such as love, friendship and the experience of nature. Best known are "Spring Celebration", "Lake Zurich" and "To My Friends", which were partly written also while he was in Copenhagen.

Valdemar Poulsen (23.11.1869–6.8.1942)

Poulsen's name is decisively linked with the development of wireless telegraphy and telephony, fields in which he held numerous important patents. This Copenhagen-born physicist constructed as early as 1898 the first workable electromagnetic sound recorder, and in 1904 he developed the "singing arc" (for the generation of radio waves), which influenced wireless transmission for years to come.

Johann Friedrich, Count von Struensee (5.8.1737–28.4.1772)

Qualifying as a doctor at the early age of twenty, Struensee became personal physician to King Christian VII of Denmark in 1769 and went to Copenhagen with the king, a degenerate and feeble-minded character. Before long he began a love-affair with Queen Caroline Mathilde and with her support he not only acquired influence over the king, but in the summer 1771 was also made a count and appointed minister in the inner cabinet. For almost sixteen months he held sway over the Danish court and country. The liberal reforms he introduced during this period anticipated the developments of the following century.
When Struensee's high-handedness became uncontrolled and his affair with the queen could no longer be concealed, a court clique opposed to him obtained a warrant for his arrest. He was arrested on Jan. 17th 1772 and executed on Jan. 28th of the same year, in accordance with the provisions of the law: his right hand was cut off while he was still alive and then his head, his body was quartered and the separate parts displayed publicly, but his head and hand were stuck on a pole. About 3000 citizens of Copenhagen witnessed this gruesome spectacle.
The English-born queen was expelled from the country.

Bertel Thorvaldsen (19.11.1768–24.3.1844)

Thorvaldsen was Denmark's greatest sculptor, for whom his native city of Copenhagen established a special museum. While still a student at the Academy of Art, he distinguished himself by winning the academy's Great Gold Medal. With the help of a travelling scholarship from the academy he was able to go to Rome in 1797. There he settled down and began to create sculpture in marble, which brought him a reputation throughout Europe and ensured that his work was much in demand. After living in Rome for 40 years he returned to Copenhagen in 1838 and was received in triumph. Between 1839 and 1848, under the direction of Gottlieb Bindesbøll, a museum was built on the Porthusgade to house the works which he had bequeathed to the city.

Bjørn Wiinblad (born 20.9.1919)

Bjørn Wiinblad, a native of Copenhagen, studied painting and illustration at the Royal Academy of Art. In addition to book illustrations, he designed posters, stage sets and costumes for the theatre. Soon, however, he became interested in different materials and techniques and started to produce tapestries, wallpaper and ceramic pieces.
He enjoyed his first great success when his ceramic work was exhibited in Copenhagen, Sweden and Norway. In 1954 he held an exhibition in New York. Among all Wiinblad's diverse creations, ceramic materials remained his preferred medium. His shapes and his decorative style create a bright, attractive effect.
As a designer, Wiinblad makes designs for table services and glassware, as well as for vases and wall plates. Sometimes he designs both shape and decoration, but sometimes either one or the other. His surfaces are covered with decoration or painted figures, or embellished with scenes from fairy tales ("1001 Nights"). As well as objects in black and white, he creates others decorated with bright colours. Wiinblad has for many years been working for the firm of Rosenthal – famous for its porcelain and ceramic ware – which has its headquarters in Selb (Bavaria).

History of Copenhagen

Prehistory	Like the rest of Denmark, the Copenhagen area was originally occupied by Indo-European hunting tribes. Evidence of their culture (tools, weapons, jewellery) can be seen in the museums of Copenhagen. Especially notable are their unusual bronze trumpets, known as "lurs" (as seen in the monument outside the town hall).
From 800	The northern Germanic Danes, known as Vikings – warriors, seamen, peasants – surge into Denmark from southern Sweden. Their kings established the first Danish state (rune-stone of Jelling in Jutland).
1167	Valdemar I, the Great, presents a fishing village called Havn to Archbishop Absalon. Ten years later Absalon fortifies the village harbour by building a castle on the site now occupied by Christiansborg Palace on Slotsholmen. The settlement which grows up around the castle acquires the name "Købmændenes Havn" ("Merchant's Harbour").
1254	First charter of municipal rights.
1397	Union of Kalmar: Denmark, Norway and Sweden are united under the rule of Erik VII of Pomerania.
1417	Erik VII grants Copenhagen royal trading privileges. The town becomes an important trading centre in the Baltic area.

Siege of Copenhagen by the Swedes in 1658

Christoffer II (of Bavaria) makes Copenhagen his capital and confirms the rights of the municipality. The town has a population of some 10,000.	1445
Coronation of Christian I – the first royal coronation in Copenhagen.	1449
Christian I founds the University. Copenhagen becomes the country's cultural centre.	1479
The Reformation reaches Denmark. King Christian III makes himself head of the Danish (Lutheran) national church.	1536
During the reign of Christian IV building of the new district of Christianshavn, the housing area of Nyboder and numerous Renaissance-style buildings.	1588–1648
Unsuccessful siege of the town by the Swedes.	1658–60
As a reward for its successful defence against the Swedish siege, Copenhagen becomes a free city and the citizens enjoy equal rights with the nobility. Introduction of an absolute hereditary monarchy, which lasts until 1848.	1660
Construction of the Citadel.	1662
Copenhagen has a population of 60,000.	1700
During the plague almost a third of the population perishes.	1711–12
A devastating fire destroys the town. Over 1670 houses are reduced to ashes.	1728

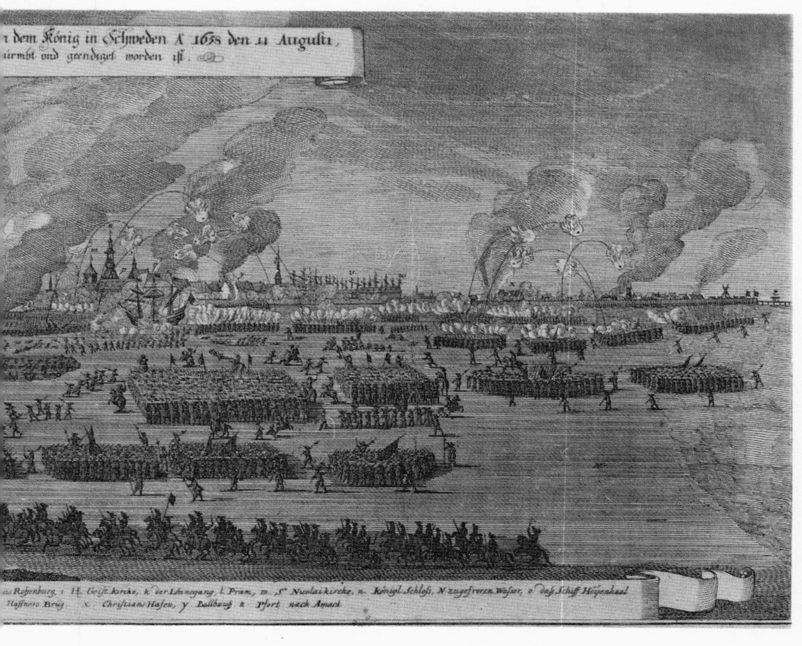

History of Copenhagen

1795	The second great fire of Copenhagen, with loss of more than 1000 houses.
1801	Copenhagen is attacked by the British fleet, in reprisal for Denmark's support of Napoleon I's continental blockade of England.
1807	Three-day bombardment of Copenhagen by the British, causing considerable destruction in the town centre.
1848	The bourgeois revolution brings the end of absolute rule. Denmark is granted a liberal constitution. Copenhagen grows out beyond its defensive walls.
1867	Demolition of the town's fortifications.
1894	The establishment of a free port gives a crucial new impetus to Copenhagen's economy.
1924	Opening of the major airport of Kastrup.
1940–45	Neutral Denmark is occupied by the German Army. There is passive resistance, in which King Christian X takes part, and the country's Jews are evacuated to Sweden.
May 4th 1945	Liberation of Copenhagen from German occupation.
1962	The pedestrian precinct of Strøget becomes one of the first traffic-free shopping streets in Europe.
1980	Meeting of the second U.N. World Conference of Women in Copenhagen.
1982	The EC Heads of State and Heads of Government meet for a summit conference in Copenhagen.
1983	Copenhagen organises Scandinavia's greatest tourism fair, the "Travel '83".
1984	A multi-phase building programme begins, designed to rebuild and extend Kastrup airport and make it (by the year 2000) one of the most modern in Europe.
1985	Reopening of the reconstructed "Gamle Scene" for ballet performances.
1987	The Danish parliament (Folketing) agrees in May to the construction of a combined bridge and tunnel connection between Halsskov (Zealand) and Nyborg (Funen/Fyn). This linkage across The Great Belt will in future make Copenhagen accessible to train and car passengers, without the need to change to a ferry. The rail stretch is due for completion by 1993, the motorway by 1996. Kastrup airport is enhanced by the addition of an elegant shopping centre opened in May.
1988	The elections – brought forward to May – result in no clear majority in the Folketing. The minority government, consisting of Conservatives, Liberals and Radical Democrats, controls only 67 out of the total 179 seats.
1989	Opening (beginning of May) of the Tycho Brahe Planetarium on the Gammel Kongevej.
1990	The 35 KSZE states, by signing the most comprehensive document on human rights and democracy since the Helsinki Declaration of 1975, commit themselves to a pluralistic democracy, a multi-party system, free elections, the preservation of law and order and the protection of national or

religious minorities. The Copenhagen document is "the first and definitive proclamation of a whole and free Europe" (June).
The Social Democrats emerge victorious from the December elections (in the Folketing) with 37.7% of the votes. Together with the Socialist People's Party, the Social Democrats now control 86 of the 179 members. Prime Minister in the new Conservative/Liberal minority government is once again Poul Schlüter.

The Danish parliament (Folketing) joins its Swedish counterpart by agreeing (on Aug. 14th) to the construction of a bridge and tunnel crossing over the Øresund (estimated cost seventeen billion Danish krone). The bridge is scheduled to be operating in 1999. 1991
In September the full democratic assembly of Christiania gives its assent to the legal recognition of the "Free State" of Copenhagen (established in 1971).

Copenhagen in Quotations

Fynes Moryson
c. 1566–1617

Elsinore and Cronenburg Castle
This is a poore village, but much frequented by sea-faring men, by reason of the straight sea, called the Sownd; where the King of Denmark hath laid so great imposition upon ships and goods comming out of the Balticke sea, or brought into the same, as this sole profit passeth all the revenues of his Kingdome. . . . In respect of the Danes scrupulous and jealous nature, I did with great difficulty (putting on a Merchants habite, and giving a greater reward then the favour deserved,) obtaine to enter Croneburg Castle, which was built foure square, and hath only one gate on the East side, where it lies upon the straight. Above this gate is a chamber in which the King useth to eat, and two chambers wherin the King and Queen lie apart. Under the fortification of the Castle round about, are stables for horses, and some roomes for like purposes. On the South-side towards the Baltich sea, is the largest roade for ships. And upon this side is the prison, and above it a short gallery. On the West side towards the village is the Church of the Castle, & above it a very faire gallery, in which the King useth to feast at solemne times. On the North side is the prospect partly upon the Iland, and partly upon the Narrow sea, which reacheth twenty foure miles to the German Ocean. And because great store of ships passe this way in great Fleets, of a hundred more or lesse together: this prospect is most pleasant to all men, but most of all to the King, seeing so many shippes, whereof not one shall passe, without adding somewhat to his treasure.
"Itinerary" 1617

William Coxe
1747–1828

Copenhagen is the best-built city of the north; for although St Petersburg excels it in superb edifices, yet as it contains no wooden houses, it does not display that striking contrast of meanness and magnificence, but in general exhibits a more equable and uniform appearance. The town is surrounded towards the land with regular ramparts and bastions, a broad ditch full of water, and a few outworks: its circumference measures between four and five miles. The streets are well-paved, with a foot-way on each side, but too narrow and inconvenient for general use. The greatest part of the buildings are of brick; and a few of free-stone brought from Germany. The houses of the nobility are in general splendid, and constructed in the Italian style of architecture. The royal palace is a magnificent pile of building of hewn stone, the wings and stable of brick stuccoed. . . .
The busy spirit of commerce is visible in Copenhagen. The haven is always crowded with merchant-ships; and the streets are intersected by broad canals, which bring the merchandize close to the warehouses that line the quays. The city owes its principal beauty to a dreadful fire in 1728, that destroyed five churches and sixty-seven streets, which have since been rebuilt in the modern style. The new part of the town, raised by the late king Frederic V, is extremely beautiful: it consists of an octagon, containing four uniform and elegant buildings of hewn stone, and of four broad streets leading to it in opposite directions.
"Travels into Poland, Russia, Sweden, etc." 1792

Mary
Woolstonecraft
1759–97

I see here nothing but heaps of ruins and only converse with people immersed in trade and sensuality
"Letter to Gilbert Imlay" 6 September 1795

Edward Daniel
Clarke
1769–1822

Our French companions complained of the bad taste by which everything in Copenhagen is characterized. To our eyes, it seemed, indeed, that a journey from London to Copenhagen might exhibit the retrogression of a century; every thing being found, in the latter city, as it existed in the former a hundred years before. . . .
"Travels" 1810–22

On Monday morning, 5th September 1819, I saw Copenhagen for the first time from the Frederiksberg Hill. I rose and with my little bundle of clothes walked through the park, the long path and the suburb into the town. . . . and put up at a small inn.

Hans Christian Andersen
1805–75

Then I went on to Copenhagen where I was to give five performances at the Court Theatre.
On our arrival, which had undoubtedly been looked forward to with great excitement, I was seized with stage-fright. When my train stopped more than two thousand people shouted "Hurrah!" so loudly that I did not know what was going on. When Monsieur de Fallesen, the director of the Court Theatre and the First Royal Chamberlain, entered my compartment I was asked to appear at the window, to pacify the understandable friendly curiosity of the public. The frightful "Hurrah!" rang out once more, and I understood.
Yet a crazy anxiety came over me. Never, no never, would I be able to fulfil the great expectations which they had of me, however much I wanted to. My tiny stature will arouse sympathy among all these fine men and these magnificent radiant women. I alighted from the train and in comparison with them was so much smaller that I had the impression of being nothing but a breath of wind. On the orders of the police the crowd split into two dense rows, leaving a broad path for my carriage. I drove through this friendly double file at a gentle trot, with the gentlemen doffing their hats respectfully while kisses and flowers were showered upon me.
In my long career as an artist I have since had many triumphs, receptions and ovations, but the welcome I received from the Danes remains one of the most memorable.
Performance of "Adrienne Lecouvreur", mid August 1880 in the Court Theatre.

Sarah Bernhardt
1844–1923

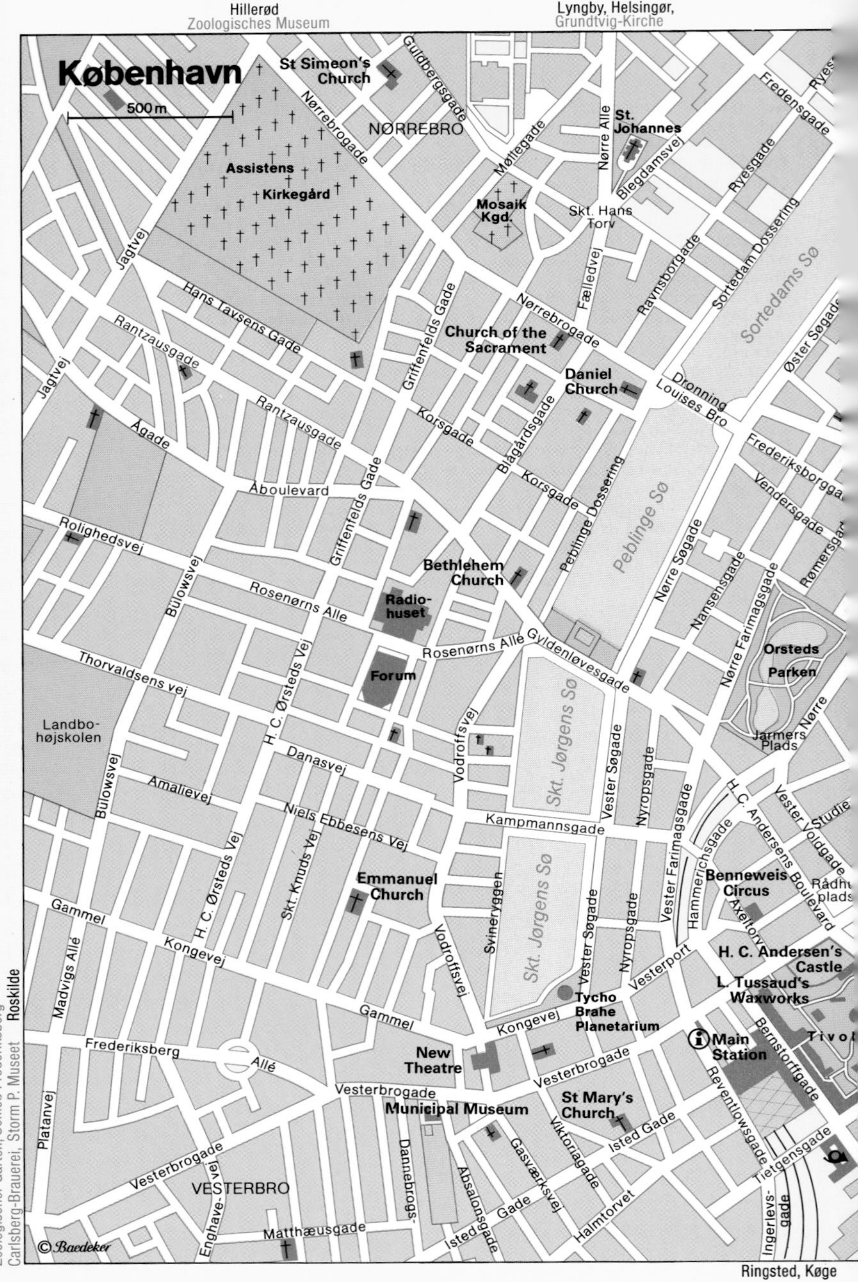
Hillerød
Zoologisches Museum
Lyngby, Helsingør,
Grundtvig-Kirche
København
500 m
St Simeon's Church
NØRREBRO
Assistens Kirkegård
Mosaik Kgd.
St. Johannes
Skt. Hans Torv
Church of the Sacrament
Daniel Church
Sortedams Sø
Peblinge Sø
Dronning Louises Bro
Bethlehem Church
Radiohuset
Forum
Orsteds Parken
Jarmers Plads
Landbohøjskolen
Skt. Jørgens Sø
Emmanuel Church
Benneweis Circus
Rådhuspladsen
H. C. Andersen's Castle
L. Tussaud's Waxworks
Tycho Brahe Planetarium
Main Station
Tivoli
New Theatre
Municipal Museum
St Mary's Church
VESTERBRO
© Baedeker
Ringsted, Køge
Roskilde
Zoologischer Garten, Schloß Frederiksberg
Carlsberg-Brauerei, Storm P. Museet
Nørrebrogade
Guldbergsgade
Møllegade
Nørre Alle
Blegdamsvej
Fredensgade
Ryesgade
Sortedam Dossering
Ravnsborggade
Fælledvej
Jagtvej
Hans Tavsens Gade
Rantzausgade
Griffenfelds Gade
Korsgade
Blågårdsgade
Øster Søgade
Frederiksborggade
Vendersgade
Rømersgade
Ågade
Åboulevard
Peblinge Dossering
Nørre Søgade
Nansensgade
Nørre Farimagsgade
Rolighedsvej
Bülowsvej
Rosenørns Alle
Gyldenløvesgade
Thorvaldsens vej
H. C. Ørsteds Vej
Vodroffsvej
Vester Søgade
Nyropsgade
Vester Farimagsgade
H. C. Andersens Boulevard
Vester Voldgade
Studiestræde
Danasvej
Amalievej
Niels Ebbesens Vej
Kampmannsgade
Hammerichsgade
Axeltorv
Skt. Knuds Vej
Svineryggen
Gammel Kongevej
Madvigs Allé
Vesterport
Frederiksberg Allé
Vesterbrogade
Bernstorffgade
Reventlowsgade
Viktoriagade
Istedgade
Gasværksvej
Absalonsgade
Dannebrogsgade
Halmtorvet
Tietgensgade
Ingerlevsgade
Platanvej
Enghavevej
Matthæusgade

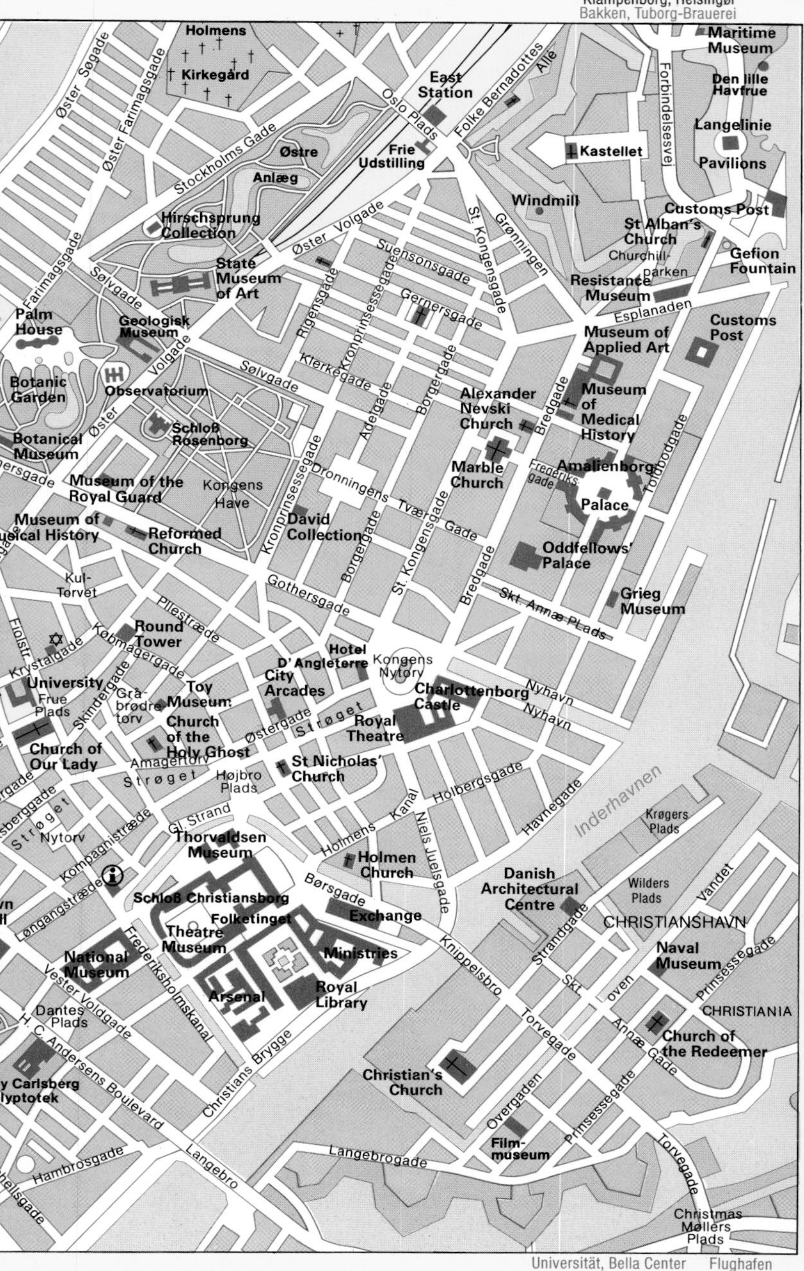
Klampenborg, Helsingør
Bakken, Tuborg-Brauerei
Holmens Kirkegård
East Station
Oslo Plads
Folke Bernadottes Allé
Maritime Museum
Den lille Havfrue
Langelinie
Pavilions
Kastellet
Forbindelsesvej
Windmill
Customs Post
St Alban's Church
Churchill-parken
Gefion Fountain
Resistance Museum
Esplanaden
Customs Post
Museum of Applied Art
Museum of Medical History
Øster Søgade
Øster Farimagsgade
Stockholms Gade
Østre Anlæg
Frie Udstilling
Hirschsprung Collection
State Museum of Art
Øster Volgade
Suensonsgade
Gernersgade
St. Kongensgade
Grønningen
Farimagsgade
Sølvgade
Palm House
Geologisk Museum
Botanic Garden
Observatorium
Øster Volgade
Rigensgade
Kronprinsessegade
Klerkegade
Borgergade
Adelgade
Alexander Nevski Church
Bredgade
Toldbodgade
Botanical Museum
Schloß Rosenborg
Marble Church
Frederiksgade
Amalienborg Palace
Gothersgade
Museum of the Royal Guard
Kongens Have
Dronningens Tværgade
Museum of Musical History
Reformed Church
David Collection
Kronprinsessegade
Oddfellows' Palace
Kul-Torvet
Gothersgade
Skt. Annæ Plads
Grieg Museum
Pilestræde
Round Tower
Købmagergade
Fiolstr.
Krystalgade
University
Frue Plads
Skindergade
Grå-brødre-torv
Toy Museum
Hotel D'Angleterre
City Arcades
Kongens Nytorv
Charlottenborg Castle
Nyhavn
Church of the Holy Ghost
Østergade
Strøget
Royal Theatre
Church of Our Lady
Amagertorv
Strøget
Højbro Plads
St Nicholas' Church
Holbergsgade
Havnegade
Inderhavnen
Strøget
Nytorv
Gl. Strand
Kompagnistræde
Thorvaldsen Museum
Holmens Kanal
Niels Juelsgade
Holmen Church
Krøgers Plads
Danish Architectural Centre
Wilders Plads
Vandet
Schloß Christiansborg
Børsgade
Exchange
Folketinget
CHRISTIANSHAVN
Løngangstræde
Theatre Museum
National Museum
Frederiksholmskanal
Ministries
Knippelsbro
Strandgade
Naval Museum
Prinsessegade
Vester Voldgade
Arsenal
Royal Library
Skt. Annæ Gade
Overgaden oven Vandet
CHRISTIANIA
Dantes Plads
H. C. Andersens Boulevard
Torvegade
Church of the Redeemer
Ny Carlsberg Glyptotek
Christians Brygge
Christian's Church
Overgaden
Prinsessegade
Film-museum
Langebro
Langebrogade
Torvegade
Hambrosgade
Christmas Møllers Plads
Universität, Bella Center
Flughafen

Copenhagen from A to Z

Suggestions for devising a programme for a short trip to Copenhagen can be found under the heading "Programme for a visit" in the section "Practical Information from A to Z" at the end of this guide. A plan of the inner city can be found on pp. 36/37

Note

*Akvarium (Aquarium; Danmarks Akvarium) H1

The Aquarium, one of the most popular museums in Copenhagen, was opened in 1939 and considerably enlarged in 1974. It is situated roughly 5km/3 miles north of the city centre just off Strandvejen in the grounds of Charlottenburg Palace and in its 90 tanks it offers a comprehensive view of freshwater and sea fish from all over the world. (Captions given only in Danish.) Its wide-ranging contents include luminous fish, sharks, electric eels, and exotic species from Asia and South America including the notorious piranhas or pirayas, huge swarms of which can reduce even fully-grown cattle to skeletons in a matter of minutes. There are about 3000 varieties of fish, as well as turtles, on view. (open: Mar.–Oct.: daily 10am–6pm; Nov.–Feb.: Mon.–Fri. 10am–4pm, Sat., Sun. 10am–5pm).

Location
Strandvejen
Charlottenlund

S-bane
Charlottenlund

Bus
6

Alexander Newski Kirke (Church) J6

Alexander Nevski Church, with its three golden onion-shaped domes, was built for the Russian Orthodox community between 1881 and 1883. At the request of the Empress Dagmar, daughter of Christian IX, Tsar Alexander III personally made a contribution to the building costs. The design for the sacred building was supplied by the Russian architect David Ivanovich Grimm of the St Petersburg Academy of Arts, while its execution was carried out by Albert Nielsen under the supervision of F. Meldahl. Its consecration in 1883 was attended by representatives of the Russian and Greek royal families as well as the Danish.

The church reflects the Moscovian style of architecture of the 17th c. Whereas the façade is built of red and grey brick, the ornamental decorations are made of sandstone. Enthroned over the bells is the Prince of Novgorod, Alexander Nevski, who in the middle of the 13th c. defeated a Swedish army by the banks of the River Neva and later fought against the German order of knights in Russia. He is patron saint of the church.

Inside the church a marble staircase leads to the upper floor where the hall of worship is situated. This contains an elaborate iconostasis with three doors, while the ceiling is adorned with Russian and Byzantine paintings. The icons show the influence of the "Romantic style", as it was interpreted in Russia at the end of the last century. Especially noteworthy is P. Bogolyobov's depiction of "Christ walking on the Sea of Galilee", where the colours cause the light not only to lend the work a compositional significance, but also a symbolic one.

Location
Bredgade 53

Buses
1, 6, 9

*Amager (Island) H–K7/8

The island of Amager, which lies to the east of the city centre of Copenhagen, is connected to it by a large bridge which can be raised and lowered

Location
in the Øresund

◄ *Old Smithy in the Frilandsmuseet*

Buses
30, 33, 73E

in a short space of time to allow a ship through. On the island, besides Copenhagen's Kastrup Airport, there is the recently established exhibition and conference centre, the Bella Center. In addition, Amager boasts a series of excellent beaches for bathing.

There are ferry services between Dragør and the Swedish town of Limhamn.

Dragør

History

Dragør, on the east side of Amager, is a picturesque little 18th c. town which has preserved its original character as a village of farmers and fishermen. By virtue of the herring fisheries in the sound, Dragør gained a position of considerable economic importance in the Middle Ages, and in 1370 was granted trading privileges and the right to salt herrings. With the eclipse of the herring fisheries Dragør declined in importance until the middle of the 16th c. when boat piloting in the sound provided a new source of income. The Dragør pilots were the first in the country to receive royal permission to discharge this service. During the 19th c. the Dragør shipping fleet enjoyed a heyday, plying not only between Copenhagen and the Danish provinces, but also between other harbours along the Baltic coasts and even to English ports. With the advent of steamships at the end of the last century the fleet's routes became restricted again to Danish waters.

Dragør Museet

Many of the houses in Dragør are protected as monuments. The oldest fisherman's house dates from 1682. It is situated by the harbour (Havne-

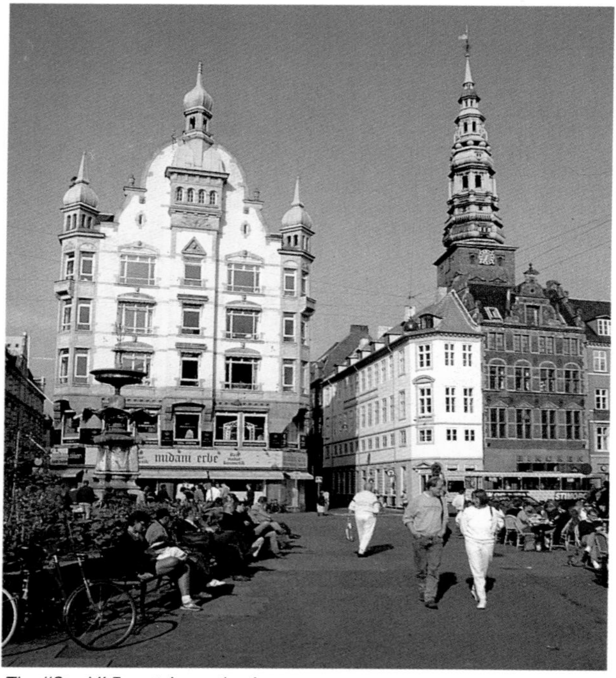

The "Stork" Fountain on the Amagertorv

pladsen) and has an exhibition showing the historical development of seafaring in that area (open: May to Sept.: Tues.–Fri. 2–5pm, Sat., Sun. noon–6pm).

Mølsteds Museet

Mølsteds Museum in the Bledersstræde (no. 1) contains paintings and drawings of Dragør from the period 1862–1930 (open: May to Sept.: Sat., Sun. 2–5pm).

Store Magleby, Amagermuseet

In the south of the island lies Store Magleby, once known as the "Dutchmen's Town". The first inhabitants of the island, who were Dutch, settled here in the early 16th c. during the reign of Christian II. They drained the land and brought it into cultivation. The Amager Museum, which occupies an old half-timbered farmhouse dating from the 18th c. (Hovedgaden 12), houses a collection of material illustrating the peasant tradition of the Dutch immigrants (open: June to Aug.: Wed.–Sun. 11am–3pm; Sept. to May: Wed., Sun. 11am–3pm).

* **Amagertorv** (Amager Market; pedestrian zone) H7

Location
Between Hyskenstræde and Østergade

Buses
8, 28, 29, 41

The Amagertorv, which runs between Hyskenstræde and Østergade and today forms part of the Strøget pedestrian zone, has been an important junction since the Middle Ages, linking the settlement at Gammeltorv with the market at Nikolaj Plads (see entry). Its name Amagertorv (Amager Market) is mentioned for the first time in 1472. In the 16th and 17th c. the street was from time to time the scene of chivalrous tournaments, even though the day-to-day occupants would have been the farmers and smallholders of Amager. As a result of the trading law enacted in 1684, all foodstuffs and flowers produced on the island of Amager (see entry) had to be sold at this market. In the adjoining buildings several merchant's shops were quickly established and at the corner of Østergade from 1656 the gentry used to drop into the fashionable inn known as "Store Lækkerbidsken" ("Large Titbits").
After Copenhagen's second Great Fire of 1795, when the Højbro Plads (see entry) was laid just to the south, a crossing was built linking it to Amagertorv. The sales stands disappeared after 1868 when the market was resited at Christianshavn (see entry).

Storkespringvandet

After the square lost its role as a market-place, the city's messengers and errand boys used to gather at the water pump at Amagertorv. The old pump was replaced in 1894 by the Storkespringvandet (stork fountain), which even today is one of the most popular meeting places of the young people of Copenhagen.

* Royal Copenhagen
* Bing & Grøndahl
* Georg Jensen

The red-brick building (no. 6), which was built in 1616 in the Dutch Renaissance style for the city councillor, later mayor, Mathias Hansen, has rich sandstone decorations. Today it houses exhibitions of goods produced by Royal Copenhagen (royal porcelain manufacturers), the Holmegaard glass works and the porcelain manufacturers Bing & Grøndahl (see Facts and Figures, Danish Design).
In the house next door (no. 4) there are salesrooms belonging to the firm of silversmiths Georg Jensen.

* W. Ø. Larsens Pipe Museum

The beautiful patrician house no. 9 was built between 1789 and 1800 for the cloth merchant J. A. Bechmann. Its façade was remodelled between 1830 and 1870. Anyone interested in smoking utensils and old pipes should pay a visit to the Pipe Museum founded in 1864 by W. Ø. Larsen (open: Mon.–Fri. 9.30am–5pm, Sat. 9.30am–1pm), which includes hand-carved meerschaum pipes, ornate tobacco tins and clay and water pipes among its treasures. Opposite, in Ole Larsen's tobacco shop, the enthusiast can choose his favourite mixture from among the many fragrant "Selected Blends" of the court purveyors of tobacco.

In Ole Larsen's pipe shop

Changing of the Guard outside Amalienborg Palace

*Illums Bolighus

In the building next door (no. 10) the visitor will find in Illums Bolighus Danish furniture of all kinds (see Facts and Figures, Danish Design).

Other buildings worth seeing

A good example of the historicist trend of the 19th c. is "Ole Haslund's House" (no. 14), which was completed in 1867. Typical of this period are the pillars crowned by busts of men, which serve as window-jambs.
No. 17 was built in 1796 for the chocolate manufacturer Joh. Fr. Treschow and had its three upper storeys added at the beginning of the 19th c. The façade was refashioned at the turn of the century.
An endowment by the Brothers Petersen enabled the "Petersen Nunnery" (no. 29) to be built at the end of the 18th c. In 1880 an extra storey was added to the front part of the building, and in 1918 the same was done to the part facing the courtyard.

**Amalienborg Slot (Amalienborg Palace) J6

Location
Amaliengade/
Amalienborg
Slotsplads

Buses
1, 6, 9

Opening times
Interior rooms not open to the public

The Rococo palace of Amalienborg, which since 1794 has been the royal residence, was built between 1749 and 1760 for King Frederik V by the famous Danish court and city architect Niels Eigtved (1701–54).
Two of the palace's four wings are occupied by the royal family, whose presence there is marked by the raising of the Dannebrog flag, whilst the other two are used for state and official functions.
Eigtved was the most celebrated architect of his time, who, besides building Amalienborg Palace and the surrounding district, was also responsible for the Prince's Palace (today the Nationalmuseet, see entry) and the Marble Bridge (see entry) on the south side of Christiansborg Palace (see entry) and thereby created an area of the city which was in a unified Rococo style. Possibly this vision of the city's architecture originated with King Frederik V, who donated land to the rich noble families of Brockdorff, Levetzau, Løvenskjold and Moltke and offered them 40 years of tax exemption to enable them to carry through their building plans. Linked to these gifts was his condition that the four mansions to be built in the middle of the new district of Frederiksstad must be based on plans by Eigtved.
Just a few decades later the palaces were taken into royal ownership after the destruction of Christiansborg Palace in the fire of 1794. In the same year

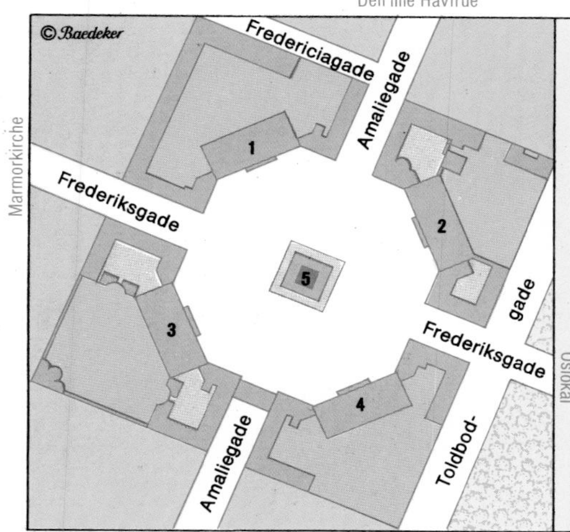

Amalienborg
Royal Palace since 1794

1 Levetzau Palace (Christian VIII, Christian X)

2 Brockdorff Palace (Frederik VIII, Frederik IX)

3 Moltke Palace (Christian VII)

4 Schack Palace (originally Løvenskjold Palace) (Frederik VI, Christian IX, Margrethe II)
5 Equestrian statue of King Frederik V (1771)

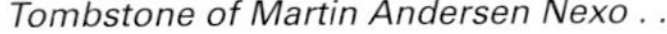

Tombstone of Martin Andersen Nexo . . . *. . . and that of Søren Kirkegaard*

Grave of Hans Christian Andersen

the colonnade designed by C. F. Harsdorff was erected – a wooden construction with Ionic columns which established a link across the Amaliengade between the two palaces.

Statue of Frederik V on horseback

Dominating the centre of Amalienborg Palace is the 12m/39ft statue of Frederik V on horseback (J. F. Saly, 1711), a present from the East India Company in acknowledgement of the Danish crown's support for their colonial conquests.

Changing of the guard

The soldiers on guard at Amalienborg Palace, who stand in front of their guard-huts in their bearskin helmets and blue, white and red uniforms, are one of Copenhagen's most photogenic attractions.
Every day, when Queen Margarethe II is in residence in Copenhagen, the changing of the guard takes place punctually at noon with music and standards. If the Queen Mother Ingrid is alone at Amalienborg, the changing of the guard takes place with music but no standards. The new soldiers march from their barracks in Kongens Have (see Rosenborg Palace) just before 11.30am. The route they take leads along the Gothersgade as far as Norrevoldgade, then on down the Frederiksborgade, the Købmagergade (see entry) and the Østergade, then over the Kongens Nytorv (see entry) and on along the Bredgade and Frederiksgade to the palace.

Arkitekturcentret Gammel Dok

See Christianshavn

*Assistens Kirkegård (Cemetery) F6

Location
Nørrebrogade/
Kapelvej

Buses
3, 5, 7, 16, 18

Copenhagen's largest and probably most interesting cemetery was laid out by royal command in 1757 following the plague epidemic of 1711. It was initially a makeshift additional cemetery, as its name indicates (Assistens Kirkegård = relief churchyard). The original brick wall with its niches, which surrounds part of the cemetery, was built by Philip de Lange, but the site was subsequently enlarged on a number of occasions. Today the Assistens Kirkegård serves at the same time as a park where people are always to be found on the grass between the graves, relaxing with a picnic or just enjoying the sun.
The cemetery and park are open from sunrise to sunset.

Graves

Many famous people are laid to rest in the cemetery; there is a board at the Nørrebrogade entrance listing their names and where they are buried.
Amongst the most famous graves is that of the poet and fairy-storyteller, Hans Christian Andersen (see Famous People), which is to be found in Section P of the cemetery. In Section B the philosopher Søren Kierkegaard (see Famous People) is buried, while in Section D there is the mausoleum of Peter von Scholten, Governor General of the former West Indian islands of St Croix, St John and St Thomas, who in 1848 on his own initiative abolished slavery on the islands following an uprising among the slaves there. Near the entrance can also be found the grave of the Danish workers' poet, Martin Andersen (see Famous People). Also worthy of special mention are the graves of the physicist and Nobel prizewinner Niels Bohr (see Famous People) and the Danish writer Poul Martin Møller (1794–1838), whose posthumous masterpiece "En dansk students eventyr" (1843), was the first fantasy novel to be written in Denmark.

*Axeltorv (Axel Market; pedestrian zone) H7

The Axeltorv, newly designed by Mogens Breyen at the end of the 1980s, and boasting a number of statues by Mogens Møller, is an example of the

Axeltorv, a pedestrian precinct

Location
Between Hammerichsgade and Vesterbrogade

S-bane
Vesterport

latest city architecture in Copenhagen. The sky is reflected in the water of the large granite pool above a Venetian mosaic symbolising the sun. The nine sculptures close by are abstract interpretations of the planets of the solar system.

At the end of the square the eye is caught by the colourful complex of the great Palad cinema-temple (no. 9; see Practical Information, Cinemas).

Scala

The new Scala shopping and entertainment centre (no. 2), alongside a row of shops and boutiques, also houses cinemas, discothèques and a fitness centre, as well as cafés and restaurants, where visitors can take a break while shopping.

*Bakken (Amusement park)

Location
Dyrehavsbakken

S-bane
Klampenborg, then on foot (10mins) or by carriage

Buses
160, 178, 188

Founded in 1583, the Dyrehavsbakken, called Bakken for short, is the oldest amusement park in the world. It lies on the edge of the Dyrehaven (see entry) in Klampenborg Park and stretches as far as the Øresund. At the end of the 16th c. visitors used to spend time at the nearby spring "Kirsten Piils Kilde", in order to find a cure for their ills. They were followed by traders and travelling entertainers who set up their stands here and on the adjoining hill; from 1746 this became a permanent fixture.

The Bakken is the popular answer to the Tivoli (see entry), with over 100 amusement rides and stalls as well as restaurants. These include the Kasperl Theatre and the Pierrot, merry-go-rounds and a giant roller-coaster, shooting-ranges, tombolas, music-halls, bars and restaurants with dancing. In the high season a children's day is held every Wednesday, when all the amusements are available at half price (open: Apr.–Aug.: daily 2pm–midnight).

Bakkan amusement park

Blixen Museet

See Karen Blixen Museet

*Bing & Grøndahl Museet (Museum) E7

This small museum, belonging to the famous porcelain manufacturers Bing & Grøndahl (see Facts and Figures, Danish Design), which used to be situated in the Vesterbrogade, is now sited directly next to the porcelain factory.
The finest examples of Copenhagen porcelain are on display, as well as a complete collection of Christmas plates (the first of the famous Christmas plates appeared in 1895) and other series (conducted tours: Mon.–Fri. 9, 10, 11am, 2pm).

Location
Smallegade 45

Buses
1, 14

Bolten's

See Kongens Nytorv

Botanisk Have (Botanical Garden) H6

The Botanical Garden between Sølvgade and Gothersgade was laid out between 1871 and 1874 according to plans by the landscape gardener H. A. Flindt. The lake was originally part of the city's defensive moat.
As well as the greenhouses with their tropical and subtropical plants (open: daily 10am–3pm), the palm house (open: daily 10am–3pm) and the cactus

Location
Gothersgade 128

S-bane
Nørreport

Buses
5, 7, 14, 16, 24, 40, 43, 84, 384

Opening times
Sept. 29th.– Mar. 28th: 8.30am–4pm; Mar. 29th– Sept. 26th: 8.30am–6pm

house (open: Sat., Sun. 1–3pm) are well worth seeing. The recently restored hothouses, made of glass, cast-iron and wood, which were probably designed by J. C. Jacobsen and Tyge Rothe, have as their model, among others, the palm house at Kew Gardens in London, designed by the English landscape gardener Joseph Paxton.

In one part of the garden it is possible to admire all the wild plants of Denmark in artificially created habitats of marsh, heath and dune. In addition there is an Alpine garden with mountain plants from all over the world.

Brøste's Samling

See Christianshavn

Burmeister and Wain Museet

See Christianshavn, B & W Museet

Københavns Bymuseum & Søren Kierkegaard Samlingen G7

(City Museum)

Location
Vesterbrogade 59

The city museum, which in all comprises 27 rooms, most of them fairly small, offers an overall view of the history of Copenhagen. Since 1956 it has been housed in the building of the Royal Copenhagen Shooting Society (built in 1787). From 1901, when it was opened, until that date it was located

The City Museum, a gouache by I. M. Wagner (1807)

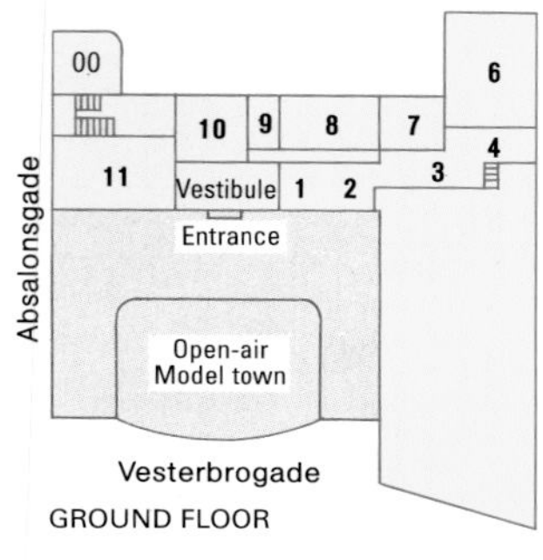

Municipal Museum

Københavns Bymuseum and Søren Kierkegaard Samlingen

Opening Times

1. 10. – 30. 4.: Di. – So. 13.00 – 16.00
1. 5. – 30. 9.: Di. – So. 10.00 – 16.00

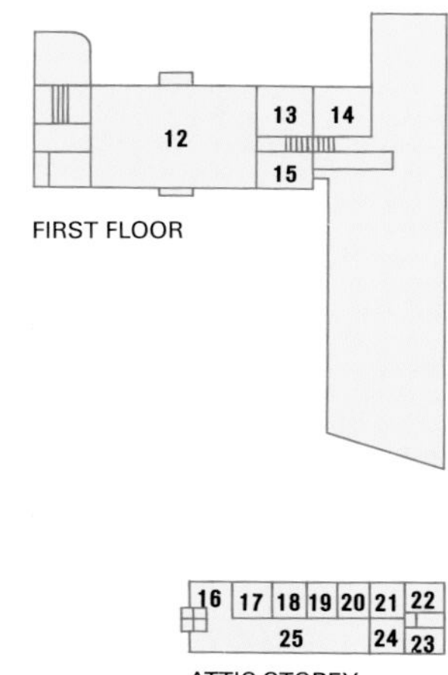

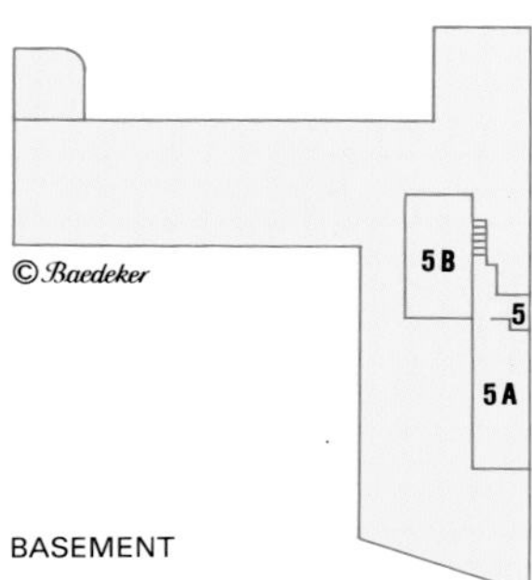

1–4 Street environment, parts of buildings, bicycles, etc.
5A–5 Middle Ages to the Great Fire of Copenhagen 1728
5B Excavations 1400–1800
6 Views of the town (18th c.)
7 Representation of the Battle of the Roadsteads (1801) and the Siege of Copenhagen in 1807
8–9 Views of the town centre (19th c.)
10 Views of the fortifications
11 View of the area outside the fortifications (19th c.)
12 Hall (for exhibitions, etc.)
13 Town Council, Copenhagen silverware
14 Søren Kirkegaard Collection
15 Furniture by the architect Th. Bindesbøll
16–21 Special exhibitions
22 Views of Copenhagen around 1900
23 Public paths, model of the Stjernen Brewery
24 Tramways
25 Fire-fighting

in the City Hall. While the individual stages in Copenhagen's history since the time of Bishop Absalon (see Famous People) are all set out, understandably it is for the last few centuries that the exhibits and documentary evidence are particularly plentiful. Thus there are rooms showing a 17th c. street during the reign of Christian IV (see Famous People), as well as the architectural changes in the street over the course of the centuries. Other themes include the city fires and subsequent rebuilding, the development of the harbour, market life, shops and public life. Anyone wanting to have a better understanding of how Copenhagen evolved will find an excellent visual account here.

Søren Kierkegaard Samlingen

Room 14 contains the Søren Kierkegaard Collection, opened in 1960, which gives an introduction to the life and works of the philosopher Søren Kierkegaard (see Famous People). On display are some pieces of furniture and

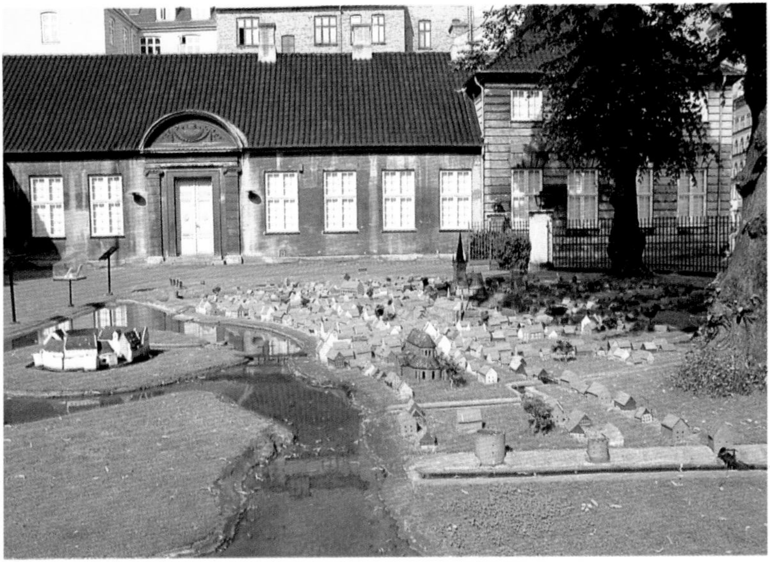

A model of Copenhagen, in the open air

The Former Exchange, one of the symbols of the city

personal mementoes, including a portrait of his parents and a picture of his friend, Regine Olsen.

Museum street

In 1980 the first 100m/325ft of the neighbouring Absalonsgade were successfully opened as a museum street, fitted out with signs, water hydrants, street lamps, letter-boxes, telephone booths and cobble-stones dating from 1850 to 1940.

City model

In front of the museum in the summer months visitors can admire a model of Copenhagen in Reformation times.

*Børsen (Old Stock Exchange) H7

Location
Børsgade

Buses
1, 2, 5, 6, 8, 9, 10, 28, 29, 31, 37, 43

On the palace island of Slotsholmen opposite Christiansborg Palace (see entry) lies the old Stock Exchange. It is one of the most beautiful buildings in Copenhagen and one of its most characteristic.

This long low Renaissance structure was built for King Christian IV (see Famous People) between 1619 and 1640 by the Dutch brothers Lorenz and Hans Steenwinckel the Younger. At the wish of the king the Exchange was given decorative gables which face at right angles on to the canal, and the roof was crowned with a 54m/177ft high tower. Its spire, completed in 1625, consists of four stylised intertwined dragon's tails, which were based on a design by the firework-maker Ludvig Heidritter. The copper roof with its patina of green is the building's other characteristic feature.

Originally there was a trading hall on the ground floor, while the upper storey – approached by a ramp on the west side and a staircase on the east – was reserved for businesses and shops. Two statues by J. C. Petzhold, "Mercury" and "Neptune", commissioned by the merchant A. Bjørn, were added to the ramp during restoration work in 1745 by the court architect Nicolai Eigtved. In the middle of the 19th c. the Exchange was taken over by the union of wholesale merchants, who had to undertake to preserve the architectural style of the building and not to alter anything without the consent of the state.
Today the exchange shops are no longer here but have been displaced to Fonnesbech House on Nikolaj Plads (no. 8; see entry). The old exchange building now belongs to and is the seat of the Chamber of Commerce of Copenhagen. As a general rule the building is not open to the public.

The mosaic work in the entrance hall on the ground floor illustrates the historical development of the Exchange. The great exchange room is spacious with pillars, wooden panelling, gilded leather-clad walls and an elaborate coffered ceiling. At the end of the room stands the bronze figure of Christian IV, the work of the sculptor Bertel Thorvaldsen (see Famous People).

Caritas Springvandet (Caritas Fountain)

Location
Gammeltorv

Bus
5

Erected in 1608 on the Gammeltorv and subsequently restored several times, the Caritas Fountain must be considered one of the most beautiful works of art of the Renaissance period. The group of figures round the copper bowl of the fountain, a pregnant woman with two children, symbolise brotherly love (Caritas = charity). At her feet are sprawled three dolphins with gargoyles. The bronze figures were made by Peter Hoffman after a wooden model by Statius Otto.

Carl Claudius' Samling

See Musikhistorisk Museum og Carl Claudius' Samling

*Carlsberg Brewery

E/F8

Location
Ny Carlsbergvey 140

Buses
6, 18

Conducted tours
Mon.–Fri.
11am, 2pm

The Carlsberg Brewery, one of the largest in the world, is also rich in tradition. Visitors to Copenhagen are not only offered a conducted tour of the brewery, but are also allowed to sample the beer in the visiting rooms of the Carlsberg Museum, which was founded in 1882.

In November 1847 J. C. Jacobsen (1811–87) produced the first Bavarian beer to be brewed in Denmark in his newly-built brewery in Valby, outside the walls of Copenhagen. The brewery was named Carlsberg by him after his son Carl, who studied brewing both in Denmark and abroad and, by extending the production capacity of the brewery in 1871, started the first Ny-Carlsberg Brewery, although he was to open his own brewery with the same name ten years later. For economic reasons the two factories were amalgamated in 1906. Because of increasing international competition Carlsberg finally merged with the Tuborg Brewery (see entry) in 1970, which resulted in the "De forenede Bryggerier A/S", now Carlsberg A/S. The various types of beer produced (see Practical Information, Food and Drink, Beer) are today exported to more than 130 countries.

The production plant of the first brewery, the "Gamle Carlsberg", was restored in 1982 and today can be visited by arrangement.

Support for the arts

The Carlsberg Brewery has for many years used a proportion of its profits to support Danish cultural life and its delivery lorries therefore boast the slogan: "Skål for Kunsten" ("a toast to the arts").

The founder of the brewery, J. C. Jacobsen, had already established a foundation for research in 1876, the aims of which also included the main-

Carlesberg Brewery: the Elephant Gate . . .

. . . and the workers' settlement

tenance of the National Historical Museum in Frederiksborg Slot (see entry). His son Carl shared his interest in the arts and, among other things, authorised the building of the spire of the Nikolaj Church (see Nikolaj Plads) and the campanile of the Jesus Church. In addition he extended the scope of the foundation and set up the Ny Carlsberg Glyptotek (see entry) with its unique collection of classical and modern art. Today the Ny Carlsberg Foundation also contributes to the upkeep of Kronborg Slot (see entry) and the Louisiana arts museum (see entry).
The company's refreshing originality is even reflected in the entrance to the brewery, which is adorned on either side by elephants fashioned out of stone.

Charlottenborg Slot

See Kongens Nytorv

Christiania J7

Location
Christianshavn district

Bus
8

The "free state" of Christiania, which was legalised in 1991, lies on the island of Amager (see entry) and belongs to the district of Christianshavn (see entry). As it was originally intended to offer protection to the royal fleet from Christianshavn, military installations were initially built on the site. In 1971 the garrison and barrack area, which amounted to 34ha/840 acres, was cleared in order to make way for dwellings and parkland. Instead of this the area was occupied by drop-outs, hippies and seekers of an alternative life-style. On November 13th 1971 they founded an independent community, the "Free State of Christiania", which was declared illegal. All attempts by the Danish authorities to get rid of them failed. In the end the place was recognised as a "social experiment", although it continued to attract controversy. Massive external pressures led to the drop-out society being legalised on its twentieth anniversary. In 1991 representatives of the grass-roots democratic full assembly of Christiania signed a long-debated agreement, in which for the first time the inhabitants of the free state undertook to meet the costs of rent and other additional services and to maintain around 150 buildings deemed worthy of preservation as well as the extensive green areas. In return the inhabitants were guaranteed usufruct by the Copenhagen authorities.
Critics still regard Christiania as a trouble-spot and a "hotbed of crime" (in the words of the Danish Justice Minister), partly because of the high poverty levels in the free state (over 50% of the adults live on social security, almost 20% are drawing a pension early or are in receipt of other benefits) and also because of the pervasive consumption of drugs such as hashish and marijuana. Supporters, however, see in the drop-outs' republic an unprecedented attempt to move towards a new type of society and point to the positive successes: since 1979, through the voluntarily set up "Junk Blockade", the consumption of hard drugs virtually no longer exists; in order to safeguard the environment, compost production, sorting of rubbish and recycling have all been introduced to car-free Christiania as part of an alternative energy strategy, and experiments have been made with solar and wind energy. In addition there is a communal child-minding service provided in the nursery and youth-club, which, together with other social services, has been financed by takings in the bars and restaurants.

**Christiansborg Slot (Christiansborg Palace) H7

Location
Christiansborg Slotplads

Christiansborg Palace, situated on the island of Slotsholmen, has been the seat of the Danish parliament since 1918 (Folketing; see Facts and Figures, Danish Parliament). In addition the Foreign Ministry and the High Court of

Chistiana, where the "alternative life style" reigns

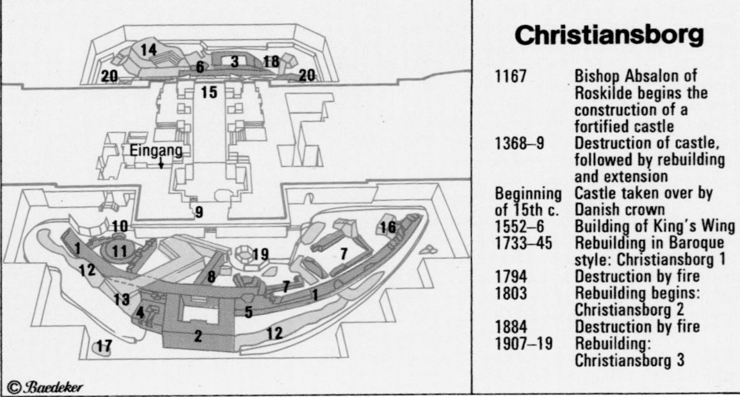

Christiansborg

1167	Bishop Absalon of Roskilde begins the construction of a fortified castle
1368–9	Destruction of castle, followed by rebuilding and extension
Beginning of 15th c.	Castle taken over by Danish crown
1552–6	Building of King's Wing
1733–45	Rebuilding in Baroque style: Christiansborg 1
1794	Destruction by fire
1803	Rebuilding begins: Christiansborg 2
1884	Destruction by fire
1907–19	Rebuilding: Christiansborg 3

Excavations

Bishop's castle (12th–14th c.)

1 Outer wall
2 West tower
3 East tower (?)
4 Privy Chamber
5 Drain from courtyard
6 House wall (ruined)
7 Small buildings
8 Two-roomed house
9 Wooden well
10 Limestone well
11 Oven

Medieval castle (14th–18th c.)

12 Outer wall
13 South gable of Knights' Hall wing
14 Foundations of Blue Tower
15 Foundation of King's Wing
16 Foundations of church wing
17 Remains of 16th c. foundations
18 Base of chimney
19 Well
20 Water supply pipe of first castle

Christianborg Palace

The Royal Stables and outbuildings

Buses
1, 2, 5, 6, 8, 9, 10, 28, 29, 31, 37, 41, 43

Justice are housed here. The royal audience rooms are also located in the castle and, like the parliament itself, can only be visited on a conducted tour.

When leaving Slotsholmen Island in the direction of the Nationalmuseet (see entry) the visitor crosses the Frederiksholms Canal by the Marble Bridge (see entry) designed by Nicolai Eigtved.

Opening times
old castle ruins

Oct.–Apr.: Tues.–Fri., Sun. 9.30am–3.30pm;
May–Sept.: daily 9.30am–3.30pm.

Conducted tours
through parliament and the palace

Danish Parliament (Folketing): Sept.–May Sun. on the hour 10am–4pm; June–Aug.: Mon.–Fri. and Sun. 20 daily from 10am–4pm.
Royal reception rooms (Conducted tours in English): Oct.–Apr.: Tues., Thur. and Sun. 11am, 1pm; May–Sept. Tues.–Sun. 11am, 1pm, 3pm.

The palace dominates the square where in the spring of 1167 Bishop Absalon (see Famous People) began the building of a fortress and founded Copenhagen. The fortifications were destroyed in 1259 by the Wends and in 1368–69 by the Lübeckers, only to be later extensively rebuilt. When the present palace was built, these ruins were left uncovered and have for some years now have been open to visitors.
The late medieval castle, which under Eric of Pomerania passed to the crown, was altered and extended several times during the 15th, 16th and 17th c. Thus the Knights' Hall was extended on the occasion of the marriage of Christoph III of Bavaria to Queen Dorothea of Brandenburg in 1445, and then in the middle of the 16th c., on the site of the dried-up moat, Christian III added a wing for the king and his bodyguards, which was to contain the second largest room in the whole castle.
The old castle buildings no longer proved adequate for the demands of Baroque grandeur in the 18th c.: after Frederik IV had as late as 1720 ordered all the wings of the castle to be brought to the same height by having additional storeys superimposed, Christian IV (see Famous People) in April 1733 laid the inaugural stone in the building of a magnificent three-storey palace. In November 1740 the royal family moved in, although it was not possible to complete the magnificent Knights' Hall until 1766. The entire kings's apartments were decorated throughout with French mirror glass and the other 348 rooms received the most elaborate fittings. For the Knights' Hall Nicolai Abilgaard contributed 22 paintings on the subject of the history of the Danish monarchy. The palace had four wings and was in the Viennese Baroque style. It was still unfinished when it burnt down in 1794. Only the buildings belonging to the riding arena survived.
In the early years of the 19th c. the second, more austerely conceived, version of the palace was built under Frederik VI to designs by the neo-classical master C. F. Hansen, with its Knights' Hall decorated by Corinthian columns and an ornate coffered ceiling. In 1849 the new parliament moved into the building, which was seldom used as a royal residence. This building also fell victim to a fire in October 1884. Those parts that remain include the palace church, built by C. F. Hansen and consecrated in 1846, the dome of which was embellished with figures of angels and statues of apostles by Bertel Thorvaldsen (see Famous People).
The design for the "third", Christianborg Palace, built between 1907 and 1928, was the work of Thorvald Jørgensen. He had the difficult task of incorporating the remaining parts of the old building into a new setting, something in which he was only partially successful. The great four-winged palace is distinguished today by its 90m/295ft high tower and the façade, imposingly clad in Bornholm granite and stone, which was provided by the Danish municipalities. The throne room and the 40m/131ft long Knights' Hall are especially worth visiting.

Statue of Frederik VII on horseback

On the square in front of the palace can be seen a statue of Frederik VII on horseback, which was created by one of Thorvaldsen's pupils, H. V. Bissen and was erected to commemorate the passing of the first Basic Law in 1849.

Folketing

In the lobby of the Folketing it is worth noticing the shrine in which the charter of the constitution is kept. From one of the central boxes in the Folketing Hall the visitor has a good view of the chamber, the dimensions of which correspond to those of the "mother of parliaments", the British House of Commons. In contrast, however, to the latter, where the members sit on benches along the length of the room, the Danish representatives are grouped in a horse-shoe shape around the central table and the seat of the parliamentary chairman, and whereas the British lower house does not have enough seats for its 650 members, the 179 representatives of the Folketing each have their own allotted seat with a desk. Following the pattern of the National Assembly which met during the French Revolution, the right-wingers are placed on the right of the chairman and the left-wingers on the left. Even though new parties and internal party regroupings have brought about changes in the seating plan, it is still the case that – looking from the chairman's position – the Conservative People's Party sits to the right of the Venstre liberal party, which in turn sits to the right of the liberal left Venstre Radical Party, itself positioned to the right of the Social Democrats. Only the Socialist People's Party sits somewhat illogically between the Liberal Left and the Social Democrats, whilst the smaller parties are usually relegated to the rear seats.
The seating of representatives is also determined by length of parliamentary service, with party leaders and political spokesmen sitting in the first row. The government is to the left of the parliamentary chairman. The front row is reserved for the Prime Minister, Foreign Minister, Finance and Justice Ministers, with the other ministers behind, their seating order being decided by length of service.
The triple podium (to the left of the speaker's desk) was carved by Anny Berntsen-Bure, daughter of the then Prime Minister Klaus Berntsen, out of a thousand-year-old trunk of oak which had served as the central structure of a mill on the island of Møn. A tapestry by Berit Hjeholt, which bears the title "Like a fleet yearning to set sail", hangs over the podium.

Kongelige Stalde og Kareter, Teatermuseet

An archway leads from the Folketingsgården to the equestrian arena and the Royal Stables (see Practical Information, Museums). Old carriages, harness and livery dating from 1778 onwards can be seen. Next door is the Teatermuseet (see entry).

*Christianshavn (City district) H-K6/7

Location
Amager Island

Buses
2, 8, 9, 31, 37

The district of Copenhagen known as Christianshavn is situated opposite Slotsholmen, on the island of Amager (see entry). King Christian IV (see Famous People), who reigned from 1588 to 1648, ordered the building of a new town here which initially did not form part of Copenhagen at all. With its parallel streets lying at right angles to its central canal, it calls to mind Amsterdam. On the side facing away from the sea the town is enclosed by thick walls.
Christianshavn is a tourist attraction in itself. It is reached by the Langebro and Knippelsbro bridges. With the building of this "city in miniature", which took place from 1618 onwards following the Dutch model of streets and canals laid at right angles to one another, King Christian IV gave to the city of Copenhagen its own personal stamp. Up until 1674 Christianshavn remained independent, but then for financial reasons it had to accept annexation to Copenhagen. That there are a striking number of old houses still preserved here is due to the fact that Christianshavn was to a large extent spared the terrible fires that Copenhagen suffered. Up to now it has been possible – despite the unavoidable renovation measures of the last few decades – to preserve in its essentials the historic fabric of buildings such as the many patrician houses and lovingly fashioned courtyards in the Strandgade, where the Danish sailor Peder Tordenskjold (1691–1720) and the educationalist and founder of adult education centres, Nicolai Frederik Severin Grundtvig (see Famous People) were born, the buildings along the

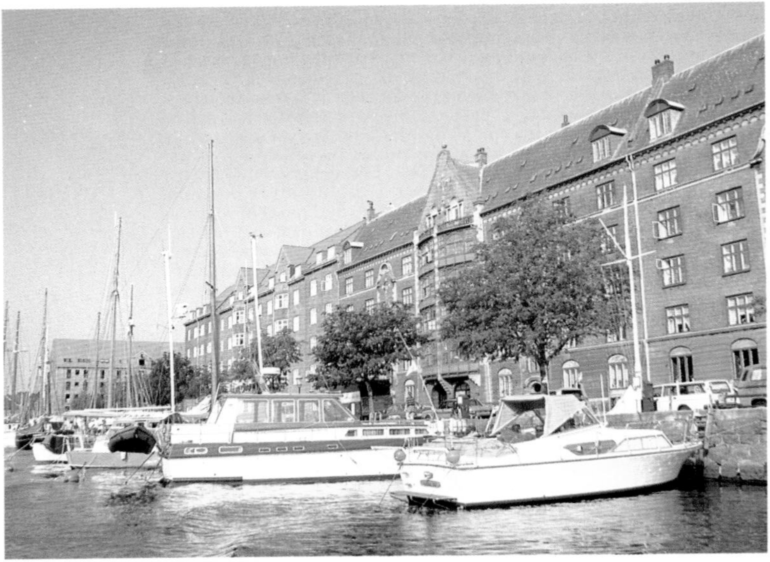

Christianshavn Canal

Gammel Dok architectural centre

Christianshavn Canal, which is included in harbour and canal boat tours, the half-timbered buildings in the Amagergade, the old ramparts, the Vor Frelser Kirke (Church of the Redeemer; see entry) and the Rococo style Christians Kirke (see entry).
Anyone coming over the Knippelsbro Bridge to Christianshavn will see first of all the unattractive building of the Foreign Ministry on the left and a bank complex on the right which was formerly the administrative offices of the shipyard Burmeister & Wain. A few minutes further on, the Christianshavn Torv (market) in the centre of the town is reached, from where a tour on foot can be made of the surrounding streets.

B & W Museet (Burmeister & Wain Museum)

In an old warehouse on the Strandgade (no. 4) Copenhagen's largest company, the shipyard Burmeister & Wain, has set up a museum in which models of ships and diesel engines are displayed (open: Mon.–Fri. and first Sun. in the month 10am–1pm).
The Burmeister & Wain shipyards are situated further north on Refshaleøen.

Arkitekturcentret Gammel Dok

The former storage house no. 27 in the Strandgade is now the home of the Gammel Dok Architecture Centre. Architectural and design exhibitions are regularly held (open: Tues., Thur.–Sun. 10am–5pm, Wed. 10am–10pm). From the windows of the café in the cultural centre the visitor can watch the ships going past in the Inderhavnen.

Christians Kirke

See entry

Brøste's Samling

Brøste's Samling in Overgaden oven Vandet (no. 10) is a museum catering for visitors to Copenhagen who are especially interested in the district of Christianshavn. It shows the genesis and development of the district with the aid of documents, paintings and objets d'art (open: May–Sept.: daily 10am–4pm; Oct.–Apr.: Mon.–Fri., Sun. 10am–4pm).

Orlogsmuseet Royal Naval Museum

Visitors who are interested in historic model ships, nautical instruments or naval uniforms (17th c. to the present-day) should pay a visit to the Royal Naval Museum (Orlogsmuseet, Over gaden Oven Vandet 58; open Tues.–Sun. noon–4pm).

Det danske Filmmuseum

The Danish Film Museum, Søndervoldstræde no. 4, offers in the form of pictures, documentation and equipment, an account of the history of the cinema from its precursors (peepshows) through to the present day, as well as an extensive library (open: June–Aug.: Mon., Tues., Thur., Fri. noon–4pm; Sept.–May: Tues. noon–9pm). In addition there are regular showings of historically important films.

Vor Frelser Kirke

See entry

Christiania

See entry

Christians Kirke (Church) 17

Location
Strandgade

Buses
2, 8, 9, 31, 37

On the west side of the Christianshavn Canal in Christianshavn stands the Christianskirke. This Rococo church, built by Nikolai Eigtved between 1755 and 1759, was the place of worship of the German Lutheran community until 1886. With the approval of King Frederik V the building costs were financed by a lottery, which earned the church the nickname of the "lottery church". Officially the church was initially known as Frederiks Tyske Kirke (Frederick's German Church), whilst it acquired its present-day name in 1901. Its tower, crowned by a sphere with a flag, dates from 1769; the stonework on the tower was the work of C. F. Stanley.
Of interest inside the church are the three-storey gallery, the font made of Norwegian marble, a baptism bowl with a German inscription dating from

1759, as well as the crypt with its 48 burial chapels, which were erected in the 18th and 19th c. (open: Mar.–Oct.: 8am–6pm; Nov.–Feb.: 8am–5pm).

Cirkusbygningen (Circus buildings) G7

Location
Jernbanegade 8

S-bane
Vesterport

The first cylinder-shaped circus and varieties building was built by the architect H. V. Brinkopff in 1885 and opened in April 1886. One of the earliest attractions was the "Black Opera" of the 1890s, a musical show which relied solely on coloured performers.
In March 1914 the circus arena fell victim to a fire, with only the stone circular wall remaining intact. The rebuilding of the circus was entrusted to the firm of Christiani & Nielsen under the direction of the architect Holger Jacobsen, while the frieze on the exterior wall, showing various scenes of classical horse-races, was the work of U. A. F. Hammeleff. The Schumann Circus then moved into the building for a number of years, until it was taken over by the permanent Benneweis Circus, a family concern founded in 1887, which has on many occasions received the accolade of being called the best circus in Europe. After extensive restoration work, which restored to the building its original appearance, the circus was able to become fully operational in the spring of 1984.
Performances take place every evening from May to October at 8pm, and there are also additional afternoon performances. Tickets can be obtained at the box office which is open between noon and 8pm (Tel. 33 15 01 11).

Citadellet Frederikshavn

See Castle

City Museum

See Københavns Bymuseum & Søren Kierkegaard Samlingen

Collegium Regium

See Regensen

Det danske Filmmuseum

See Christianshavn

C. L. Davids Samling (Museum of art) H6

Location
Kronprinsesse-
gade 30

Buses
7, 10, 43

Opening times
Tues.-Sun. 1–4pm

The former private art collection of C. L. David is housed in an old patrician house built in 1807 by J. H. Rawert. Both the works of art and the building, rather plain in appearance from the outside, were bequeathed to the Danish state in 1945 by the lawyer C. L. David.
The museum has on show outstanding examples of Islamic art from Persia and the surrounding countries dating from the 8th to the 16th c. (brocades, carpets, glassware, ceramics, manuscripts, miniatures and silver tableware). The collection also includes pieces of English furniture, a French Rococo sopraporte by François Boucher, furniture from the workshop of

Crown Prince Frederik (1787 . . . *. . . and an Indian miniature drawing (16th c.)*

David Roentgen, paintings, in particular Danish painters of the 19th c., Danish silver from 17th and 18th c., and a collection of porcelain from the early period of Royal Danish factory (see Facts and Figures, Danish Design).

Dragor

See Amager

Dukketeatermuseet, Priors Papirteater (Puppet Theatre Museum) H6

The Dukketeatermuseet, which is situated in a pedestrian zone on the Købmagergade (see entry) near the Rundetårn (see entry), shows the art of puppet theatre from various periods and countries. Companies from Denmark, Germany, England and France cover a diverse repertoire, ranging from fairy tales to Shakespeare. Both large and small-scale puppet theatres can also be bought here – there is no obligation to buy, although the temptation to do so can be considerable (open: May–Mar.: Mon., Wed.–Fri. 12.30–5pm).

Location
Købmagergade 52

S-bane
Nørreport

Buses
5, 7, 14, 16, 24, 43, 84

*Dyrehaven (Deer park)

Dyrehaven Nature Park, which adjoins the highly popular amusement park of Bakken (see entry), is where herds of several hundred deer and sika live in a wooded area of about 10sq.km/4sq.miles (hunting rights exclusively belong to the Queen).
The "Hermitage", a Rococo hunting lodge displaying rich ornamental and sculptured decoration, was built by Laurids de Thura for King Christian V in

Location
Klampenborg (10km/6 miles to the north of the city centre)

S-bane
Klampenborg

Opening times
All day

1734–36. It is only roused from its "Sleeping Beauty" slumber by the presence of the Queen.
At the S-bane station at Klampenborg a horse-drawn carriage can be hired in order to cross the park – just as the Danish kings used to.
Theodor Fontane, the German writer and theatre critic, describes this enchanted castle in the middle of the game park in his novel of 1891, "Unwiederbringlich" ("Gone for ever"):
"The path which they had to take lay along the edge of the park near the village, for the most part under tall-trunked plane trees, whose dangling branches covered in yellow foliage obscured their view with the result that it was only on emerging from this avenue of trees that they became aware of the "Hermitage" standing in the middle of its bright woodland glade . . . Holk and the woman . . . came to an involuntary halt and stared, almost in consternation, at the castle, towering in the distance in the clear autumnal sky, enveloped in the spell cast by its very seclusion. No smoke was rising and only the sun lay over the wide flat expanse of thick, lush grass, whilst up in the steely blue sky hundreds of sea-gulls hovered, and, in a long column, flew over from the sound in the direction of their long-favoured destination which lay further inland, Fura Water . . . Already, in the background, the whole wide silvan canvas was coming alive, and likewise, just as hitherto only isolated herds had darted out from those spots nearest to them, now from the furthermost depths of the woodland emerged hundreds of deer, which, not wishing to fail to appear on the parade ground directly in front of them, started up a lively trot, at first in a wild and almost crazed confusion, until, on drawing nearer, they all formed orderly groups and in sections now filed past the Hermitage."

*Eksperimentarium (Museum) H3

Location
Hellerup,
Tuborg Havnevej 7

Bus
6

In 1991 the Danish Science Centre Eksperimentarium was opened in the old bottling hall of the Tuborg Brewery (see entry). The building was renovated at a cost of 125 million krone and in its workshops and experiment rooms the new museum offers research opportunities in natural sciences and new technologies. In 335 experiments – ranging across such topics as magnetism, aerodynamics, polarised light and gyroscopics, sources of energy, anatomy, astronomy and environmental influences – the visitor is enabled in an easily understandable way to draw nearer to the processes and laws of science and technology. The experimentarium is seen as a point of contact between the general public and organisations concerned with trade, industry and research, which, by means of lectures and presentations of new discoveries, are constantly bringing up to date and enlarging the scientific information available within the museum (open: Mon., Wed., Fri. 9am–6pm; Tues., Thur. 9am–9pm; Sat., Sun. 11am–6pm.)

Fiskerkone

See Gammel Strand

Folketing

See Christiansborg Slot

**Fredensborg Slot (Fredensborg Palace)

Location
40km/25 miles north of Copenhagen

This spring and autumn residence of the royal family, situated on the Esrumsø, was built between 1719 and 1722 by J. C. Krieger in the Italian Baroque style. King Frederik IV gave the palace the name "Fredensborg" in memory of the peace which ended the 2nd Nordic War (1700–20). The

Scientific experimental rooms in the Eksperimentarium

Frederiksborg Palace

Railway station
Fredensborg

Buses
336, 384

present appearance of the palace with its classical façade goes back to the architect Caspar Frederik Harsdorff.
If the Queen is present a changing of the guard takes place every day at noon. The palace can only be visited during the month of July (daily 1–5pm).
In the palace park stretching north-westwards to Lake Esrum, Frederik IV had 69 statues of artisans, farmers and fishermen ("Nordmandsdalen") erected. These are perfectly preserved even today. With its avenues and statues, the palace park, which is open all the year round, is considered one of the most beautiful parks in Denmark.

*Frederiksborg Have (Park) E7

Location
Roskildevej/Pile Allé/Allégade, Frederiksborg

Buses
18, 28, 41

Opening times
All day

Close to the Zoologisk Have (Zoo) lies Frederiksborg Palace in the middle of a picturesque park criss-crossed by canals. In former times members of the court used to arrange boating parties here; today Frederiksborg Have is a popular destination for weekend outings with the people of Copenhagen. Inside the park, the crowning attraction of which is an avenue of linden trees 270 years old, there is a succession of bars and cafés where visitors can also consume food they have brought with them.
One of the peculiarities of Copenhagen is that, although it is not far from the city centre, Frederiksborg is an independent municipality with its own council. This affluent suburb of Copenhagen has its own coat of arms and its citizens pay fewer taxes than the people of Copenhagen itself.

Frederiksborg Slot

Frederiksborg Palace dates from 1732–38 during the reign of King Christian VI, although a start had already been made on the building of a summer residence back in 1699. Laurids de Thurah built the symmetrically conceived palace on Valby Hill (today Frederiksborg Hill) in the baroque style of an Italian mansion. The rooms contain massive baroque paintings by the Danes, Coffre and Krock, encircled with stucco decorations by Italian masters such as Carbonetti, Quadri and Rigas, as well as tapestries and wall hangings. In 1770 the palace was renovated and some of the rooms redesigned, the Knights' Hall acquiring the appearance that it still has to this day with wall decorations coming from Hersdorff. Since 1869 the palace has been the home of the military academy, founded in 1713 by Frederik IV (the Hærens Officersskole). Only the palace chapel in the east wing, now restored with all its original features, is open to the public.

Frederiksborg Have

The palace garden was originally laid out in 1711 by Hans Henrik Bruhn. Its design was geometric, following French models, with a large number of fountains, statues and exotic plants. Between 1789 and 1800 it was completely relandscaped by Peter Petersen. He inclined to the English tradition and created a romantically scenic park with tiny islands and meandering rivulets. He left intact the two main avenues lined with linden trees, but replaced the others with small groups of trees.
A tour by rowing-boat is recommended: these are provided by Flemming Svendsen – the only person to have royal permission to do so.

**Frederiksborg Slot (Frederiksborg Palace; National Historical Museum)

Location
Hillerød (35km/22 miles north of Copenhagen)

S-bane
Hillerød;
then bus 701, 703

Since 1884 the National Historical Museum has been housed in the most beautiful Renaissance palace in Denmark, situated on three islands in the middle of the tiny Frederiksborg Lake. The palace was built for King Christian IV (see Famous People) between 1602 and 1620 by the Fleming Hans van Steenwinkel the Elder and his son Hans van Steenwinkel the Younger. It was erected on the site of an older castle belonging to Frederik II and after a fire in 1859 was restored in the old style.

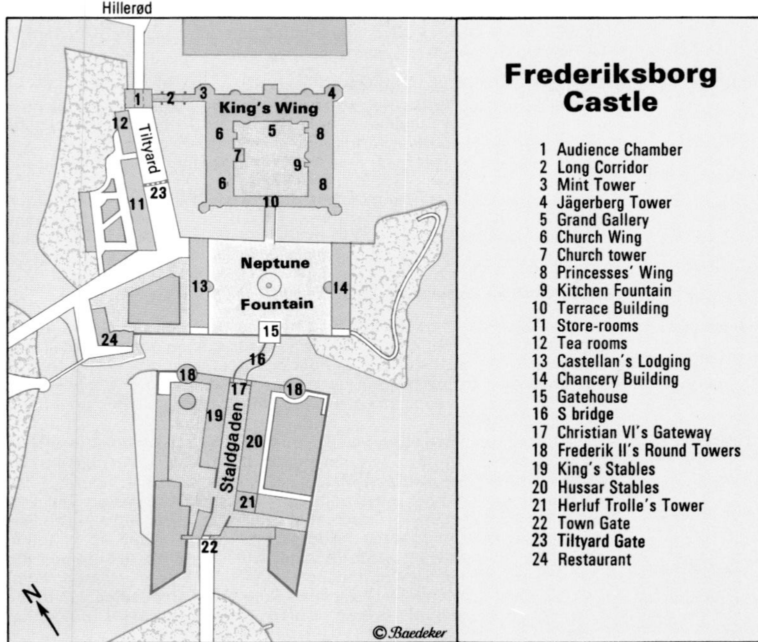

Opening times
Apr., Oct.:
daily 10am–4pm
May–Sept.:
daily 10am–5pm
Nov.–Mar.:
daily 11am–3pm

Until Fredensborg Palace was built, the palace at Frederiksborg provided the Danish monarchs with a fitting venue for their coronation ceremonies. All the absolute monarchs during the period 1671 to 1840 initiated their reign here in the palace church. Moreover the Order of the Elephant was newly established in Frederiksborg Palace, the Dannebrog Order introduced in 1671 and in 1693 the palace church was promoted to the role of chapel of the Order of Knights, a role which it still has to this day. After the Second Nordic War it was at Frederiksborg that the peace treaty between Denmark and Sweden was signed in 1720, ending centuries of enmity between the two countries.

In the 1820s J. C. Krieger began the task of laying a garden to the north of the palace. In 1737–40 the living quarters were modernised. With the completion of Fredensborg Palace, Frederiksborg began to take on the air of a museum in the latter part of the 18th c. and the 19th c. The Knights' Chamber was turned into an art gallery and in 1812 Frederik VI set up a portrait collection. Frederik VII made the palace a royal residence once more and, after a fire in December 1859, had it extensively restored under the direction of Ferdinand Meldahl. After his death the state had no more use for the palace and on April 5th 1878, at the instigation of the brewer J. C. Jakobsen (see Carlsberg Brewery), it was officially designated by the king as a museum of Danish history. By 1884 the Knights' Chamber, king's wing and prince's wing and the church had been restored, and in 1907 the audience room was made part of the museum, while Christian IX and Frederik VIII used the palace rooms on isolated occasions for receptions. The size of the collection of valuable furniture and historically important objets d'art can be ascribed to the fact that at that time there was no other museum for arts and crafts in Denmark and therefore everything of any worth was brought here. Even the existing portrait collection of Frederik VI was incorporated into the museum and added to.

Palace grounds

In its architectural style the whole palace complex shows itself heavily influenced by the Dutch Renaissance. From the southernmost island a continuation of the Staldgaden is linked by an S-shaped bridge to the outermost palace courtyard. This is reached through a massive gatetower which was built by Hans van Steenwinkel the Younger between 1618 and 1623.

Between the chancellery and the lord of the castle's house there has stood since 1888 in the forecourt of the second island a copy of a Neptune fountain made by Adrian de Vries in 1623, which was taken to Sweden in 1658; the original bronze figures were stolen by the Swedes during the siege of Copenhagen in 1660 and today are to be found in the grounds of Drøttningholm Castle outside Stockholm.

Main building

On the third island the actual castle is reached. The oldest part is the king's wing at the north end; of later date is the church wing on the west side as well as the church tower and the princess's wing on the east side. The middle island is connected by a low terraced building. As a link between the mint tower and the audience house the Long Passage, built in grey brick, was added in 1613.

**Palace church

The palace church, which survived the fire of 1859 unscathed, is located in the west wing. The nave, with its Gothic stellar vaults, is supported by golden sandstone buttresses. Marble marquetry, alabaster figures, inlay work in ebony and other rare woods complete the grand design. The altar and pulpit, also of ebony, are decorated with silver reliefs depicting biblical scenes by the Hamburg artist Jakob Mores. The silver font was made in 1920, based on a drawing by Mores dating from the 16th c. At the end of the church the shields of the Order of the Elephant can be seen – among them the shield of the atomic physicist Niels Bohr (see Famous People), at the sides hang the shields of the Knights of the Grand Cross of the Dannebrog Order.

The organ, one of the most valuable in Europe, was made in 1617 by the Brunswick organ builder Esaias Compenius. It was dismantled in 1693 and left until 1868, but is now played again, and is even used for concerts (every Thursday 1.30–2pm). Its thousand pipes and its sound, still as splendid as ever, have made it famous all over the world.

*Knights' Hall

The Riddersalen (Knights' Hall), is a 50m/160ft long room situated over the palace church which was rebuilt after the fire of 1859. In the time of Christian IV it was aptly named the "Ballroom". The king ordered it to be decorated with magnificent ornaments and silver figures and there are marvellous wood carvings on the ceiling. Originally there were also a series of wall tapestries depicting the coronation in 1596, woven by Karel von Mander in Delft: these unfortunately were destroyed in the 1859 fire. The wooden ceiling has been faithfully restored to the original and shows a water mill, nautical instuments, a printing works, a clockmaker's, a foundry for cans and mugs and finally the royal coat of arms with the motto "Regna firmat pietas" ("Fear of God strengthens the earthly realms"). The walls are covered with Gobelin tapestries depicting scenes from the Kalmar War and the coronation procession of 1596. The fireplace is made of black Belgian marble and dates from 1880, while the patterns on the marble floor have also been reconstructed according to the originals. The great chandeliers were designed around 1900 by the architect Carl Brummer. In addition there are portraits of Christian IX and his ruling descendants.

Other rooms

The ceiling painting in the Angels' Hall (no. 37) is a small-scale version of a ceiling in the Doge's Palace in Venice. Its carvings, which are by Franz Schwartz and date from 1883, depict Frederik III surrounded by the four estates of the kingdom and by "War" and "Peace". The great wall painting of 1879–83 deals with the Swedish War and the introduction of absolutism.

Frederiksborg Palace: a magnificent bed

Portraits from time of Frederik VI

Frederiksborg Palace: the Knights' Hall

The furniture in Room 42 provides a highly impressive example of the grandiose displays of splendour which were seen as befitting an absolute monarch. The focal point is a large ebony-carved four-poster bed which was made for the wedding of Count Danneskiold-Samsøe to Christine Catharine von Holstein in 1724 in Paris. The walls are covered with luxurious Gobelin tapestries, while in the two wardrobes on the narrow side of the room there is a collection of silver on display dating from around 1700. The beginning of the 19th c. was a period when Danish literature, art and science flourished. Pictures of important figures from this time, when Frederik VI was on the throne, are to be seen in Room 55, among them the sculptor Bertel Thorvaldsen (see Famous People), the poet Adam Oehlenschläger (whose own memorial room is no. 60), the physicist H. C. Ørsted, the discoverer of electromagnetism, and the adult educationalist Nicolai Frederik Severin Grundtvig (see Famous People); the pictures of the royal couple were painted by W. Eckersberg in 1825 and 1826. Of especial interest is also the painting of the inauguration session of the constituent royal assembly on October 23rd 1848, which takes up a whole wall in Room 61. At this assembly the king relinquished absolute power. Opposite hang portraits of Danish politicians. The neighbouring room no. 62 is devoted to three men who were to have a profound influence on Danish religious life during the 19th c.: Mynster, Søren Kierkegaard (see Famous People) and Nicolai Frederik Severin Grundtvig (see Famous People).

Frederikskirken

See Marmorkirken

Frihedsmuseet (Museet for Danmarks Frihedskamp 1940 bis 1945; Museum for Denmark's Freedom Struggle 1940 to 1945) J6

Location
Churchillparken

S-bane
Østerport

Buses
1, 6, 9

The Museum for Denmark's Freedom Struggle from 1940 to 1945 is situated on the esplanade in the Churchillparken. An early exhibition, "Denmark at War", which was held on July 21st 1945 at the Copenhagen masonic lodge, was later taken to Sweden, London and Moscow. To finance the building of the museum a nationwide lottery was held, the proceeds of which came to over 500,000 kroner, with the result that in October 1957 the museum could be inaugurated. The architect Hans Hansen was responsible for the design of the building.
The museum today has a series of outlying branches both in Denmark and further afield. Thus there are permanent exhibitions in such places as the Frøslev camp (Sønderjyllan), from where many Danes were sent to concentration camps, in the Polish concentration camp of Auschwitz and in the concentration camp at Sachsenhausen near Berlin.

Opening times

May 1st–Sept. 15th: Tues.–Sat. 10am–4pm, Sun. 10am–5pm; Sept. 16th–Apr. 30th: Tues.–Sat. 11am–3pm, Sun. 11am–4pm.

Exhibition

The Museum of Freedom documents the period of the German occupation and Danish resistance between 1940 and 1945 by means of a comprehensive collection of historic photographs, pictures, newspaper articles, letters, weapons and other mementoes. The exhibition is subdivided as follows: Germany's attack on Denmark in April 1940 (Displays 1 and 2); passive resistance by the Danish population (Displays 3–5); the Danes serving with the Allies (Displays 6–11); blackouts and the printing of illegal papers (Displays 12–15); illegal printing (Display 16); radio connections with England (Displays 17–19); illegal arms and sabotage (Displays 20–30); August 29th 1943 (Germany's attack on Denmark's armed forces and fleet, followed by the resignation of the Danish government) (Displays 31–32);

the Germans in Denmark (Displays 33–37); prison cell in Vestre Fængsel, Copenhagen (Display 38); prisoner-of-war camp at Horserød in North Sjælland (Display 39); police prison camp at Frøslev in North Schleswig (Display 39); persecutions of Jews (Displays 40–41); organisations in Sweden (Displays 42–44); German concentration camps in which there were Danish prisoners (Displays 45–47); arrest of Danish policemen (Display 48); Nazi organisations in Denmark (Display 49); measures taken against Danish informers (Display 50); strike of the Danish population on July 5th 1944 (Displays 51–53); Greenland (Display 54); Freedom Council and Danish council in London (Display 55); attacks on Gestapo headquarters (Displays 56–57); news service (Display 58); illegal work (Display 59); the "white buses" (Display 60); the liberation of Denmark in May 1945 (Displays 61, 72); Bornholm (Displays 63–66); the fallen (Displays 67–71); organisation of the resistance movement (Display 73).

Lassen Memorial

Memorial to A. Lassen

In front of the museum there is a memorial to Major Anders Lassen who died in 1945.

The Frihedsmuseet documents Denmark's resistance from 1940 to 1945

**Frilandsmuseet (Open air museum)

Location
Lyngby,
Kongevejen 100

S-bane
Sorgenfri

Bus
184

Opening times
May 1st–Sept. 30th:
Tues.–Sun.
10am–5pm;
Oct. 1st–Nov. 14th:
Tues.–Sun.
10am–3pm

The Frilandsmuseet (open air museum), which is affiliated to the Nationalmuseet (see entry) (Danish National Museum), is situated 8km/5 miles north of Copenhagen in Lyngby. It covers an area of 35ha/86 acres which the visitor can walk round on foot by means of a circular path 3km/2 miles long. The rural buildings, which date from the 17th to the 19th century, are grouped together according to their geographical origin. In order to get a picture of the various types of houses it is a good idea to visit at least one example of each group. For a walk round the whole museum site and a short visit to four buildings an hour should be allowed, whereas a visit to nine or ten houses can take just under two hours. In the summer there are also folk music performances from time to time, the exact dates of which may be ascertained by consulting the various entertainment announcements in the press. Tours round the park by horse-drawn carriage begin at the 1832 windmill tower (no. 6). Because of the fire risk smoking is strictly prohibited anywhere on the site.

The aim of the Open Air Museum is to document traditional living and working conditions in rural Denmark and its exhibits comprise old farmhouses, cottages, sailor's houses, mills, forges, etc., which have been brought together from their original locations throughout the regions of Denmark and the former Danish provinces in Southern Sweden and Southern Schleswig. The interiors of the buildings have been fitted out with the appropriate old furniture, utensils and working tools. In the parkland surrounding the houses indigenous wild plants can be found, while the gardens of the houses boast traditional types of flowers, colourful vegetable patches and old fruit trees. The range and number of buildings is continually being increased.

Tower windmill of the Dutch type

An old loom (Fünen)

Frilandsmuseet

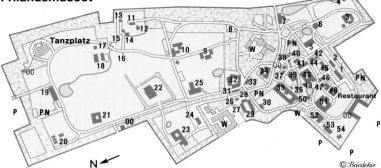

P – Parking, PN – Picnic areas, W – Workshops and stores, 00 – Toilets

© Baedeker

1 Fisherman's house, Agger, N Jutland
2 Seaman's house, Fanø
3 Farmhouse (early 19th c.), Øster Larsker, Bornholm
4 Watermill, Pedersker, Bornholm
5 Peasant house (end of 16th c.), Ostenfeld, S Schleswig (Germany)
6 Tower windmill, erected on its present site in 1832, in use until 1906
7 Watermill (before 1800), Ellested, Funen (Fyn)
8 Boundary stone (1734), Løve, Central Jutland
9 Farmhouse (*c.* 1850), Karup Heath, Central Jutland
10 Farmhouse (from 1736). Læsø, Kattegat
11 Peasant house (1866), Múla, Bordoy, Faroes
12 Store hut, Viderejde, Vidoy, Faroes
13 Watermill for domestic use, Sandur, Sandoy, Faroes
14 Buckwheat drying kiln, Múla, Bordoy, Faroes
15 Stone used in weight-lifting contests, Múla, Bordoy, Faroes
16 Milestone (2nd half of 17th c.), Holstebro district, W Jutland
17 Quarry (2nd half of 18th c.), Smedevad, near Holstebro, W Jutland
18 Farmhouse (from 1770), Vemb, W Jutland
19 Barn (originally *c.* 1600) from a farm at Fjellerup/Djursland, E Jutland
20 Fishermen's houses, Nymindegab, W Jutland
21 Farmhouse (1803), Lønnestak, W Jutland
22 Peasant house (1653), Eiderstedt, SW Schleswig (Germany)
23 Farmhouse (originally 17th c.), Sønder Sejerslev, N Schleswig
24 Pillow-lace-making school (19th c.), Nørre Sejerslev, N Schleswig
25 Crofter's house (18th c.), Rømø
26 Fuel shed, Sode, NE Schleswig
27 Barn (17th c.), Øsby, NE Schleswig
28 Barn (1605), Grønninghoved, NE Schleswig
29 Peasant house (1766), Barsø, NE Schleswig
30 Cottage from Dyndred (2nd half of 18th c.), Alsen, N Schleswig
31 Peasant house with shoemaker's workshop, Ødis Bramdrup, near Kolding, E Jutland
32 Farmhouse (18th c.), True, E Jutland
33 Potter's workshop (1844), Sorring, E Jutland
34 Farmhouse (originally 2nd half of 17th c.), Halland (Sweden)
35 Double farm (18th c.), Göinge, Skåne (Sweden)
36 Bath House, Småland (Sweden)
37 Two-storey storehouse, SE Småland (Sweden)
38 Small watermill, W Småland (Sweden)
39 Smallholder's steading (18th c.), Dörröd. Skåne (Sweden)
40 Weaver's house, Tystrup, Zealand
41 Houses of country craftsmen (17th–19th c.), Kalvehave, Zealand
42 Farm worker's house, Englerup, Zealand
43 Farmhouse (before 1800), Pebringe, Zealand
44 Almshouse (1710), Greve, Zealand
45 Boundary stone (1757), Virum, Zealand
46 Fire station (*c.* 1850), Kirke Såby, Zealand
47 Small farm (19th c.), Årup, Funen (Fyn)
48 Wooden shoe maker's house (19th c.), Kirke-Søby, Fünen
49 Village green with place of assembly
50 Village smithy (*c.* 1845), Ørbæk, Funen (Fyn)
51 Farmhouse (1747), Lundager, Funen (Fyn)
52 Small farmhouse, Dannemare, Lolland
53 Small farmhouse (before 1800), Tågense, Lolland
54 Post-mill (*c.* 1662), Karlstrup, Zealand (no access)

A rural brewhouse (Fünen)

A thatched seafarer's house (Fanø)

Gammel Bryghus (Old Brewery) H7

Location
Christians Brygge

Buses
1, 2, 5, 6, 8, 9, 10, 31, 37, 43

The Old Brewery Building (or Royal Brewhouse), which is distinguished by its prominent tiled roof, is among those buildings which were erected under King Christian IV (see Famous People).
The brewery, built between 1616 and 1618 on the south-western fortified wall with three gables and a tiled roof, had to be rebuilt twice, following fires in 1632 and 1767. Today it constitutes one of the oldest industrial concerns in Denmark, although the building was used from the 19th c. as a military depot.

Gammel Dok

See Christianshavn

Gammel Strand (Old Beach) H7

Location
To the west of Højbro Plads

Buses
1, 2, 6, 8, 10, 28, 29, 41

Situated opposite Slotsholmen (the palace island), and separated by the canal, is Gammel Strand, where long rows of fishwives once offered for sale fresh fish and other marine produce from Tårbæk and Skovshoved.
At the beginning of the middle ages the coastline still ran along the present-day Løngangsstræde, Magstræde, Snaregade and Fortunstræde. It is assumed that this was where the fishing boats unloaded their catches; in 1337 the area was for the first time mentioned as being "propre mare" (near the sea). From the 15th c. the references varied between "ved Stran-

den" (on the beach) and "Strandgade" (beach road), while the name "Gammel Strand" was only used for the first time in 1716.
A reminder of the fish market which up until a few years ago was still active is provided by the fishwife's memorial, the stone "Fiskerkone", which was erected in 1940. Its special feature is the fisherman's basket tied to the fishwife's back, in which the women used to carry their husband's catch to the town.

Today boats going on the harbour tour or the canal trip to "Den lille Havfrue" (little mermaid) leave from Gammel Strand. Opposite the mooring place is one of the city's best fish restaurants, Krogs Fiskerestaurant.

*Gefion Springvandet (Gefion Fountain) J6

The Gefion Fountain, built in 1909 by the sculptor Anders Bundgaard for the Carlsberg foundation (see Carlsberg Brewery) in what is today the Churchillparken, is one of the most impressive fountains in Copenhagen. Its powerful jets of water can be seen in action from April 15th to October 31st.

Location
Churchillparken

S-bane
Østerport

Buses
1, 6, 9

It owes its conception to the Old Norse saga, the "Ynglingesaga der Heimskringla". According to this, the goddess Gefion, who had been ordered by Odin to obtain land, was promised by King Gylfe of Sweden as much land as she could plough up in one night. The goddess thereupon betook herself to Jotunheim where she bore a giant four sons, whom she turned into bulls. With these she ploughed up an area the size of Zealand. The ploughed land was lifted up out of Sweden and set down in the Baltic (the "hole" left behind is the Vänern Lake): this was how Zealand was formed.

The Gefion Fountain

Grundtvig Church

Glyptotheque

See Ny Carlsberg Glyptotek

*Grundtvigs Kirke (Church) E4

Location
På Bjerget, district of Bispebjerg

Buses
10, 16, 19, 43

This church is named in honour of Bishop Nicolai Frederik Severin Grundtvig (see Famous People), the father of the adult education movement, which was the first to be established in Europe.
This modern church was built between 1921 and 1940 on the Bispebjerg, in brick, in an unusual style reminiscent of an organ. Its proportions are massive: inside length 76m/249ft, inside width 35m/115ft, inside height 22m/72ft, exterior height 30m/98ft. Its nave can accommodate 1800 people. 6000 bricks, all yellow, a typical Danish building material, were used for the construction of the church, which employed the six best masons in Denmark for 19 years. The architect was P. V. Jensen-Klint, whose son Kaare completed the building after his father's death. The great Marcus organ is used for concerts throughout the year.

Opening times

May 15th–Sept. 14th: Mon.–Sat. 9am–4.45pm, Sun. noon–4pm; Sept. 15th–May 14th: Mon.–Sat. 9am–4pm, Sun. noon–1pm.

*Den lille Havfrue (The little mermaid) J5

Location
Langelinie

The statue of the little mermaid, sitting on a stone on the harbourside at Langelinie, was erected in 1913, based on the character of the fairy tale of

The Little Mermaid ▶

Buses
1, 6, 9, June 15th–Sept. 1st: special buses from the Rådhuspladsen (city hall)

S-bane
Østerport

the same name, written in 1837 by Hans Christian Andersen (see Famous People). The immediate inspiration for the statue was the premiere in 1909 of the ballet about the little water nymph with the fish's tail, who once upon a time came up out of the depths of the sea, because she loved a prince, and who, as Andersen portrayed in his story, had to forsake the world of humans once more, because the prince did not return her love. During the performance in the Royal Theatre, the brewery proprietor, Carl Jakobsen (see Carlsberg Brewery) had the idea of presenting Copenhagen with a statue of the legendary creature. The model was to have been the prima ballerina, Ellen Price, who had danced the fairy tale heroine. As she was predictably little inclined to pose nude as a model for the sculptor Edward Eriksen, he based only the face of the bronze sculpture on Ellen Price and for its body used that of his beautiful wife. His patron wanted the mermaid to be given a fish's tail but Eriksen had read Andersen's story very thoroughly and knew that the little sea nymph had given the old sea witch her golden hair and her sweet voice in order to gain two legs like a human. As a compromise Eriksen designed a veil-like tail within which two legs were easily recognisable.
The statue of the little mermaid rapidly developed into a much visited symbol of the city and became one of its most sought-after photographic subjects. When on the night of April 24th 1964 some unknown hands sawed off the head of the statue the whole of Copenhagen was outraged. Luckily the old moulds which had been used back in 1913 were still to hand and the mermaid was able to receive a new head.

*Helligåndskirken (Church of the Holy Spirit) H7

Location
Amagertorv

Buses
28, 29, 41

Opening times
daily noon–4pm

The oldest church in Copenhagen dates back as a monastery church to the year 1400 when a basilica with three naves was built here in brick. After it was partially destroyed by a fire in 1728 it was rebuilt in 1880 in the New Renaissance style.
The sandstone entrance portal, originally intended for the Old Stock Exchange building (see Børse), dates back to 1620. The altar, donated in 1732 by Christian VI, was the work of Didrik Gercken, the sculptures are by Just Wiedewelt, the altarpiece depicting the ascension of Christ by Hendrick Krock. On the north side of the church is the burial chapel of a Danish minister of state, which was erected in 1670.

In the tiny churchyard there is a memorial honouring the Danish victims of Nazi concentration camps. Behind the church stands the House of the Holy Ghost, dating from about 1300, and part of the monastery of the Holy Ghost.

*Hirschsprungske Samling (Hirschsprung art collection) H6

Location
Stockholmsgade 20

Buses
10, 14, 24, 40, 43, 84

Opening times
Wed.–Sat. 1–4pm, Sun. 11am–4pm

The Hirschsprung art collection, which was assembled in the 1940s, comprises 600 paintings, 200 sculptures and well over 1000 watercolours and drawings from the period 1800 to 1910.
It brings together the works of many Danish artists of this period and is also highly informative in the way it mirrors the Danish way of life at this time. Among the main representatives of this period are C. W. Eckersberg and his pupils C. Kobke, P. C. Skovgaard and Constantin Hansen as well as the Skagen painters P. S. Kroyer and Anna and Michael Ancher, who represent the "modern breakthrough" which came about 1880. There is also work on display by Vilhelm Hammershøj, Ejnar Nielsen and L. A. Ring.
The collection goes back to a foundation by Heinrich Hirschsprung, a famous Copenhagen cigarette manufacturer, who in 1902 left his works of

art to the Danish state. A picture of Hirschsprung, together with his wife Pauline, their daughter and four sons, hangs in the second room. It was painted by P. S. Krøyer, who enjoyed Hirschsprung's patronage.
The building in which the collection is housed was completed in 1911 and has a main façade which juts forward like the front of an ancient temple. Its triangular gable is decorated by a relief which was created by the artist Kai Nielsen.

*Holmens Kirke (Church) H7

Location
Holmens Kanal

Buses
1, 2, 6, 8, 9, 10, 31, 37, 43

Opening times
May 15th–Sept. 15th: Mon.–Fri. 9am–2pm, Sat. 9am–noon; Sept. 16th–May 14th: Mon.–Sat. 9am–noon

The Holmenskirke was built in 1619 by the canal of the same name under King Christian IV (see Famous People) by converting an anchor smithy which had been set up by Christian II. In the middle of the 17th c. Leonhard Blasius added the transepts to the Renaissance building. The splendid main portal on the east side (the "King's Portal", 17th c.) came originally from the cathedral in Roskilde (see entry).
The king had the church built specially for sailors, but today it is also used by the royal family. In 1967 Queen Margrethe II and Prince Henrik were married here.
The long chapel added in 1705–08 is dedicated to Denmark's sea heroes and contains two models of ships hanging from the ceiling. Of especial artistic value is also the superb brass screen in the interior of the church, with its 38 balusters, which separates the choir from the nave, as well as the brilliantly carved altar and the oak pulpit extending right up to the roof – the largest in Copenhagen. Both of these were completed in the second half of the 17th c. by Abel Schrøder the Younger.

Holmens Kirke

*Højbro Plads (High Bridge Square) H7

Location
by Gammel Strand

Buses
1, 2, 6, 8, 10.28, 29, 41

The spaciously laid out Højbro Plads, situated at the end of the Amagertorv, is one of the most frequented squares in Copenhagen.

In the centre stands a monument erected in 1901 for Bishop Absalon (see Famous People), which represents the founder of the city as a powerfully armed knight. This statue on horseback was the work of Ch. G. Vilhelm Bissen, while the plinth is by Martin Nyrop and bears the inscription "He was courageous, wise and far-sighted – a friend of scholarship – in the intensity of his striving a true son of Denmark".

The Højbro Plads looks out on to the island of Slotsholmen and Christiansborg Slot (see entry), the Børsen and Thorvaldsens Museum (see entries), while there are also views of Holmens Kirke and Gammel Strand (see entries).

Statue of Absolon

House nameplates

House nameplate

Before 1771, when house numbers were introduced in Copenhagen – following the French model – by the Count of Struensee (see Famous People), citizens and visitors had to find their way around by means of nameplates which made some reference to the profession of the owner, or to plants, animals or celestial bodies, etc. in pictorial form and were fixed to the outside of the houses. While simple signs were used in the Middle Ages, the wrought-iron ones of the 17th and 18th c, displayed elaborate shapes and embellishments – for example, the richly decorated house sign of the hatmaker, N. Jørgensen, in Vandkusten, made in 1723, with a golden hat symbolising the business that was pursued there. Under Christian II inns had already had to make the nature of their trade explicit by means of a sign displaying the name of the hostelry or tavern. In the 18th c., especially after the appalling fire of 1728, there was a trend towards stone signs, bearing the emblem of the building and placed over the entrance portal or door.

Karen Blixen Museet (Museum)

Location
Rungstedlund
Rungstedstrandvej 111

Opening times
May 1st–Sept. 30th: daily 10am–5pm; Oct. 1st–Apr. 30th Mon., Wed.–Sun. 1–4pm

In May 1991 a museum dedicated to Karen Blixen (see Famous People) was opened in the manor house on her parents' estate. The Danish writer was born here and also lived here after her return from Africa until her death in 1962.

Karen Blixen wrote her first stories here at Rungstedlund, before she went out to East Africa with her husband, the Swedish Baron Bror von Blixen-Finecke, to manage a coffee plantation there for 17 years. Even during this period the authoress returned to Denmark on numerous occasions. In 1958 she presented the estate to the Rungstedlund foundation, which in 1991 set up the museum.

In the rooms of the house furniture and mementoes from Kenya are to be

Karen Blixen: portraits of a man and woman of the Kikuyu tribe

seen, such as the gramophone mentioned in her book "Out of Africa", a present from her friend Denys Finch Hatton.
Of particular interest are her portraits of members of the Kikuyu tribe. The picture "The History of the Kingdom of Denmark", in which the work of the same name by the Danish dramatist Ludvig Holberg (see Famous People) is depicted with a decoratively placed toucan bird, was painted by her in Africa and given by her there to Denys Finch Hatton. After his death in 1931 Karen Blixen received the painting back.

***Kastellet** (Castle; Citadellet Frederikshavn) H5/6

The castle on the Langelinie, which today houses the Livjäger Museum and the Royal Garrison Library, was built under Frederik III by the Dutchman Henrik Ruse in 1662–63, in the place where under Christian IV (see Famous People) in 1629 the St Annæ entrenchment had been established. The five-cornered fortress was erected with a double moat and was given the name of Citadellet Frederikshavn after its founder. Between 1662 and 1725 the fortification was considerably enlarged by Frederik's successors.
The buildings comprise the main police station, the prison of 1725, in which, among others, Johann Friedrich Count of Struensee (see Famous People) was held prisoner before his execution; the two-storey commandant's house, also built in 1725 to plans by E. D. Häusser; old storehouses as well as two fine fortress portals: the Zealand Gate at the south end of the castle, built in 1663 (the Sjællandsporten), which is adorned by a bust of King Frederik III by the sculptor fr. Dieussart, and the Norway Gate (Norgesporten), completed in the same year, which was blown up by the Germans in 1940, but later rebuilt. The church, consecrated in 1704, was conceived in such a way that the prisoners were able to follow the service without entering the church. The park and lawns around the castle are open daily from 6am until dusk.

Location
Langelinie

S-bane
Østerport

Buses
1, 6, 9

Kastellet: the Commandant's House

Kierkegaard Samlingen

See Københavns Bymuseum & Søren Kierkegaard Samlingen

Kongelige Teater

See Kongens Nytorv

Kongens Have

See Rosenborg Slot

**Kongens Nytorv (New Royal Market) H/J6

Location
on the Strøget

Buses
1, 4H, 6, 7, 9, 10, 10H, 28, 29, 31, 41

Kongens Nytorv, which is reached from the Rådhuspladsen (City Hall Square) at the end of the Strøget (see entry) pedestrian zone, is Copenhagen's largest square. A dozen or so streets lead off it.
This important traffic junction was laid out in 1680 by King Christian V. From here it is only a very short walk to the museum ships at Nyhavn (see entry).

Charlottenborg Slot

In the direction of the New Port stands the palace of Charlottenborg (Kongens Nytorv 1). It was built between 1672 and 1683 for the half-brother of Christian V and governor of Norway, Ulf Frederik Gyldenløve in the Baroque Dutch Palladian style. Today it is the home of the Academy of Arts and is used for exhibitions. Opening times: daily 10am–5pm.

Harsdorffs House

This building, Kongens Nytorv no. 3, was designed by the architect Caspar Harsdorff in 1777 in the classical style. It has been made a listed building for preservation purposes and today houses the school of architects.

Thotts Palais

On the north-east side of Kongens Nytorv is situated Thotts Palais (no. 4), which was built in 1685–86 in the Dutch Palladian style for Admiral Niels Juel and which since 1930 has housed the French Embassy. After Count Otto Thott acquired the building in 1760, the wall pillars of the main façade were given Corinthian capitals and the balustrade, crowned with figures and a cartouche with a coat of arms, was added.

*Kongelige Teater (Theatre Royal)

The south-east side of the square is dominated by the Theatre Royal, founded in 1748, in which plays, operas and ballets are presented (see Practical Information, Music).The present-day building was erected in 1872–74 to designs by Vilhelm Dahlerup and Ove Petersen in the New Renaissance style. The inscription on the main façade "Ei blot til lyst" ("Not just for pleasure") goes back to the original building erected in 1748 by Nicolai Eigtved, while the decorations in the auditorium (1500 seats) are the work of the painter C. Hansen. In 1931 the theatre had an additional auditorium created, the "New Scene" (1050 seats), designed by the architect H. Jacobsen.

Memorials to L. Hohlberg and A. Oehlenschläger

The two statues on either side of the main entrance are of the poets Ludvig Hohlberg (see Famous People) and Adam Oehlenschläger (1779–1850). Oehlenschläger is considered to be Denmark's national poet, having written the Danish National Anthem as well as many plays.

Magasin du Nord

The main building belonging to the department store Magasin du Nord is also situated on Kongens Nytorv. It was built in 1893–94 in the French "chateau" style by A. Ch. Jensen and H. Glæsel on the site of the elegant "Hotel du grand Nord" which had been opened in 1796.

Equestrian statue of Christian V on Kongens Nytorv

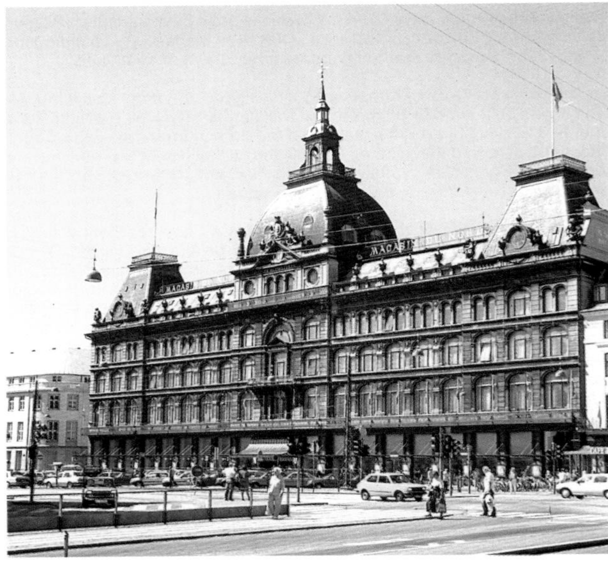

The Magasin du Nord department store

*Hotel d'Angleterre

The Hotel d'Angleterre, which lies on Kongens Nytorv (no. 34), must be considered one of Copenhagen's leading and best established hotels. The High Chancellor Frederik Ahlefeld had a palace built here under Christian V, which in 1795 was taken over by the gastronome Gottfried Rau who turned it into the Hotel d'Angleterre. Later the hotel came into the possession of the Tietgens building company, which had the buildings extended by V. Dahlerup and G. E. W. Møller. In 1903 the façade was given the appearance it still has today.

Statue of Christian V on horseback

In the middle of the square is the statue of Christian V on horseback (1687), the work of the French sculptor Abraham-César Lamoureux, which is almost concealed by a garden which was laid out in 1855–56. It depicts the king in the robes of a Roman emperor. At his feet are Minerva symbolising wisdom, Alexander the Great symbolising courage, Hercules symbolising strength and Artemis symbolising honour.

Cultural Centre Bolten's

Musical events and temporary exhibitions are also offered on Kongens Nytorv by the new Copenhagen Cultural Centre Bolten's, where there are also several cafés and restaurants (open 10am–5pm).

**Kronborg Slot (Kronborg Castle)

Location
Helsingør

Railway station
Helsingør

Within Kronborg Castle there are today 27 rooms devoted to a trade and seafaring museum (Handels- og Søfartsmuseet), which documents the history of Danish seafaring, as well as displaying exhibits from earlier Danish settlements in Greenland and the West Indies.

As early as 1420 Erich the Pomeranian had established a castle called the "Krogen" ("hook") here at the narrowest point in the Øresund, where a sandy tongue of land protrudes close to the coast of Schonen in Sweden,

Kronborg Castle

with the express purpose of demanding a toll on ships passing through the sound – a substantial source of revenue for the king.

In 1558–59 Christian II had the wall encircling the castle strengthened with corner bastions under the direction of the Saxon fortress builder Hans von Dieskow. In 1574–85 under Frederik II the site was converted into a magnificent four-winged Renaissance castle under the Dutchmen Hans van Paeschen and Antonius van Opbergen and was given the name "Kronborg". After a fire in September 1629, in which only the church was left unscathed, Christian IV (see Famous People) had the castle rebuilt by Hans van Steenwinckel the Younger in 1635–40 without any alterations. When the Swedes took the castle in 1659 they carried off many treasures, among them the famous "table canopy" of Frederik II, woven from gold and silver thread by Hans Knieper, which is today to be found in the National Museum in Stockholm. Under succeeding kings the castle received further extensions and alterations and between 1785 and 1922 it was used as a barracks.

Between 1924 and 1935 the castle was completely restored by J. Magdahl-Nielsen and refurbished in the style of Frederik II and Christian IV.

The upkeep of the palace has been subsidised for many years by the Ny-Carlsberg Foundation (see Carlsberg Brewery), while the collection of paintings from the 16th and 17th c. is continually supplemented by loans from the Copenhagen Statens Museum (see entry) and the National Historical Museum at Frederiksborg Palace (see entry) in Hillerød.

Opening times
May–Sept.: daily 10.30am–5pm; Nov.–Mar.: Tues.–Sun. 11am–3pm; Apr. and Oct. 11am–4pm

"Hamlet's Castle"

Shakespeare's play "Hamlet" is set in Helsingør (Elsinore) and thus Kronborg has become "Hamlet's Castle". Even if this is not really historically correct, the castle courtyard makes an outstanding backdrop for the occasional festival performance of the play.

Tour of the castle

Over the main entrance portal there is an inscription confirming that Frederik II had the castle built in 1577 and named it "Kronborg". Above can be seen the oriel belonging to the royal apartment.

The former royal apartments with superb ceiling paintings dating from the middle of the 17th c. are situated in the north wing. Of the original fittings and furnishings scarcely anything remains, the greater part of the furniture on display there having been made in the 17th c.
The Knights' Hall or ballroom with its 62×11m/203×36ft proportions is the largest and also one of the most beautiful Renaissance rooms in the whole of Northern Europe. Its enormous paintings were originally intended by Christian IV for Rosenborg Palace (see entry), as were the pictures in the queen's gallery. The theme running through the pictures is that of the power of the planets over the course of the lives of mortals.
In the west wing the Small Hall, besides its Renaissance furniture, still boasts seven of the original fourteen magnificent Gobelin tapestries dating from 1582 which used to decorate the ballroom. The other seven wall hangings are now to be found in the Nationalmuseet (see entry).
The south wing contains the castle chapel, consecrated in 1582, which by virtue of its stone vaulting was able to withstand the fire of 1629. Its sumptuous Renaissance interior fittings dating from the 16th c., with elaborate wood carvings by German masters, are well worth seeing. The golden alabaster relief of the "Crucifixion" over the altar was completed in 1587, while the valance covering the lower part of the altar was provided by the clothmakers Kirsten and John Becker in 1982.
Finally the visitor also has access to the castle casemates with their gloomy dungeons.

From the south-west "trumpeters' tower" (approached by a spiral staircase with 145 steps) a wonderful view across the Øresund can be enjoyed. A walk along the western bastions is equally rewarding for the wealth of views which it affords.

*Kunstindustrimuseet (Museum of Decorative and Applied Art) J6

Location
Bredgade 68

S-bane
Østerport

Buses
1, 6, 9

Opening times
Tues.–Sun. 1–4pm

The Museum of Decorative and Applied Art encompasses European arts and crafts from the Middle Ages up to the present time, as well as material from China and Japan. Its collections are housed in nearly 60 rooms, three of them, with the Rococo and silver collection, on the first floor. The main emphasis of the exhibits is on living room furniture and fittings. Thus there are carpets, 18th c. crockery from the royal porcelain manufacturers, faience, Danish silver, chinoiserie, Art nouveau work, glass, textiles, furniture, jewelry and scientific instruments. Modern Danish design is also represented.

The museum is housed in the Rococo building of the former Frederik Hospital which was built in 1757 by Niels Eigtved and Laurids de Thura. The museum was set up in 1890 by the Ny-Carlsberg Foundation (see Carlsberg Brewery) and has been located here since 1926.

Garden

The house has a garden which is open to visitors. A series of sculptures are to be found there, including "The Sea Horse" (1916) by Niels Skovgaard and a "Figure of a Woman" and a "Vase" (about 1750) by J. C. Petzold.

Købmagergade (Pedestrian zone) H6/7

Location
Between Kultorvet and Højbro Plads

Buses
1, 2, 5, 6, 7, 8, 10, 14, 16, 17, 24, 28, 29, 41, 43, 84

The Købmagergade pedestrianised zone which runs between Kultorvet and Højbro Plads (see entry) was very likely from the 13th c. onwards part of the main thoroughfare between Roskilde (see entry) and the "Købmændenes Havn" (merchant port). In the 15th c. the butchers (kødmangere) of Copenhagen settled here and gave the street its name "Købmagergade". In the middle of the 16th c. the butchers moved to the Skindergade, but the street retained the original name, albeit in its present

Articles of modern furniture in the Kunstindustrimuseet

Museum of Arts and Crafts: "Seahorse" . . .

. . . and Delft tiles (c.1729)

Model boutique in the Købmagergade

slightly altered form. Today the Købmagergade is a lively pedestrian area with many shops, fashion boutiques, restaurants, bars and cafés.

*Rundetårn

See entry

Royal Porcelain Factory

The Royal Porcelain Factory had its first premises between 1775 and 1882 at Købmagergade no. 5. Within only a few years of its opening it had become internationally renowned for its dinner and tea services, vases and porcelain busts and figures. Conducted tours: Mon.–Fri. 9, 10 and 11am, also 1 and 2pm May 15th–Sept. 15th.

Statue of Mercury

From the roof of the red-brick house at no. 42 (1896) the visitor is greeted by a statue of Mercury, the Old Roman god of trade and crafts who was based on the Greek god Hermes.

Legetøjsmuseet (Toy Museum) H6

Location
Valkendorfsgade 13

S-bane
Nørreport

Buses
2, 5, 14, 16, 43

The little toy museum on the Valkendorfsgade was set up on the initiative of Fritz Hartz, who assembled the first exhibits from antique markets in London. Since then the museum's stock has been enlarged by numerous donations from private collectors of old toys.
The childhood dreams of past times are mirrored in the two lovingly assembled rooms which make up the museum. Here can be seen old dolls, tin soldiers, a wide variety of Danish Father Christmases, marionettes, toy cars, doll's prams, fairy tale characters ranging from "Hänsel and Gretel" to "Snow White", stuffed animals and a toy chest dating from 1880 containing cardboard hens, bears, zebras and pigs, which King Frederik VIII, as a little prince, was given by his father King Christian IX and which he later gave to his own children (open: Mon.–Thur. 9am–4pm; Sat., Sun. 10am–4pm).

*Lejre Forsøgscenter (Lejre historical and archaeological research centre: "Prehistoric dwelling places")

At the Lejre historical and archaeological research centre the aim is to bring the past back to life. The "social and material culture of prehistoric times" is represented here with the main attraction a reconstructed "ice-age village" set in attractive scenery, the tour of which is just under 3km/2 miles long. Historically authentic prehistoric workplaces have been set up: a forge, pottery, brickworks and weaving, as well as stalls for domestic animals – especially popular with children. At the "valley of fire" the visitor has the opportunity to bring meat or bread and roast it over prehistoric hearths.

Location
Slangeallé 2,
Lejre
(38km/24 miles south-west of Roskilde)

Railway station
Lejre;
then bus 233

Opening times
May 1st–Sept. 29th, Oct. 12th–20th:
daily 10am–5pm

Beyond the grounds of the museum, the estate of Ravnshøjgård was also acquired by the research centre. On this old farm the type of agriculture practised before the Second World War has been revived.

Nearby there are stone settings in the form of ships: according to Viking belief, when a person died he went to the Kingdom of the Dead in one of these vessels.

**Louisiana (Art museum and cultural centre)

The Louisiana Museum of Art and Cultural Centre is situated in the little town of Humlebæk, 35km/22 miles to the north of Copenhagen and about 10km/6 miles south of Helsingør. It was founded in 1958 by the businessman and art lover, Knud W. Jensen, who had a bright airy museum complex built by Jørgen Bo and Vilhelm Wohlert which since then has had to be extended several times to house the constantly increasing number of acquisitions. Most recently in 1990–91 a basement graphics wing was opened, which turned what had until then been a semi-circular set of buildings into a closed complex. The new buildings were designed by the architects Jørgen Bo, Vilhelm Wohlert and Claus Wohlert and the surrounding gardens by Vibeke Holscher and Lea Nørgaard.

Location
Humlebæk,
Gl. Strandvej 13
(35km/22 miles north of Copenhagen)

Railway station
Humlebæk;
then bus 388

Opening times
daily 10am–5pm

For lovers of modern art a visit to Louisiana is strongly recommended. As an acknowledgement of its extraordinary commitment to this field the centre was awarded the European prize "Museum of the Year" in Paris in 1984.

Visit

The main building of the modern art collection is a patrician house built in 1860 whose previous owner was married successively to three women named Louise, hence the name of the collection "Louisiana". To the original manorial house the exhibition pavilions have been built on, tactfully and harmoniously integrated into the surrounding parkland.

In the glass-covered pavilions there are displays of international as well as Danish artists of the 20th c. – the latter group represented above all by those who, as members of the Cobra group, put their stamp on European art after the Second World War. The following artists have works displayed: Alberto Giacometti, Josef Albers, Pierre Alechinsky, Alice Aycokk, Shusaku Arakawa, Georg Baselitz, Mark Rothko, Asger Jorn, Bram van Velde, Max Bill, Eduardo Chillida, Franciska Clausen, Enzo Cucchi, Ad Dekkers, Marcel Duchamp, Sonia Delaunay, Sam Francis, Alexander Exter, Jackie Ferrara, Dan Flavin, Linda Francis, Franz Kline, Barnett Newmann, Mark Tobey, Jan Groth, Richard Hamilton, David Hockney, Robert Rauschenberg, Jasper Johns, Andy Warhol, Will Insley, Mimmo Paladino, Per Kirkeby, Walter Pichler, Svend Wiig Hansen, Nigel Hall, Joel Shapiro, Richard Mortensen, Richard Serra, A. R. Penck, Moshe Kupfermann, Roy Lichtenstein, Pablo

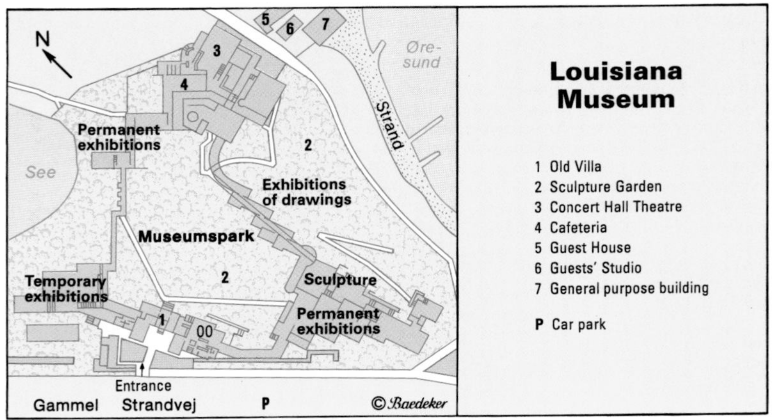

Picasso, Jean Tinguely, Anselm Kiefer, Frank Stella, Georg Grosz, Chuck Close, Markus Lüpertz and Cindy Shermann.

The parkland by the Øresund is embellished with outstanding sculptures, including numerous works by Henry Moore, Hans Arp, Alexander Calder, Max Ernst, Alberto Giacometti and Jean Tinguely.

Special exhibitions of abstract and modern art from all over the world are brought here – mainly in the winter months. In addition events such as

Louisiana Art Museum: Andy Warhol and contemporaries

Louisiana: a work by Roy Lichtenstein . . .

. . . and a sculpture in the museum park

concerts and film shows are organised. A bookshop, cafeteria, and play-room for children complete the range of facilities.

Marble Bridge (New Bridge, Main Bridge, Palace Bridge) H7

Location
Frederiksholms Kanal

Buses
1, 2, 5, 6, 10

The marble bridge which spans the Frederikskanal between the island of Slotsholmen and the National Museum (see entry) is considered one of the masterpieces of Nicolai Eigtved. King Christian VI had issued instructions for the building of the bridge in 1739 but it was not possible to finish the sculpture work until 1745. From a technical point of view the bridge's special advantage lay in the flat construction of its arches which meant that the road over the bridge could be almost completely horizontal.

The central pillars bear elegant classical portrait medallions with Rococo decorations, while the central arch is adorned with a head of Medusa. The French sculptor Louis-Augustin le Clerc, also hard at work at Christiansborg Palace (see entry), was given the task of carrying out all this decorative work on the bridge. In his workshop he created out of Saxon sandstone the heavily symbolic portraits which, framed by reeds, rocaille and two foam-belching sea monsters, offer homage to the sea. Whether they actually represent the ancient gods Poseidon, Amphitrite, Oceanos and Tethys is debatable.

Officially the bridge is actually called the New Bridge, Main Bridge or Palace Bridge, although the name it is unofficially known by is the "Marble Bridge" on account of its marble-surfaced pavements. At the beginning of the 1970s a comprehensive restoration of the bridge was initiated under the direction of Erik Erlandsen and this continued until 1983.

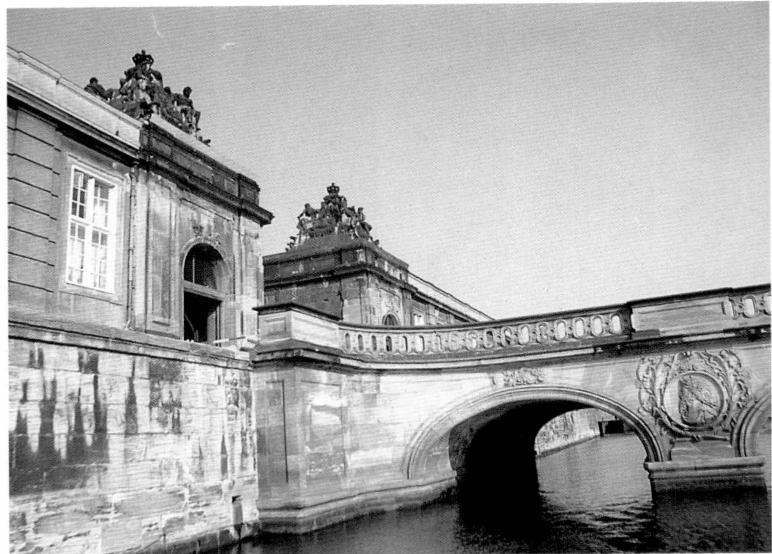

The Marble Bridge over the Frederikskanal

*Marmorkirken (Marble Church; Frederikskirken) J6

Location
Frederiksgade 4

Buses
1, 6, 9

Opening times
Mon.–Sat.
11am–2pm;
Sun. 10.30am

Officially called the "Frederikskirken", the place of worship which has always been known by the people of Copenhagen as just the "Marble Church" was designed in 1740 as the central church for the new city district of Frederiksstad by the famous court architect Nicolai Eigtved, who died in 1754 during the course of its construction. King Frederik V laid the foundation stone in October 1749, but work on the building was brought to a halt in 1770 by Count von Struensee (see Famous People) on account of the high costs. Its eventual completion, using Danish limestone instead of the expensive Norwegian marble, did not come about until 1894, after the great industrialist C. F. Tietgen had bought the ruin with the proviso that the church should be finished.

Eigtved's original building plan was now altered by the architect Ferdinand Meldahl, who added a 46m/151ft high cupola in the Roman baroque style. The cupola has a diameter of 33m/108ft and is one of the largest in Europe. Inside the rotunda are 12 towering marble pillars and coloured frescos in blue, gold and green. Particularly worth noticing are an ivory crucifix in the choir, a German oak relief of the Descent from the Cross in the front chapel, a marble font by Joakom Skovgård, Grundtvig's seven-armed gold chandelier and a relief by Niels Skovgård which commemorates C. F. Tietgen and his wife. The church is lined with statues of famous Danes from church life, including Søren Kierkegaard (see Famous People), St Ansgar, Denmark's patron saint, the reformer Martin Luther and the priest Nicolai Frederik Severin Grundtvig (see Famous People). The figures are by, among others, H. V. Bissen, J. F. Willumsen and K. Nellemose. On the roof projection there can also be seen enthroned 12 sculptures of famous representatives of religious and ecclesiastical history.

Grundtvig monument . . .

. . . outside the Marble Church

The Marble Church: interior of the Rotunda

Mindelunden (Memorial to Danish resistance fighters) G3

Location
Tuborgvej, Ryparken

S-bane
Hellerup

Buses
21, 23

The Mindelunden memorial is dedicated to all Danes who were killed in the struggle for their country's freedom during the German occupation from 1940 to 1945. On the Mindelunden site the corpses of 199 executed resistance fighters were found after the Second World War.
A commemorative wall designed by Axel Poulsen bears their names together with a poem by the Dane, Kaj Munk, who himself became a victim of fascism. In the small wood behind the memorial there are 31 graves which bear witness to those who were killed in German concentration camps. In the pergola which lies to the east, 141 memorial tablets have been erected to victims of the Nazi tyranny who disappeared without trace. On August 20th 1945, after the German withdrawal, the first interments took place and the official opening of Mindelunden followed on May 5th 1950. The subsequent artistic design of the remembrance groves was carried out by Kaj Gottlob, while the landscaping of the park was entrusted to Axel Andersen from Gentofte.

Opening times

Dec., Jan.: 10am–4pm; Nov., Feb.: 10am–5pm; Mar., Oct.: 10am–6pm; Apr., Sept.: 10am–7pm; May, Aug.: 10am–8pm; June, July: 10am–9pm.

*Musikhistorisk Museum og Carl Claudius' Samling H6

(Museum of Musical History)

Location
Åbenrå 30

S-bane
Nørreport

Buses
5, 7, 14, 16, 43, 73E, 184

Opening times
Tues., Wed. 10am–1pm, Fri.–Sun. 1–4pm

The Museum of Musical History, which was originally attached to the Museum of Industrial Art (see Kunstindustrimuseet), was founded in 1898. Since 1966 it has been located in its present home, a two-storey building restored between 1963 and 1966 by Jørgen Bo and Vilhelm Wohlert. The comprehensive collection comprises some 2000 historical instruments of various types, including a harmonium belonging to King Christian VII, a violin belonging to Niels W. Gades and a piano from the collection of Carl Nielsens. In 1941 the museum received an extensive addition of instuments bequeathed by the Consul General, Carl August Claudius. There is a library joined to the museum with a wide-ranging collection of musical literature.
On certain Saturdays and Tuesdays (see announcements) the museum arranges concerts on historical instuments.

Nationalhistoriske Museum

See Frederiksborg Slot

**Nationalmuseet (National Museum) H7

Location
Frederiksholms Kanal 12; Ny Vestergade 12

Buses
1, 2, 5, 6, 10

The Copenhagen National Museum is situated on the Frederiksholms Kanal opposite the island of Slotsholmen and Christiansborg Slot (see entry), which can be reached from here by crossing the Marble Bridge (see entry).
The museum complex comprises the Prince's Palace, which was built by Nicolai Eigtved in 1743–44 and wings of the palace added on at a later date which are on the Stormgade, the Ny Vestergade and the Vester Voldgade, as well as several departments located outside the main site.

Since 1989 the National Museum has been completely modernised and considerably enlarged. After the projected completion of the work (set for 1992) the museum will have, in addition to its existing collections, now

Model of the new National Museum

newly refurbished, a 1000sq.m/10,700sq.ft hall for special exhibitions and an information centre where, with the help of modern technology (videos and computers), visitors can find out more about the museum's exhibits. Two sections of the museum, the Danish Folk Museum and the antiques collection, are scheduled to reopen in the middle of this decade when renovation work has been completed.

Opening times

Prehistoric period, Middle Ages until 1750, Modern Age from 1750, Oriental and classical antiquities, coin and medal collection:
June 16th–Sept. 15th: Tues.–Sun. 10am–4pm; Sept. 16th–June 15th: Tues.–Fri. 11am–3pm, Sat., Sun. noon–4pm (alterations to these times are possible because of renovation work).

Collections

The main area on the ground floor comprises a comprehensive collection from Nordic prehistory. Especially interesting are the sun cart from Trundholm (*c.* 1200 B.C.), the reproduction of a cult vehicle with a gold sun-screen, and finds from the Viking age.
In the Middle Ages section there are gold altars on show, including the gold altar of Lisbjerg, Romanesque and Gothic church fittings, tools and furniture, as well as seven Gobelin tapestries, which were designed in 1582 for the decoration of the Knights' Hall at Kronborg Slot. The period after 1660 is represented by a series of living rooms belonging to the upper middle classes, for example a room in Ålborg dating from *c.* 1680, Rococo rooms and rooms directly planned for the Prince's Palace, as well as Danish ceramics and silver.
The collection of antiques has exhibits on display which Danish scientists on Rhodes and in Hama (Syria) have excavated, while the coin and medal collection concentrates above all on work from Denmark and the other Scandinavian countries.
The folk collection, entitled "Danish Farming" displays agricultural implements, tools, furniture, ceramics and clothes, as well as rooms set out as they would have looked in the 18th and 19th c.

National Museum: A middle-class room of the 18th century

In the ethnographic collection, the oldest in the world, the most striking section is the one dealing with the way of life of the Eskimos in Greenland, Canada and Alaska. There are also sections on Asia, Africa, Oceania and the culture of the Indians.

Victorian House

Finally a visit should be made to the Victorian House, built in 1851–52, in which can be seen the contents of an upper-class household of 1890 belonging to the Danish businessman Rudolph Christensen (Conducted tours: June 16th–Sept. 15th: Thur.–Sun. noon–3pm on the hour; Sept. 16th–June 15th: Sat., Sun. noon–3pm on the hour).

New Bridge

See Marble Bridge

New Port

See Nyhavn

Nikolaj Plads (Nicholas Square) H7

Location
East of Højbro Plads

Nikolaj Plads takes its name from the massive Nicholas Church (Nikolaj Kirke), built in the 13th c., which was completely burnt down in the great conflagration of 1795, except for the tower. Subsequently the butchers of Højbro Plads set up their stalls or "Maven" (stomachs) in the abandoned churchyard. The use of the area as a market did not come to an end until

View of Saint Nicholas' Church

1917 when the rebuilt Nicholas Church which we know today was opened. The spire of the new church, which was completed in 1910, was financed by a donation from the brewery owner Carl Jacobsen (see Carlsberg Brewery).

Buses
1, 2, 6, 8, 10, 28, 29, 41

Today the Nicholas Church is no longer used for religious services, but instead is a venue for concerts and art exhibitions. The building also has a small restaurant.

Nicolaj Kirke

In the summer months Nikolaj Plads is the setting for theatrical and musical events, in particular the Copenhagen Jazz Festival: one of its most famous venues is the bar, "De tre Musketérer" ("Three Musketeers"), at no.25 in the square.

**Ny Carlsberg Glyptotek (Glyptotheque) H7

The Ny Carlsberg Glyptothek is situated on Dantes Plads with its ancient Dante column which was presented as a gift by the city of Rome. It houses the collections of the brewer Carl Jacobsen and his wife Ottilia (see Carlsberg Brewery), which they donated to the nation in 1888. The museum was built to designs by Vilhelm Dahlerup and opened in 1897 and has been continuously developed and extended right up to the present day through the Carlsberg Foundation. Thus the original collections of Etruscan, Egyptian, Greek and Roman sculptures have been joined by a remarkably large selection of works by Rodin and also works by Gerhard Henning, Kai Nielsen and other modern Danish sculptors. In the 1920s French paintings from the 19th c. were added to the collections with the result that the glyptotheque is also rich in works by Gauguin, Degas and other painters from this period.

Location
Dantes Plads 7

S-bane
Main railway station

Buses
1, 2, 5, 10, 14, 16, 28, 29, 30, 32, 33, 34, 41

Opening times

May–Aug.: Tues.–Sun. 10am–4pm; Sept.–Apr.: Tues.–Sat. noon–3pm, Sun. 10am–4pm.

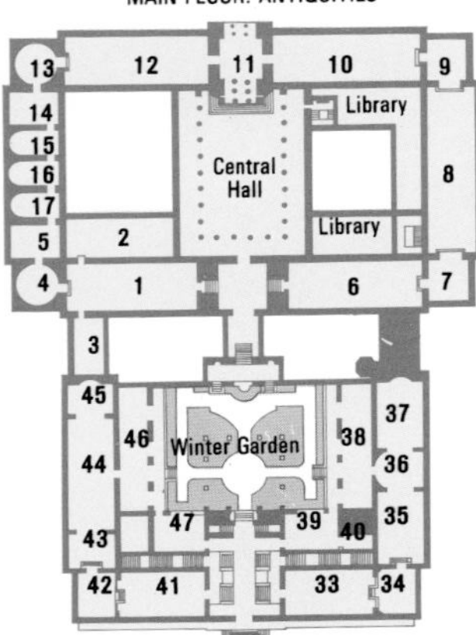

Ny Carlsberg Glyptotek

MAIN FLOOR: ANTIQUITIES
Entrance through Winter Garden

1–4 Egyptian art and craft
5 Ancient Oriental art
6–9 Greek archaic, classical and Hellenistic art
10 Greek portraits
11–17 Roman portraits

GROUND FLOOR: MODERN COLLECTION
Entrance through Entrance Hall or Winter Garden

33–37 French sculptors (Carpeaux and Rodin; Kai Nielsen)
38 Cafeteria
39 Sales area (catalogues, postcards)
40 Lift
41–46 Danish sculptors of 19th and 20th c. (H. V. Bissen, J. A. Jerichau)
47 Sculpture by C. Meunier

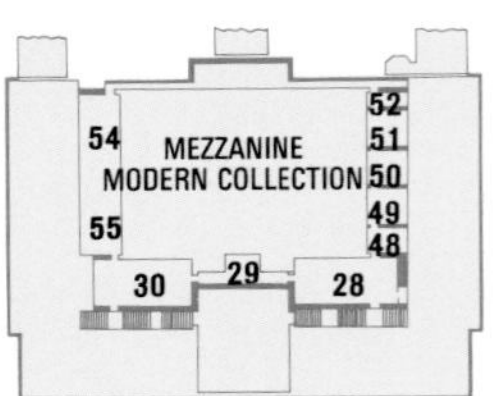

GROUND FLOOR: ANTIQUITIES
Entrance through Central Hall

19–23 Etruscan art
24–25 Palmyra collection
S Study collections

MEZZANINE: MODERN COLLECTION
Stairs from Entrance Hall or lift from Room 40

28–30 French Impressionists and their followers (29 Degas bronzes)
48–52 Danish paintings from J. Juel (early 19th c.)
53 Sculpture by H. E. Freund
54–55 Danish painting and sculpture 19th–20th c. (from Th. Philipsen to N. L. Stevns, E. Weie and K. Isakson)

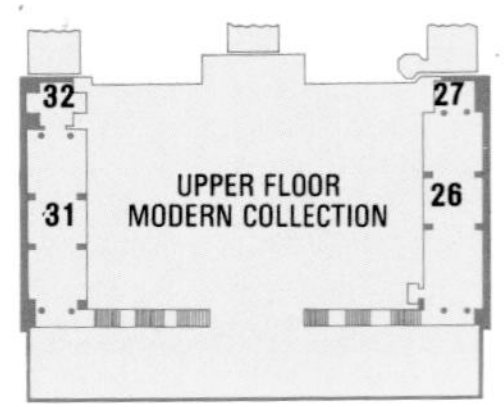

UPPER FLOOR: MODERN COLLECTION
Stairs from Entrance Hall or lift from Room 40

26 French painting from David to Manet
27 French sculpture
31–32 French painting from Gauguin to Toulouse-Lautrec

Visit

Winter garden

The central point of the museum is a wonderful winter garden with a Mediterranean climate, which is intended to convey to the visitor the atmosphere in which a substantial part of the works on display were created. In the centre of the room in addition to other portraits can be seen the picture by the Dane Kai Nielsen entitled "Water mother with children".

The front building contains the modern section (Rooms 33–47).
To the left of the entrance hall are the rooms devoted to the Danish sculptors, especially the two Thorvaldsen pupils H. W. Bissen (1798–1868) and J. A. Jerichau (1816–83); to the right are the French rooms in which a collection, unrivalled outside France, of works by the sculptor Auguste Rodin (1840–1917) is to be found.

In the middle and top storeys of the front building, together with more sculpture (an important collection of bronzes by E. Degas), there is a collection of paintings by French impressionists and their contemporaries (Rooms 26–32) and Scandinavian masters of the 19th and 20th c. (Rooms 48–55). These collections include the following: J. K. David ("Portrait of the Comte de Turenne", 1816), Camille Corot ("View of Grand Trianon", 1866), Gustave Courbet ("Three English girls", 1865), Paul Cézanne ("Self-portrait", 1888), Edouard Manet ("Shooting of Emperor Maximilian I of Mexico", 1867), Paul Gauguin ("Girl from Tahiti", 1891) and Vincent van Gogh ("Landscape at St Rémy", 1889), as well as representatives of the "Danish Golden Age", the artists C. W. Eckersberg ("Double portrait of Preben Pille-Brahe and Johanne Caroline Wilhemine f. Falbe", 1817) and Jens Juel ("Mother and son", 1800).

The antiques section (Rooms 6–17) in the rear building, which to a large extent was assembled with the help of the German archaeologists W. Helbig and P. Arndt, can claim to be one of the finest north of the Alps: its

Sculpture by pupils of Thorvaldsen, H. W. Bissen and A. Jerichau

Egyptian grave drawings (c. 480 B.C.)

Paul Gaugin: "Girl from Tahiti" (1891)

wealth of Roman portrait statues and busts could scarcely be surpassed even in Rome itself.

Among the Greek statues there are excellent originals of archaic art of the 6th and 5th c. B.C. as well as Roman copies of the famous Greek sculptures and busts of Myron, Phidias, Polyklet, Kresilas, Agorakritos, Praxiteles, Skopas and Lysippos.

The Egyptian and Etruscan sections are also notable.

The major part of the Etruscan collection (Rooms 19–23) was already in the glyptotheque at the time of Carl Jacobsen. The oldest exhibits include an urn, the cover of which is fashioned in the form of a head, and a cube-shaped gravestone (Cippus) with elaborate relief decorations depicting a burial ritual (both from Chiusi; 6th c. B.C.). Vases and bronzes found in noble Etruscan graves date from the same period.

In the Egyptian collection (Rooms 1–4), which mainly consists of burial art, all early periods of Egyptian art are represented. Especially worthy of mention is the beautifully wrought head of an Egyptian princess (*c.* 1360 B. C.).

Room 5 is devoted to antique art of the Near East. The oldest piece on display here is the sitting figure of a Sumerian, which can be dated to about 2500 B.C. In addition the visitor will find Assyrian, Persian, Phoenician and Cyprian sculptures.

In Room 18, which also serves as a hall for concerts and lectures, there are numerous portrait statues and Roman copies to see, as well as a series of sarcophagi from the period of the Roman Empire.

**Nyhavn (New harbour) J6/7

Location
Kongens Nytorv

Buses
1, 6, 7, 9, 10, 28, 29, 31, 41

The Nyhavn is the name of a canal which was dug between 1671 and 1673 in order to connect the port of Copenhagen with the Kongens Nytorv (see entry). The harbour promenade of the same name runs along it and on the north side it is today a pedestrian zone and one of the most popular places in the whole city. In summer the Nytorv is especially "hyggelig", as the Danes say, which means more or less "very friendly" but furthermore conveys the charming atmosphere of this colourful harbourside street.
Nyhavn, where the writer Hans Christian Andersen (see Famous People) once lived (in nos. 18, 20 and 67), used to be considered a kind of counterpart to the Hamburg Reeperbahn. On what was formerly the "seedy" side, in the now extensively restored brightly painted old gabled houses on the quayside, a large number of restaurants have been set up. They offer the visitor not only the traditional Danish "Kolde Bord" but also superb fish dishes and foreign specialities. On summer evenings the people of Copenhagen like to meet on the Nyhavn "just for a glass of beer", with which they can relax on the quayside and enjoy the romantic view of the old sailing ships mirrored in the water.
One of the curiosities to be found among the small shops which have grown up here is the studio belonging to Ole, the "King of Tattooists", which is in the cellar of no. 17.

Sailors' Memorial

An anchor was placed at the end of the Nyhavn as a memorial to Danish sailors who lost their lives during the Second World War.

Museum harbour

Nyhavn is a "museum harbour" for the picturesque museum ships of the National Museum (see entry) and other lovingly restored ships. There is also a lightship at anchor here dating from 1885 (Fyrskib XVII) which once did service as the "Gedser Riff" lightship.

The "hyggelige" (pleasant) atmosphere of the Nyhavn

Harbour and canal trips

From Nyhavn the visitor can take harbour and canal trips to the Little Mermaid (see Den lille Havfrue) and Christianshavn (see entry). See also Practical Information, Boat trips.

Orlogsmuseet

See Christianshavn

Peblinge Sø

See Sankt Jørgens Sø · Peblinge Sø · Sortedams Sø

Reformert Kirke (Reformed Church) H6

Location
Gothersgade 111

Buses
7, 17, 43

After the German, French and Dutch Calvinists were given the right to freedom of religious worship in 1685, building of the Dutch–French Reformed Church was begun in 1688 and was completed just a year later. The stonemason Henrik Brockham was the architect of the rectangular Baroque building made with red Dutch bricks. The church suffered severe damage in the fires of 1728 and 1731 but was afterward completely restored.
Inside the church, special attention should be given to the wonderful carved pulpit by Friedrich Ehbisch, the galleries and the monarch's throne. The placing of the altar and the pulpit on the same side and the lack of any figurative decorations are characteristic of buildings of the Reformed Church.

Regensen (Collegium Regium; students' college) H6

Location
Store Kannikestræde 2

Buses
5, 7, 14, 16, 17, 24, 43, 84

In 1569, in order to help students with inadequate means, Frederik II founded a society offering 100 free scholarship places. The Regensen students' college was built between 1623 and 1628 in red brick under Christian IV (see Famous People). The royal benefactor is remembered by a plaque on the Købmagergade (see entry). The hostel, which was able to accommodate just under 100 students in 48 rooms, was officially called Collegium Regium in 1628 but within a year the name Regensen came into use.
The only part of the building to survive the great fire of 1728 was the wing on the Store Kannikestræde, the rest being rebuilt in 1731. Further additions and alterations to the building followed at the end of the 18th c. and the beginning of the 20th c.

In the courtyard of the Collegium, which is still used today as a students' hostel, there is a linden tree, which was planted in the 1950s. It replaced the famous linden tree which was planted by the Regensen provost A. C. Hviid on May 12th 1785, the anniversary of which is celebrated every year.

**Rosenborg Slot (Rosenborg Palace) H6

Location
Øster Voldgade 4A

Since 1833 the collections of the Danish kings have been on display to the public in Rosenborg Palace, which was built at the same time as Frederiksborg Palace (see entry).

Rosenborg Castle

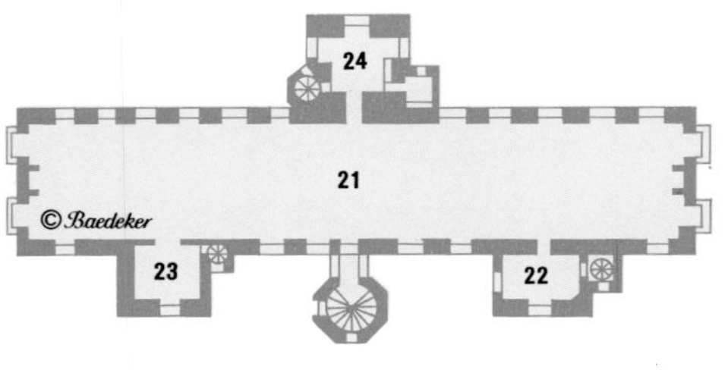

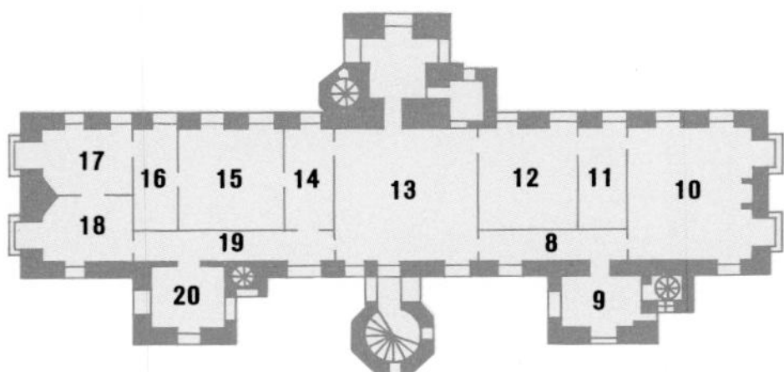

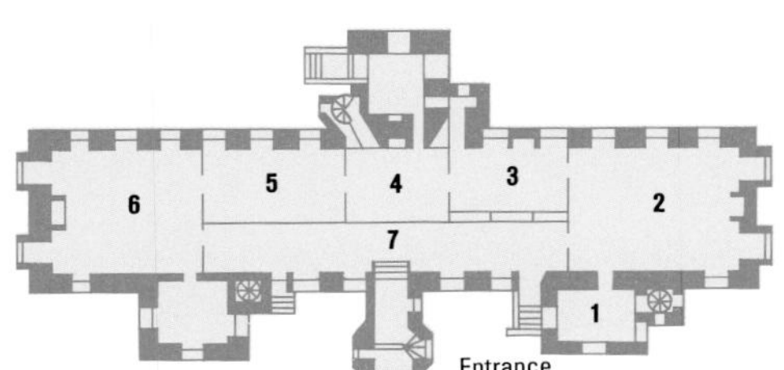

SECOND FLOOR

21 Long Room
22 Glass Chamber
23 Porcelain Chamber
24 Regalia Room (at present closed)

FIRST FLOOR

8 Frederick IV Corridor
9 Lacquer Cabinet of Princess Sophie Hedwig
10 Frederick IV's Apartment
11 Frederick IV's Study
12 Christian VI's Apartment
13 "The Rose" Anteroom Mirror Cabinet
14 Frederick VI's Study
15 Christian VII's Chamber
16 Frederick IV's Chamber
17 Christian VIII's Chamber
18 Frederick VII's Chamber
19 Corridor of Christian VII and Frederick VI
20 Bronze Room

GROUND FLOOR

1 Christian IV's writing cabinet
2 Christian IV's Winter Room
3 Christian IV's Bedroom
4 Dark Room
5 Frederick III's Marble Room
6 Royal Chamber of Christian V
7 Stone Passage

S-bane
Nørreport

Buses
5, 7, 10, 14, 16, 17, 24, 43, 84

The palace dates back to the reign of Christian IV (see Famous People), who initially had the south part built in 1606–07 and then in 1613–17 had it considerably extended by the addition of the square west tower designed by Bertel Lange. Between 1633 and 1634 the eight-sided staircase tower was added on the front of the east façade, most likely by Hans van Steenwinckel the Younger. The palace was built in the Dutch Renaissance style as a spring and autumn residence of the Danish kings and was used as such until the middle of the 18th c.

Opening times

May 1st–May 31st, Sept. 1st–Oct. 21st: daily 11am–3pm; June 1st–Aug. 31st: daily 10am–4pm; Oct. 22nd–Apr. 30th: Tues., Fri. and Sun. 11am–2pm.

Visit

Rosenborg Slot today contains, in the 24 rooms on show, a wealth of objets d'art associated with the Danish royal house, as well as the unusually charming original furniture, which contributes to the palace's immense appeal.
The following are especially worth seeing: Christian IV's study, decorated with elaborate panels and ceiling paintings, where the king carried out his extensive correspondence sitting at a gold-painted writing cabinet made in 1580 in Augsburg; the Winter Room of Charles IV, in the panelling of which

Christian IV's study . . .

. . . in Rosenborg Palace

Dutch paintings from Antwerp have been inset; Frederik III's Marble Room, originally the bedchamber of Christian IV's consort, decked out in a very formal baroque style; the King's Chamber, with Dutch Gobelin tapestries by M. Wauters and formal portraits of King Christian V and Queen Charlotte Amalie (both paintings by J. D'Agar); the painted chamber, decorated in 1663–65 for Sophie Amalie, the wife of Frederik III, with sumptious chinoiserie, turquoise and mother-of-pearl; the hall of Frederik IV, adorned with gobelins from Audenarde of (*c.* 1700); the "Rose" ante-chamber, with paintings and furniture from the time of Frederik V; the mirror chamber, fitted out in 1700 for Frederik IV following the model of Versailles; a 24-arm amber chandelier made in 1743–56 by L. Spengler; the Flora Danica dinner service for 100 people, produced in 1803 by the Royal Porcelain Factory, the floral decoration of which is from a design by G. C. Oeders; the Glass Chamber, fitted out with Venetian glass in 1714 by Frederik IV after his tour of Europe; and the Long Banqueting or Knights' Hall. It was the last room to be completed in 1624. Only two fireplaces remain from the original fittings. The stucco ceiling, installed at the beginning of the 18th c. by Frederik IV, shows the royal coat of arms, flanked by the Order of the Elephant and the Dannenborg Order.

Treasure Chamber

Occupying three well-secured rooms in the vaults is the Treasure Chamber, opened in 1975 and now on show to the public. Here are to be found the imperial regalia, which have been held in Rosenborg Palace for safe keeping since the end of the 17th c., as well as other royal treasures, including the golden crown of the absolute monarchy, made in 1670 by Poul Kurtz in Copenhagen with diamonds, sapphires and rubies, which was worn by the kings of Denmark for 170 years and which even today is placed on the sarcophagus of a monarch lying in state. In addition the crown of Christian IV, made in 1595–96 by the goldsmith Dirk Fyring in Odense, can be seen, as well as various crown jewels, an enamelled silver drinking horn of 1465 and the symbol of the Order of the Garter, founded in 1348 by Edward III, with its

A royal apartment in Rosenborg Palace

famous motto "Honi soit qui mal y pense". There is also the saddle of Christian IV, embroidered with gold, jewels and pearls, and finally the imperial regalia, made in 1648 for the coronation of Frederik III. The sceptre symbolises authority and power, while the orb with its cross symbolises the earthly ball, with God's anointed ruler at the head of its church.

Kongens Have

Forming part of the palace is the Kongens Have (also called Rosenborg Have), which was laid out in 1606 under Christian IV and is the oldest park in Copenhagen. It contains many statues, including one of Hans Christian Andersen (see Famous People) surrounded by eagerly listening children. The barracks of the Royal Guards are also situated here and the new guard leaves here shortly before 11.30am for the changing of the guard at Amalienborg Palace (see entry). The historical collection of the Royal Guards is also housed in the barracks (see Practical Information, Museums, Livgårdens historiske Samling).

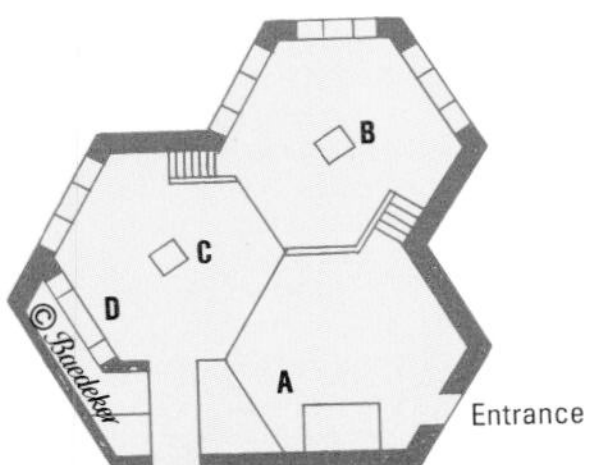

Treasury
Rosenborg Castle

A Christian IV's Collection

B Christian IV's Royal Crown

C Royal Crown from Christian V to Christian VII

D Crown Jewels and Regalia

Roskilde

Location
30km 19 miles west of Copenhagen

Railway station
Roskilde

Location
Town centre

Opening times
Apr. Sat. 11.30am–5.45pm, Sun. 12.30–3.45pm; May–Sept.: Mon.–Fri. 9am–5.45pm, Sat. 11.30am–5.45pm, Sun. 12.30–5.45pm; Oct.–Mar.: Mon.–Fri. 10am–3.45pm

The town of Roskilde lies on the fjord of the same name, which cuts deep into the island of Sjælland (Zealand). Founded according to legend by King Ro, but in point of fact by the Vikings in 980, the town became the seat of the Zealand bishops in about 1020 and rapidly developed into a centre of royal power. It was also from time to time used as the town of residence of the royal family. Today Roskilde is the largest provincial town in Zealand and is the seat of a university.

** Roskilde Domkirke (Cathedral)

The Cathedral of St Luke at Roskilde is one of Denmark's national monuments. The imposing building of red brick faces across the fjord from its slight elevation. Its main features date from the time of Bishop Absalon (see Famous People). Building of the cathedral was begun in 1170 in the Romanesque style at the place where earlier around 1000 under Harold Bluetooth a wooden church had stood. In 1200 the church was extended in the Northern French Gothic style while in the chapels and entrance halls which were added later, various other directions of Danish architecture can

Roskilde Cathedral

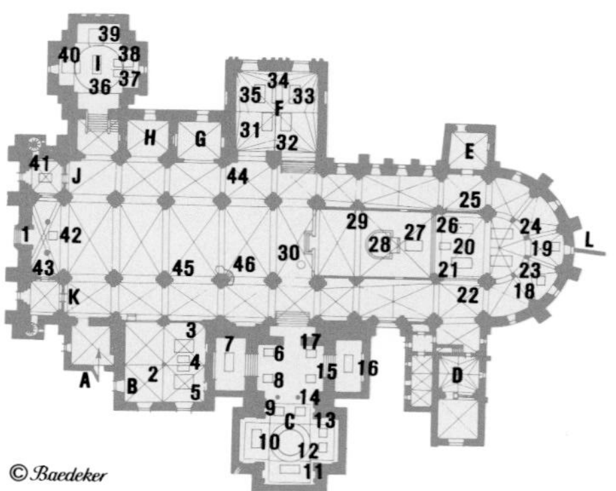

A Entrance
B Christian I's Chapel (chapel of the three kings)
C Frederik V's Chapel
D Chapterhouse
E Oluf Mortensen's Porch
F Christian IV's Chapel
G St Andrew's Chapel
H St Birgitte's Chapel
J N Tower Chapel
K S Tower Chapel
L Absalon's Arch

1 Main entrance
2 Royal Column
3 Monument of Christian III and Queen Dorothea
4 Tombs of Christian I and Queen Dorothea
5 Monument of Frederik II and Queen Sophie
6 Tomb of Caroline Amalie
7 Tomb of Sophie Magdalene
8 Tomb of Christian VIII
9 Tomb of Marie Sophie Frederike
10 Tomb of Queen Louise
11 Tomb of Frederick V
12 Tomb of Juliane Marie
13 Tomb of Christian VII
14 Tomb of Frederik VI
15 Tomb of Louise Charlotte
16 Tomb of Chritian VI
17 Tomb of Frederik VII
18 Helhestens Sten
19 Gravestone of Bishop Peder Jensen Lodehal
20 Monument of Duke Christopher
21 Tomb of Frederik IV
22 Pillar with remains of Svend Estridsen
23 Tomb of Christian V
24 Tomb of Charlotte Amalie
25 Pillar with remains of Estrid, Knud the Great's sister
26 Tomb of Queen Louise
27 Tomb of Queen Margaret
28 High altar
29 Choir-stalls (1420)
30 Font
31 Tomb of Frederik III
32 Tomb of Sophie Amalie
33 Tomb of Anne Catherine
34 Tomb of Christian IV
35 Tomb of Prince Christian
36 Tomb of Frederik IX
37 Tomb of Queen Alexandrine
38 Tomb of Christian X
39 Double tomb of Christian IX and Queen Louise
40 Double tomb of Frederik VIII and Queen Louise
41 Tomb of Anne Sophie Reventlow
42 Kirsten Kimer, Per Døver and St Jørgen
43 Vincentz Hahn's armour
44 Royal Gallery
45 Organ
46 Pulpit (17th c.)

be observed. The two west towers were added in the 14th c., their slim, copper-covered helm roofs dating from 1635–36. The basilica is 85m/280ft long, with three naves, and inside has a height of 24m/79ft. The royal door between the two west towers is only opened for royal funerals, so visitors enter through the side-door on the south side.

Visit

The cathedral is the final place of rest for the Danish monarchs of the last 400 years. The alabaster and marble gravestones of 38 Danish queens and kings buried here – from Margarete I (d. 1412) to Frederik IX (d. 1972) – are one of the main attractions of the church. Inside the church the superb 15th c. carved choir stalls are especially worth seeing.

Above the choir stalls there are wooden reliefs with pictures from the Old Testament (south side) and the New Testament (north side) with a noteworthy depiction of the Ascension.

The great golden winged altar (16th c.) comes from Antwerp and was originally intended for the church of Frederiksborg Palace (see entry). The altar was faultlessly restored after a fire in 1968.

Among other contents of the cathedral which on no account should be missed are the following:

The royal throne with sumptuous decoration dating from the 17th c. (on the canopy), a figure of St John from the early 16th c. (in the middle one of the three chapels in the north transept), the pulpit (1609) made of sandstone, alabaster, marble and black limestone, and the bronze font of 1602.

The royal tombs in the burial chapel (which can be reached from inside) offer a unique basis for comparing the various fashions in monumental art from the early 15th c. to the present century.

The most valuable piece is the supine statue of Queen Margarethe I, behind the high altar, a Gothic piece in alabaster made in 1414 by the Lübeck artist, Johannes Junge.

The burial chapel of Christian IV (on the north side), with its massive ogival vaulting, displays wall paintings by Wilhelm Marstrand and a bronze statue

Roskilde Cathedral

**Rådhus and Rådhuspladsen (City Hall and City Hall Square) G/H7

Location
in the south-west of the city centre

Buses
1, 2, 6, 8, 14, 16, 19, 28, 29, 30, 32, 33, 34, 35, 41, 63, 64, 68

Copenhagen City Hall, seat of the city's administration, is easily reached from the Vesterport and main railway station S-bane stations. It is the fifth in the city's history. It took 13 years to build and was opened in 1905. The architect was Professor Martin Nyrop (1849–1921), himself a member of the city administration.

The city hall covers an area of 7000 sq.m/75,350 sq.ft. Within its rectangular plan are located a covered central hall and also an open courtyard planted with flowers. The administrative offices are to be found in three wings of the building (open: Mon.–Fri. 10am–3pm; conducted tours: Mon.–Fri. 3pm, Sat. 10am).

Flanked by six stone guards the Danish flag today flutters on the ridged roof of the front part of the building. Above a small balcony on the façade is the golden statue of the founder of the city, Bishop Absalon (see Famous People).

Conducted tours of the city hall start in the central hall, which has an area of 44×24m/144×79ft and a height of 9m/30ft and has a glazed roof as well as balconies and galleries on the upper floors. The hall serves as a polling station for elections to the City Council Assembly and for the Folketing, but it is also used as a concert and exhibition hall. It contains busts of four famous Danes and freemen of the city: the first shows the architect of the building, the others the sculptor Bertel Thorvaldsen, the physicist Niels Bohr and the writer Hans Christian Andersen (see notes on all three under Famous People). The oak banisters of the staircase boast 17 balusters which, according to an old Danish children's rhyme, represent the architect and the craftsmen entering the city hall. The magistrate's session room, a large banqueting hall with the coats of arms of Danish cities, the city council chamber and a library complete the city's "seat of government".

Town Hall Square: the Dragon Fountain . . .

. . . and lure blowers

Jens Olsens Verdensur

From the entrance hall there is access to the room housing Jens Olsens' famous world clock, which he worked at for 27 years and which was set going in 1955. It is a miracle of astronomy, showing times throughout the world, the paths of the stars (in particular, the planets) and the dates of the Gregorian and Julian calendars (open: Mon.–Fri. 10am–4pm, Sat. 10am–1pm; conducted tours: Mon.–Fri. 11am, 1.30pm, 2.30pm, Sat. 11am).

Tower

The city hall tower, at 106m/346ft Denmark's highest tower, offers the most panoramic view of Copenhagen. The visitor must first climb nearly 300 steps to reach the balcony and then proceed along narrow passageways to the foot of the spire. The peal of bells in the tower is used as a time signal by the Danish radio service. (Conducted tours: Oct.–May: Mon.–Sat. noon; June–Sept.: Mon.–Fri. 10am, noon, 2pm, Sat. noon.)

Dragon's Leap Fountain

On the imposing square in front of the city hall stands the Dragon's Leap Fountain, the statue of which depicts a bull fighting with a dragon. The bronze statue was made by Joachim Skovgaard in 1923.

Lure Blowers

Between the city hall and the Palace Hotel can be seen two bronze lure blowers by the sculptor Siegfried Wagner which were erected here in 1914. Their bronze horns, bent into an S shape, are 1.70m/5½ft and 1.80m/6ft long. During the Bronze Age in Northern Europe the lures were sacred musical instruments. More than 30 of such instruments were found in Denmark, 18 of which can now be seen in the National Museum (see entry).

Bronze basin

In front of the city hall there also stands a bronze basin made by Martin Nyrop in 1908 which bears the inscription "A beautiful city, you our mother, you look tenderly on the sound. Your mouth smiles lovingly on your children, both big and small."

Andersen Monument

On the square in front of the city hall there is also a monument to the writer Hans Christian Andersen (see Famous People).

Jens Olsen's World Clock

Saint Alban's Church J6

Location
Esplanaden

Buses
1, 6, 9

The Anglican Saint Alban's Church is situated between the Frihedsmuseet and Gefion Springvandet (see entries). It was built in 1885–87 in the English Gothic style to a design by the English architect A. W. Blomfield. English language services have been held here right up to the present day.

In the adjacent Churchillparken there is a monument to the British politician Sir Winston Churchill (1874–1965).

Sankt Ansgar Kirke (Church) J6

Location
Bredgade 64

S-bane
Østerport

Buses
1, 6, 9

The Roman Catholic St Ansgar Church was built in 1841–42 in the Neo-Romanesque style next to the Kunstindustrimuseet (see entry). Since Catholics were not granted permission to ring the bells for mass until the Constitution of 1849, the church originally possessed no tower. The present bell-tower was added in 1943. Of note are the statues of saints over the main doorway and the richly decorated interior (open: Tues.–Sun. 9am–5pm).

Sankt Jørgens Sø

See Sankt Jørgens Sø · Peblinge Sø · Sortedams Sø

Sankt Nikolaj Kirke

See Nikolaj Plads

Sankt Petri Kirke (Church) H6

Location
Nørregade/
St Peders Stræde

Bus
5

Conducted tours
Tues., Wed.
10–11am

Built in 1450, the Sankt Petri Kirke is the church of the German community, which King Frederik II transferred to the Germans resident in Copenhagen back in 1585. From 1681 to 1683 Hans van Steenwinckel the Younger undertook alterations to the building, in the course of which the choir received a Baroque gable. Most of the fittings in the church fell victim to the great fire of 1728, but in 1730–31 the church was rebuilt by J. C. Krieger. Its 78m/256ft tower topped by a spire was added by Boye Junge in 1757. During the bombardment by the English in 1807 the church suffered severe damage but was subsequently completely restored.
Inside the building there are valuable burial chapels, the contents of which include works by the Neo-classical artist, Johannes Wiedevelt (open: June–Aug.: Fri., Sat. 10am–noon, Sun. 11am–noon).

Sankt Jørgens Sø · Peblinge Sø · Sortedams Sø (Lakes) G7–H5

Location
North-west of the city centre

Three lakes (søerne) form a semi-circle round the centre of Copenhagen, the tree-lined streets that pass along their banks being connected by four bridges. In summer it is possible to sail or row on the lakes, in winter skaters are to be seen skimming across the ice. To the west of this girdle of lakes – going from south to north – extend the city districts of Vesterbro, Nørrebro and Østerbro.
The southernmost lake is St Jørgens Sø, on the southern bank of which is situated the Tycho Brahe Planetarium (see entry). In front of the bridge

St Alban's Church

Churchill Monument

(Gyldenløvesgade), which separates off the neighbouring Peblinge Sø, the towers of the Restaurant Søpravillonen (no. 24) dominate the skyline. By the northernmost lake, the Sørtedams Sø, the visitor can stop at "Den franske Café" for coffee and cakes.

Skala

See Axeltorv

Sortedams Sø

See Sankt Jørgens Sø · Peblinge Sø · Sortedams Sø

*Statens Museum for Kunst (State Art Museum) H6

Location
Sølvgade 48–50

S-bane
Nørreport,
Østerport

Buses
10, 24, 43, 84

Opening times
Tues.–Sun.
10am–4.30pm

The State Art Museum consists of a main building in which paintings and sculptures are housed, additional rooms for drawings, graphics and engravings, and a separate building (Kastelsvej 18) which has a succession of temporary exhibitions. The collection was originally derived from the paintings and sculptures belonging to the Danish kings in Christiansborg Palace (see entry), which after the fire of 1894 needed new museum space. The present-day complex was built between 1889 and 1896 by Vilhelm Dahlerup and E. V. Møller in the Italian Renaissance style.
In the painting collection the visitor can see a representative sample of European art from the 13th to the 18th c. The Italian section contains important works by Titian, Bassano and Tintoretto; the Dutch and Flemish

State Museum of Art Statens Museum for Kunst

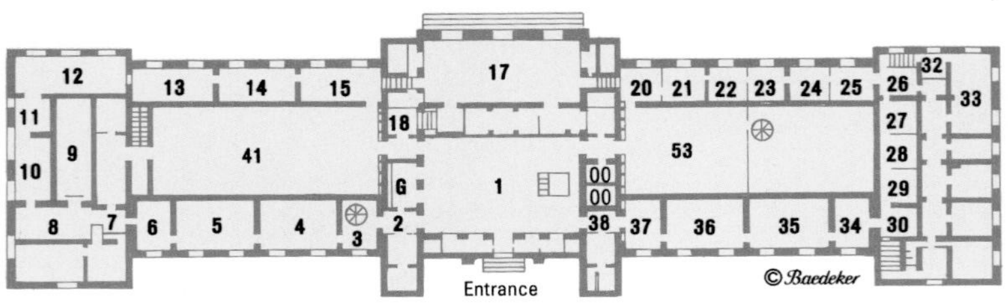

GROUND FLOOR
1 Entrance hall; 20th c. Danish art
2 Information kiosk
3 Cafeteria
4–10 European art (1st half of 20th c.) (including Munch, Matisse, Maillol, Braque, Picasso, J. Gris, Modigliani, E. Nolde)
11–18 Danish art (1st half of 20th c.) (including J. A. Jerichau, K. Nielsen, H. Giersing, J. Søndergaard, G. Henning)
20–30 Exhibition rooms; Print Room
30 Entrance to Museum Library
33 Study room for prints
34–37 Danish art of the 20th c. (temporary exhibitions)
41–53 Danish and international art of the 20th c. (including R. Mortensen, R. Jacobsen, V. Lindstrom, V. Freddie, E. Bile, M. Ernst, Cobra, Poliakoff, M. Andersen, Chagall)

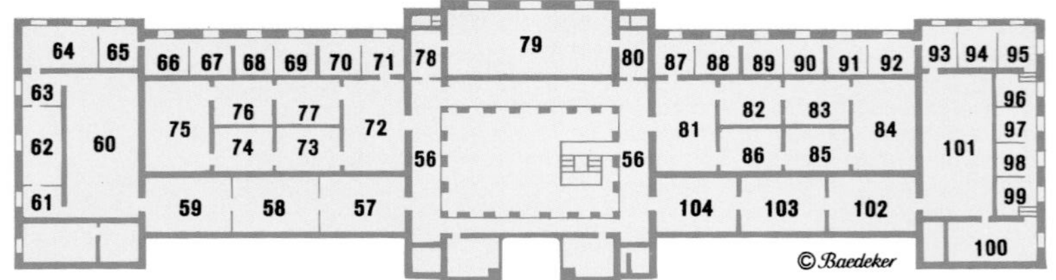

FIRST FLOOR
57–71 Flemish, Dutch and German art of the 15th–18th c. (including P. Breugel, Valchenborch, Rembrandt, Franz Hals, Rubens, Gijsbrechts, J. de Momper, Pieter de Hooch, de Vreis, E van de Welde, Jan Both, Hans Memling, Lukas Cranach the Elder)
56, 72–75 Italian art of the 14th–18th c. (including S. Rosa, Mantegna, Titian, Tintoretto, El Greco, Bernini, Tiepolo, Guardi)
76–77 French art of the 17th and 18th c. (including Poussin, Clodion, H. Robert Claude)
81–104 Danish and Scandinavian art of the 18th and 19th c. (including Jens, Juel, Lungby, C. W. Eckersberg, C. A. I. C. Dahl, Niels Skovgaard, P. S. Krøyer, Anna Ancher, Strindberg, Ch. Købke, Abildgaard V, Hammershøi, Larsen Stevns, Th. Philipsen, P. Hansen, Zahrtmann)

schools are represented by Rubens, Bruegel the Older, Mostaert, Hans Memling, Frans Hals, Rembrandt, van de Velde, van Goyen, Jacob Ruisdael, Jan Steen, Pieter Lastman and Jacob Jordaens. In the German collection can be seen paintings by Lucas Cranach the Older, his studio and his successors. The French section includes, most notably, works by Poussin and Fragonard. There is also a particularly extensive collection of Danish Biedermeier painting, as well as Danish works of the first decade of the 20th c., though relatively only a few painters of the modern school. The Danish artists of the 18th c. include Nicolai A. Abildgaard and Jens Juel, while the "Golden Age" of the early 19th c. is represented by C. W. Eckersberg and his pupils Christen Kobke and Constantin Hansen. Among the landscape painters of the second half of the 19th c. Lundbye, Dreyer and Skovgaard are the most outstanding. Of interest is also a private collection

State Art Museum

Museum of the humourist artist Robert Storm Petersen

donated to the museum of works by French painters of the 20th c. including Braque, Matisse, Rouault and Picasso.

Gallery of engravings

The gallery of engravings, which has been moved here from the Royal Library (Det Kongelige Bibliotek, see Practical Information, Libraries), contains about 100,000 European drawings and examples of graphic art from the middle of the 16th c. to the present day (including etchings and engravings by A. Dürer).

Storkespringvandet

See Amagertorv

Storm P.-Museet (Storm P.-Museum) E7

Location
Frederiksberg Runddel

S-bane
Frederiksberg

Buses
18, 27, 28, 41

This museum, opened in September 1977 at Frederiksberg Runddel, shows the artistic development of the humorous artist Robert Storm Petersen. The collection gained its name from the signature on his works, which was Storm P. (open: May–Aug.: Tues.–Sun. 10am–4pm; Sept.–Apr.: Wed., Sat., Sun. 10am–4pm).

The first room presents the artist's early creative period, influenced by symbolism and Art Nouveau, while the second room contains works on the theme of "the circus", including the work "Green Clown", dating from 1940. The third room is given over to Storm P.'s modern paintings. The drawings in the fourth room are derived from two series, begun in 1916 and 1922, created for the Copenhagen newspaper "Berlingske Tidende". In the fifth room, the reading room, is housed the library. Stage designs by the artist are also set out here.

**Strøget (Pedestrian zone) H6/7

Location
in the centre between Rådhuspladsen and Kongens Nytorv

Buses
Rådhuspladsen:
1, 2, 6, 8, 14, 16, 19, 28, 29, 30, 32, 33, 34, 35, 41, 50, 63, 64, 68, 75E
Kongens Nytorv:
1, 4H, 6, 7, 9, 10, 10H, 28, 29, 31, 41

The name Strøget, which basically means "stripe" or "stroke", is today to be found over the signs of the five streets which form the most famous shopping mile in Denmark and longest pedestrian zone in Europe. The popular name given to the 1.8km/1 mile long traffic artery linking Rådhuspladsen and Kongens Nytorv (see entries) was not recognised officially until the 1980s. Strøget is Copenhagen's most popular shopping street, and the one with the widest range of goods (see Practical Information, Shopping). Many restaurants, bierkellers and cafés have also been set up here.

The five streets which make up the Strøget were declared a pedestrian zone in November 1962 in spite of considerable misgivings among the residents. The names of the historic thoroughfares leading from the Rådhuspladsen are: Frederiksberggade, Nygade, Vimmelskaftet, Amagertorv (see entry) and Østergade. The two squares, Gammeltorv and Nytorv, with their green spaces and fountains, of which Gammeltorv with the Caritas Fountain (see entry) has the oldest, add to the appeal of the Strøget. Alongside many elegant shops, fashion boutiques, jewellers, booksellers, attractive souvenir shops, delicatessen and specialist shops there are the large department stores of Illum and Magasin du Nord, as well as salesrooms belonging to the Copenhagen Porcelain Factory, the Holmegaard Glassworks and the silversmiths, Georg Jensens (see Facts and Figures, Danish Design). Strøget is the epitome of Copenhagen, typical not just of the city itself, but also of its total informality.

Youthful fashions . . .

. . . in the pedestrianised Strøget

Søren Kierkegaard Samlingen

See Københavns Bymuseum & Søren Kierkegaard Samlingen

Teatermuseet (Theatre Museum) H7

The theatre museum is situated in the south wing of Christiansborg Slot (see entry), directly over the royal stables in the rooms which were fitted out by N. H. Jardin in 1766 to form the former Royal Court Theatre.
The theatre can look back on an eventful past. For instance, it was here that Count von Struensee (see Famous People), a powerful minister and lover of Queen Caroline Mathilde, was arrested at a masked ball on January 16th 1772. A short time later he had to pay for his relationship with the queen with his life. In 1842 Jørgen Hansen Koch modernised the auditorium, which had remained unaltered up to then.

Location
Christiansborg, Ridebane 18

Buses
1, 2, 6, 8, 10, 28, 29, 41

Opening times
Wed. 2–4pm, Sun. noon–4pm

The museum, set up in 1922, illustrates the history of Danish and international theatre from the time of Ludvig Holberg (see Famous People) to the present day. There are photographs, prints, costumes and programmes on display.

**Thorvaldsens Museum H7

This museum, which is devoted to the most famous of Danish sculptors, Bertel Thorvaldsen (see Famous People), was founded by the sculptor himself in 1837. However it could only be opened after his death in September 1848 (memorial slab to Thorvaldsen in the inner courtyard). The plot of

Location
Porthusgade 2

Thorvaldsen's Museum

Buses
1, 2, 6, 8, 10, 28, 29, 41

Opening times
Tues.–Sun.
10am–5pm

Amor and the three Graces

land used for the museum was a gift from Frederik VI, while Thorvaldsen donated the extensive collection which was formed from his own works and those he had collected. Gottlieb Bindesboll was chosen as architect for the museum and he designed a building in the historicist style, enhancing it with bright colours both inside and outside. His design gave the outer walls a vivid pictorial frieze, which on the side looking on to the canal depicts Thorvaldsen's triumphant return from Rome in 1838, while on the other two walls the unloading of the frigate "Rota" and the transporting of Thorvaldsen's sculptures into the museum are portrayed. The main entrance is dominated by a four-horsed chariot driven by the goddess of victory which was executed by Thorvaldsen's pupil H. V. Bissen to plans by the master. The bronze group was a present from King Christian VIII.
The ceiling decorations inside the building, which follow antique models, were entrusted by Bindesboll to several artists, including G. C. Hilker, Christian Købke and Jorgen Sonne; the floors were covered with elaborate mosaics and terrazzo work.

Collection

The museum contains a wide-ranging collection of antique figures, sculptures – partly originals, partly models – and details about Throvaldsen's life, such as a demonstration of the artist's methods of working. Thorvaldsen's own collections of paintings and classical antiquities are also on display.

Thotts Palais

See Kongens Nytorv

**Tivoli G/H7

Location
Vesterbrogade 3

S-bane
Main railway station

Buses
Rådhuspladsen: 1, 2, 6, 8, 14, 16, 19, 28, 29, 30, 32, 33, 34, 35, 41, 50, 63, 64, 68, 75E

Opening times
Apr. 24th–Sept. 15th: daily 10am–midnight

The Tivoli amusement park is the most famous tourist attraction in Copenhagen. It lies right in the city centre, only a stone's throw from the Rådhuspladsen (see entry) and the main railway station.

From the very first season it opened the Tivoli has been both a fairground and a cultural centre rolled into one. Using the argument "If the people are kept amused, then they do not get involved in politics", the Algiers-born Georg Carstensen (1812–57) persuaded King Christian VIII in 1843 to construct the park. For an annual rent of 472 thalers Carstensen obtained the 8ha/20 acre site, with its lakes, which are the remains of the moats which once surrounded the old city. Even on its inauguration day in August 1843 the Tivoli attracted 16,000 visitors. In a very short time it developed into the amusement park where – something which was quite unusual for that time – all social classes could mix together. It fast became a world attraction which, since its opening has been visited by over 260 million people. Even today the Tivoli manages to combine in a unique way amusing and exciting entertainment with architectural beauty and a spirit of adventure.

The park is thought to have got its name from a similar amusement park called Tivoli in Paris, which in turn took its name from the Italian city near Rome which is famous for its fountains.

As well as the main entrance on the Vesterbrogade there is another entrance at the Hans Christian Andersen Castle, in which there is also an information office, the museum of holographs (see Practical Information, Museums) and L. Tussaud's Wax Museum (see entry).

Carstensen Memorial

Entering through the main entrance on the Vesterbrogade the visitor will notice a few steps ahead on the right-hand side a bronze statue of Georg Carstensen, extending a cordial greeting with his top-hat and stick. Carstensen's life was however a good deal less cordial: the creator of the Tivoli was to quarrel with his shareholders within a very short space of time. After the unsuccessful opening of another amusement park called Alhambra, Carstensen went abroad for some time, returning to Copenhagen in 1855 embittered and bankrupt, only to die there two years' later at the relatively young age of 45. Yet, even today, the spirit and inspiration of the Tivoli's founder can still be found in the many perfectly preserved original buildings, whose imaginative architecture reflects the oriental influence of Carstensen's childhood and his passion for the Far East.

**Attractions

The wide-ranging entertainment available to the visitor comprises 25 different attractions, including roller-coasters, roundabouts, a mountain railway, hall of mirrors, chamber of horrors, ferris wheel, flying carpet, electric, rowing and pedal boats, as well as the Valmuen puppet theatre. Refreshments are provided by 28 restaurants at prices to suit every pocket, with menus ranging from a simple sandwich with beer through traditional home cooking to exclusive haute cuisine.

An afternoon or evening visit is especially delightful when the 100,000 lamps of every colour (neon-lights are not allowed) which light up the old

Tivoli Amusement Park

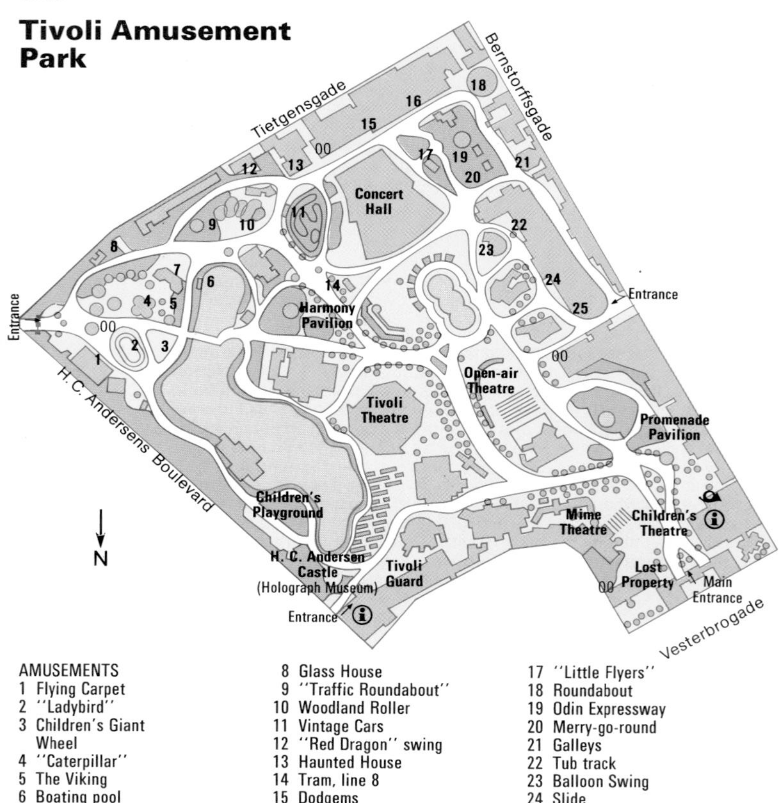

buildings, the wonderful flower arrangements, ornate fountains and the reflections on the surfaces of the lakes combine to make the Tivoli an illuminated dream-world.

*Pantomime theatre

Since political theatre was forbidden in absolutist Denmark, Carstensen allowed pantomime to find its home here. The pantomime theatre, which is protected by a preservation order, is the home every evening to – something unique in the whole world – performances of the traditional Italian commedia dell'arte, with the innocent white-painted clown Pierrot appearing on stage with Columbine and Harlequin.

Concert hall

In the concert hall internationally known artists appear regularly as guests with the Tivoli's symphony orchestra. Wind music, jazz sessions and festival concerts can be heard and performances from visiting ballet companies are also arranged.

Chinese Tower reflected in the Tivoli lake ▶

Oriental architecture in Tivoli . . . *. . . and the pantomime theatre*

Open-air stage

International stars also provide the entertainment on the great open-air stage of the "Plænen" theatre, which has space for 50,000 spectators (performances: Tues.–Sun.: 7pm and 10.30pm, at week-ends also 5pm).

Less well known artists perform on several smaller stages located round the park.

**Fireworks

Particularly impressive are the firework displays which take place on Wednesdays, Fridays and Saturdays at 11.45pm and also on Sundays at 11.30pm on the lake.

*Tivoli Guards

An important symbol of the Tivoli Gardens are the Tivoli Guards, founded in 1844. They consist of 110 boys aged between 9 and 16 drawn from all social classes. Like the Royal Guards they have their own uniform, music corps, flagbearers, marine artillery and a golden coach, in which a tiny prince sits with his tiny princess. The Tivoli Guards march through the park on Saturdays and Sundays at 6.30 and 8.30pm.

Trinitatis Kirke

See Rundetårn

*Tuborg Brewery H3

Location
Hellerup,
Strandvejen 50

A tour of the internationally renowned Tuborg Brewery (Tuborgs Bryggerier A/S), which was founded in 1873, provides the visitor with an excellent introduction into how beer is produced. The tour starts at the historic oak barrel which dates back to when the brewery was founded; the visitor is then taken round the brewing installations where he can follow the production process, starting with the soaking of the barley, which turns into green malt which is then dried into brewer's malt. The tour then proceeds to the brewing room and the mash pans, where the spent hops are separated from the wort, and then finishes up at the bottling plant. Free beer tasting is also then provided.

Tuborg, which has been amalgamated with the Carlsberg Brewery (see entry) since 1970, produces over 17 million litres of beer and exports to over 130 countries.

On the 34ha/84 acre factory site there is a 26m/85ft high beer bottle, which was made for the Nordic industrial exhibition of 1888 at the Tivoli Gardens and which then had a lift operating inside it. Its capacity is the equivalent of 1·5 million bottles of beer!

In the former bottling hall of the brewery the Eksperimentarium (see entry), a museum for natural sciences and new technology, was opened in 1991.

The Turborg "beer-bottle"

Bus
1

Conducted tours
Mon.–Fri.
10am, 12.30 and 2.30pm (and by arrangement, tel. 31 29 33 11)

*L. Tussaud's Wax Museum (waxworks) G7

The idea and art of waxworks in the form we know it today came about in the 17th c. and spread from Paris to London and Amsterdam. A great-grandson of the famous Madame Marie Tussaud, called Louis Joseph Tussaud (1875–1940), who had already set up his own waxworks museums in London and Liverpool, brought the art of wax portraits to Copenhagen. The waxworks building, which was opened in 1894, has been renovated and extended on several occasions, the last time in 1988, when additional galleries were added on to make space for further sections of the museum.

The waxworks museum contains likenesses of over 200 personalities from the worlds of politics, the arts, science, the cinema and other areas of public life. These include the oldest king "Gorm den Gamle", the Viking Knut the Great and his successor Knud the Holy, the English princess Caroline Mathilde, who became famous because of her liaison with the Count of Struensee (see Famous People), many Danish monarchs, including King Christian VI (see Famous People), international politicians from more recent history, (including Adolf Hitler, Sir Winston Churchill, Mao Tse-Tung, Emperor Hirohito, Indira Gandhi, former Prime Minister of Britain, Margaret Thatcher, the United States Presidents Reagan and Bush and the former Soviet President Mikhail Gorbachev), the Danish philisopher Søren Kierkegaard (see Famous People), the artists Pablo Picasso, Vincent van Gogh and Salvador Dalí, the composers Mozart, Beethoven, Edvard Grieg and H. C. Lumbye, the writers Ernest Hemingway, Henrik Ibsen and Karen Blixen (see Famous People), the Danish poet Hans Christian Andersen (see Famous People), surrounded by his fairy-tale characters, the physicists Albert Einstein and Niels Bohr (see Famous People), the Wright brothers, famous as pioneer aviators, stars of theatre and screen, such as Charlie Chaplin, Marilyn Monroe, Jean Harlow, the "Goddess" Greta Garbo, Elizabeth Taylor, Peter Sellers, Liv Ullmann, John Wayne, Ingrid Bergman and Humphrey Bogart in the café in "Casablanca" and great names of the music scene, including Elvis Presley, the Beatles and Charles Aznavour.

Location
H. C. Andersen Boulevard 22

S-bane
Main railway station

Buses
1, 2, 6, 8, 14, 16, 19, 28, 29, 30, 32, 33, 34, 35, 41, 63, 64, 68

Opening times
Sept. 16th–Apr. 28th: daily 10am–4.30pm; Apr. 29th–Sept. 13th: daily 10am–11pm

Christian II and Christian IV . . .

. . . and the "heavenly" Greta Garbo

Chamber of Horrors

In the basement there is a "Chamber of Horrors", where Madame Tussaud is to be seen at work, making death masks from the heads of guillotine victims during the French Revolution. Also on display here are the "Phantom of the Opera", Alfred Hitchcock's "Psycho" cellar, Frankenstein and Count Dracula, as well as Queen Marie Antoinette on the way to her execution.

*Tycho Brahe Planetarium — G7

Location
Gl. Kongevej 10

Buses
1, 14

Opening times
daily 10.30am–9pm

This planetarium, which was opened at the beginning of November 1989, owes its name to the great Danish astronomer Tycho Brahe (see Famous People). Over 400,000 visitors come every year to what is to date the largest planetarium in Western Europe. Its cylinder-shaped building was built to designs by the Danish architect Knud Munk.

In the planetarium's permanent and temporary exhibitions, which are accompanied by explanations in Danish and English, the visitor has the opportunity to become acquainted with the fascinating variety of the universe. With the help of a computer-assisted Zeiss projector, a night sky with around 9000 planets, galaxies, comets and stars can be projected on to the roof of the planetarium, which functions as a colossal screen. The visitor can sit back in his "flight seat" and gaze at the complete panorama.
Apart from these public presentations, there are also astronomy courses, an information centre and the "Cassopeia" restaurant, situated on the bank of St Jørgens Sø and named after the constellation in the northern sky where in 1572 Tycho Brahe discovered a new star, the Nova Cassopeia.

Hven Island

On the tiny island of Hven, which lies in the Øresund to the north-east of Copenhagen and today belongs to Sweden, archaeologists have un-

Niels Bohr and Albert Einstein in wax

Exhibition in the Tycho Brahe Planetarium

covered the remains of the observatories of Stjerneborg and Uraniborg, where Tycho Brahe carried out his earliest astronomical researches. The possible restoration of the ruins, which today can be visited, is under discussion. The local museum on Hven provides an interesting overview of the astronomer's life and work. In winter the island can only be reached by ferry from Landskrona in Sweden, but in summer there are daily crossings by hydrofoil from Copenhagen.

Tøjhusmuseet (Arsenal museum) H7

Location
Tøjhusgade 3

Buses
1, 2, 5, 6, 8, 10, 31, 37, 43

This museum of military history, which was set up in 1928, is housed in the Royal Arsenal, which was built in 1598–1604 under King Christian IV (see Famous People) following Italian models, in particular the arsenal in Venice. Its ground floor consists of a cannon hall, in which aeroplanes can also be seen; its first floor has a hall of weapons and a collection of uniforms. The exhibits are gathered together under the following themes: handguns, armour (including that of Duke Adolf von Gottorf, 1560) and swords from 1400, cannons, flags, coats of arms and uniforms (open: Sept. 16th–June 14th Tues.–Sat. 1–3pm, Sun. noon–4pm; June 15th–Sept. 15th Tues.–Sat. 1–4pm, Sun. 10am–4pm).
The ground floor of the arsenal forms the longest vaulted hall in the whole of Europe: 163m/535ft long, 24m/79ft wide, 27m/89ft high, with the cross vault being supported by 16 central pillars.

Universitet (University) H6

Location
Frue Plads

Bus
5

Bust of Niels Bohr

The old buildings of the university, which was set up in 1479 by Christian I, are situated opposite the Vor Frue Kirke (see entry) in the centre of the old Latin quarter, which with its little alleys full of corners is very reminiscent of the Quartier Latin in Paris. Even today the students of the university continue to put their stamp on the surroundings and ambience of this quarter, although in point of fact most of the university departments have been moved to the island of Amager (see entry).
The university complex has been destroyed by fire on several occasions during the course of its history. The present main building, in which Peter Malling combined classical architectural trends with Neo-Gothic stylism, dates from 1831–36, as a Latin inscription on the façade proves: "Fredericus sextus instauravit anno MDCCCXXXVI" (opened by Frederik VI in 1836). It was built on the ruins of a medieval bishop's palace. At the instigation of the theologist Matthias Hagen Hohlenberg, an enormous eagle was placed over the main entrance to the university with the inscription: "Coelestem adspicit lucem" ("He saw the heavenly light"). On the neighbouring Frue Plads there is a row of busts commemorating distinguished graduates of the university, including one of the physicist and Nobel prizewinner Niels Bohr (see Famous People). Inside the main building the visitor should make a special note of the old university banqueting hall with its historic paintings, the entrance hall with its painted frescoes and the Gobelin hall with Belgian Gobelin tapestries of the 17th c.

University library

Only a short walk away in the Fiolstræde (no. 1) is the university library (open: Mon.–Fri. 9am–6pm, Sat. 9am–4pm), which was moved from its original home in the Trinitatis Kirke (see Rundetårn) in 1862. The red-brick building was erected by J. D. Herholdt between 1857 and 1861. The decorations in the reading room were the work of Georg Hilker.

*Vor Frelser Kirke (Church of the Redeemer) J7

Location
St Annægade

Buses
2, 8, 9, 31, 37, 72E, 73E, 79E

Opening times
Mar. 15th–May 31st: Mon.–Sat. 9am–3.30pm, Sun. noon–3.30pm; June 1st–Aug. 31st: Mon.–Sat. 9am–4.30pm, Sun. noon–4.30pm; Nov. 1st–Mar. 14th: Mon.–Fri. 10am–1.30pm, Sat., Sun. noon–1.30pm

Situated in the district of Christianshavn (see entry), the Church of the Redeemer was built between 1682 and 1696 out of sandstone and brick under the direction of the royal architect, Lambert van Haven. However the upper part of the tower with the external spiral staircase was added later in 1752 by Laurids de Thura, whose inspiration for this addition was the Baroque church of Sant' Ivo alla Sapienza in Rome. The top of the tower is crowned by a globe with a 3m/10ft high golden figure of Christ, which was made by the coppersmith Jacob Høvinghoff.

A visit to the tower involves an ascent of more than 400 steps, of which a third are on the outside of the tower and should only really be negotiated in good weather. There is no truth in the story that the builder of the tower plunged to his death because he had designed the spiral incorrectly!

The interior of the church is just as worthy of attention as the ascent of the tower is spectacular. The high altar, designed in the Italian Baroque style by Nicodemus Tessin the Younger, is elaborately decorated with figures and cherubs. Other outstanding features are the choir screen with its carved angels, a baptismal font of white marble and the organ, begun in 1698 by Christian Nerger, with its carved wooden casing. The gallery of the church with its two-storey organ is supported by two magnificent stucco elephants.

Church of the Redeemer

Church of our Lady

Vor Frue Kirke (Church of Our Lady) H7

Location
Nørregade 8

Bus
5

Copenhagen's "cathedral" is the sixth church to have been built on this site. After the fifth church was burnt down during the bombardment of the city in 1807, C. F. Hansen was given the task of rebuilding the church, which he did between 1811 and 1829 in the neo-classical style with a well-defined design. The triangular gable on the temple-like front facing on to the Nørregade is decorated by a group of statues by Thorvaldsen (see Famous People). The interior, spanned by massive whitewashed barrel-vaulting, contains further examples of works by Thorvaldsen (see Thorvaldsens Museum). Especially noteworthy are the figure of Christ behind the altar, twelve apostles on the walls and the font with its kneeling angel. The characteristic square tower is flat-roofed and is topped by a gleaming cross. (open: June–Aug.: Mon.–Sat. 9am–5pm, Sun. noon–4.30pm; Sept.–May: Sat. noon–4.30pm, Sun. 2.30–4.30pm).
The square adjoining the university (see Universitet) is often the venue in summertime for open-air dramatic and musical performances.

**Zoologisk Have (Zoo) E7

Location
Roskildevej 32

Buses
28, 39, 41, 175

Opening times
Daily 9am–5pm;
June–Aug.
9am–6pm;
Nov.–Mar.
9am–4pm

Copenhagen's zoo is one of the oldest in Europe and, with over 2500 animals, one of the largest. The zoo was founded in 1859 by the ornithologist Niels Kjærbølling. Most of the present stock of animals were either born in Copenhagen or in other zoos. Their enclosures are laid out in such a way that as far as possible they approximate to their natural environment in the wild. Information signs and boards provide the visitor with details about the origins of the individual species.
The zoo has been extensively modernised during the last few years and further alterations and innovations are planned for the future, including the construction of a new house for tropical animals. Consequently the visitor will find modern open-plan enclosures alongside less appropriate older buildings.
A general survey of the zoo can be had from the top of the 44m/144ft viewing tower, situated at the entrance. Prams, etc. can be hired and in addition it is possible to cross the zoo on a miniature railway.

Animals

The zoo consists of the following sections: the reptile house (including giant snakes, tiger pythons, iguanas, poisonous gila lizards, swamp turtles); the gibbon island and the bird lake with storks, pelicans and geese; the lions' enclosure; the parkland with its pink flamingoes; the enclosure for animal species from the far north, such as seals, polar bears, musk-oxen and reindeer; those for pandas, marabous, capybaras; the giraffe house, in which between 1982 and 1987 six new calves were born; the aviary where pheasants and scarlet ibisses from South America can be admired; the tigers' open enclosure; the cages for the snow-leopards and black panthers; the enclosures for shabrack tapirs, boars, gaurs, antelopes, okapis, zebras, ant-eaters, rhinoceroses, gnus, hippopotamuses, sea-lions, camels, pampas, kangaroos and prairie dogs; the nocturnal zoo with bats, South American armadillos, African galagos; next to the parrots's aviary the tropical house with Asiatic birds, sloths, white-tufted apes, Nile crocodiles and tortoises; the house for smaller mammals (including mandrills, tree kangaroos, Brazza seacats, spider monkeys and sacred baboons), in the cellars of which insects and other articulates are housed; and the elephant house, known for its breeding successes. Since 1984 the chimpanzees and gorillas have lived in a new ape house, which with its tropical forest vegetation, tropical temperatures and high humidity simulates a jungle atmosphere. In the Søndermark section it was possible by 1987 to complete a new 4500sq.m/5380sq.yd enclosure for African savanna animals, and in addition there is a children's zoo here with pony rides and other attractions.

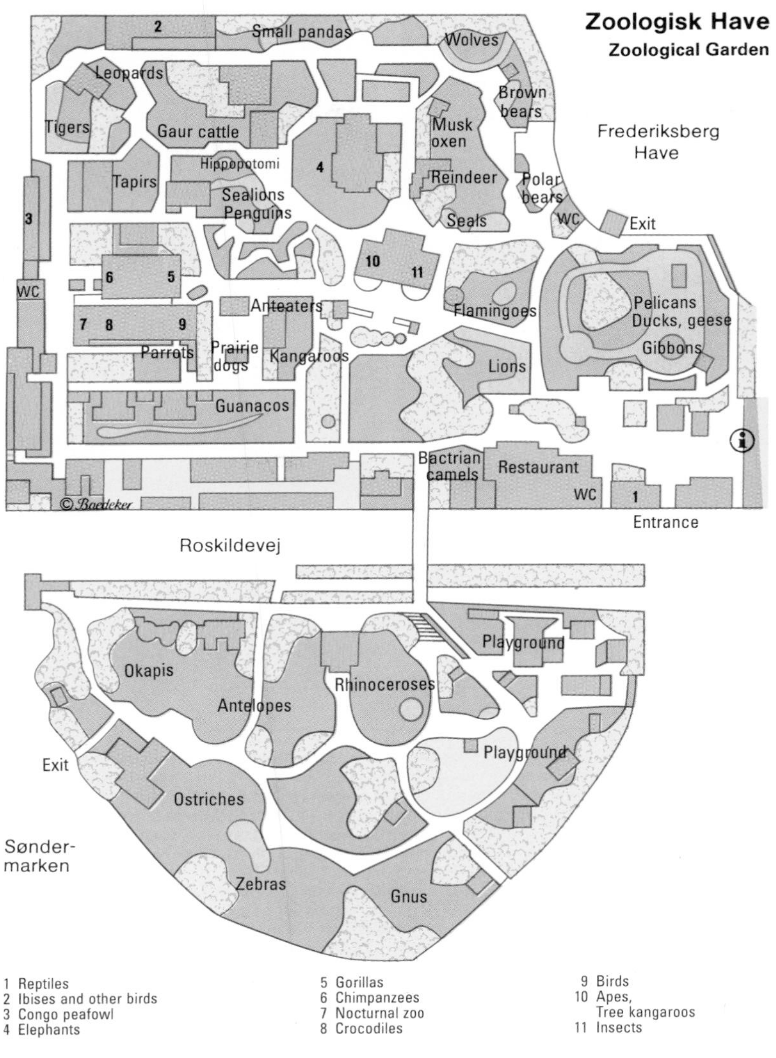

1 Reptiles
2 Ibises and other birds
3 Congo peafowl
4 Elephants
5 Gorillas
6 Chimpanzees
7 Nocturnal zoo
8 Crocodiles
9 Birds
10 Apes, Tree kangaroos
11 Insects

The Zoo: polar bears . . .

. . . and pink flamingoes

At the same time all kinds of activities have been devised for the occupants of the zoo. Thus the ant-eaters for example can dig down in artificial ant-hills for their favoured syrup-like food, and in the climbing trees and rigging frames of the monkey house there hang wooden blocks, the hollows of which are stuffed with dainties which the monkeys can tease out for themselves.

**Zoologisk Museum (Zoological Museum) G5

Location
Universitetsparken 15

Buses
18, 45, 184, 173E, 175E

Opening times
Tues.–Sun.
11am–5pm

The Zoological Museum is one of the most popular museums in Copenhagen among visitors. The reason for this is the up-to-date and highly impressive representation of animals in their natural environment, which for visitors both young and old is an extremely interesting experience.
An early zoological collection was assembled in Copenhagen over 300 years ago by Ole Worm (1588–1654). This museum was taken over by Frederik III and incorporated in his "Royal Chamber of Arts", which existed for around 200 years and in part is preserved today in the Zoological Museum. Around 1770 the university assembled a zoological collection of its own which was not made accessible to the general public until the first half of the 19th c. when it was amalgamated with the "Royal Natural Science Museum". This museum was closed in 1967 and its stock transferred to the new exhibition building in the university park.
The Zoological Museum is divided into two large parts: "Denmark's Animal Kingdom" begins with the migration of the various animal species into Denmark at the end of the last ice age around 15,000 years ago and covers not only the individual natural Danish habitats with their typical flora and fauna, but also the animal species to be found in the urban areas. The section "From pole to pole" outlines the animal world to be found in the various types of natural landscape across the entire planet. Thus the living

conditions of animals is shown not just in the proximity of the North and South poles, but in the endless expanses of the tundra; life is documented in coastal areas, on islands, in the vast forest regions of the northern hemisphere, in mountain areas, deserts, steppelands and tropical rain forests; information is given about the special features of freshwater species as well as about the distinctive forms of life to be found in the ocean (from its uppermost layers to its depths).
The museum is manned by students who can give detailed information and explanations to visitors. In addition a list of the names of Danish animals with translations is available.

Practical Information

Advance Booking Offices

Tickets can be obtained from theatres or concert-halls, or through the following agencies:

Engstrom + Sodring
Palægade 6; tel. 33 14 32 28

Huset
Rådhusstræde 13; tel. 33 32 00 66

Jazzhaus Montmartre
Norregade 41; tel. 33 13 69 66

Saga Ticket Office
Vesterbrogade 25; tel. 31 23 88 00

Tivoli Ticket Centre
Vesterbrogade 3; tel. 33 15 10 12

Tickets at half price for the theatre and concerts on the same day can be obtained from:
Nørreport
Fiolstræde/Nørregade opposite the Nørreport underground station
Open: Mon.–Fri. noon–7pm, Sat. noon–3pm.

Theatres

See entry

Circus

See A–Z, Benneweis Circus

Airlines

Scandinavian Airlines System (SAS)
SAS Building, Hammerichsgade 1–5
Domestic sevices; tel. 33 15 52 66
Europe; tel. 33 15 48 77

British Airways
Vesterbrogade 2; tel. 33 14 60 00

Airport

Kastrup Airport

Copenhagen's airport at Kastrup is on the island of Amager, some 10km/6 miles from the city centre.
In recent years the airport has been made far more attractive, mainly through the construction of a highly modern shopping zone in the depar-

◀ *Ny Carlsberg Glyptotek: the winter garden*

ture and transit area. The duty-free shop has also been enlarged and is now one of the cheapest in Europe.

Domestic flights

There are services from Copenhagen to Billund, Esbjerg, Karup, Skrydstrup, Stauning, Sønderborg, Thisted, Ålborg and Århus (Tirstrup) in Jutland; Odense (Beldringe) on Funen (Fyn); and Rønne on the island of Bornholm (40–60 minutes).

Air taxis

There are air taxis to the islands of Anholt, Læso, Samsø and Ærø.

Air terminal

From the Air Terminal at the main railway station opposite the Tivoli buses leave every fifteen to twenty minutes between 6.15am and 10.45pm, and every ten minutes between 7.40am and 10am and between 3.10pm and 5.30pm; the journey takes about 25 minutes. For information regarding bus times telephone 32 52 00 66.

Flight information

For flight information from Kastrup telephone 31 54 17 01.

Hiring aircraft

Information on private air-fields and the hiring of aircraft (with or without pilot) can be obtained from the Kongelig Dansk Aeroclub, Lufthavnsvej 28, DK-4000 Roskilde.

Antique Dealers

Antiques

Copenhagen is a happy hunting ground for those interested in antiques. There are, of course, many different kinds of antique shops: some are mere junk-shops, others decidedly up-market, and there is a wide range in between. Fortunately for the antique-hunter, however, the dealers tend to be concentrated in certain particular streets, so that it is easy for prospective buyers to look around and make comparisons. Among the most favoured streets are a number running parallel to Strøget (see entry) – Favergade, Kompagnistræde, Læderstræde and Hyskenstræde.

The green-painted house at Kompagnistræde 12, built in 1797–98, is now the home of Denmark's oldest glass company, that of C. E. Fritzsche. purveyors of glass to the Danish Court. Established in 1788, it is still owned by the same family.

At Royal Copenhagen Antiques, Bredgade 12, will be found old Danish silver and jewellery from the workshops of Georg Jensen and A. Michelsen, as well as Holmegaard glass and tableware made by the Royal Porcelain Factory.

Hand-blown glass from the Holmegaard factory can, of course, also be purchased at the emporium of the same name at Østergade 15. A little further along, at No. 40, valuable items from the Georg Jensen silversmiths are on display. We also recommend a visit to the English Silver House at Pilestræde 4. Old porcelain at affordable prices can be found at Mønstuen's at Vester Voldgade 21, and work by the Danish Rosenthal artist Bjørn Winblads (see Famous People) is exhibited at Winblads Hus, Østergade 11.

Antique enthusiasts will also find a number of interesting antique shops in the popular Nyhavn (see A to Z) district.

During the summer months a stroll through the flea-markets (held on Saturdays from 8am–2pm), especially on Israel Plads, can be most rewarding.

Antiquarian and secondhand books

There are many secondhand bookshops (see Shopping) in the University quarter (Studiestræde, Fiolstræde), and altogether Copenhagen boasts some 700–800 such shops, with almost 5000 people engaged in the trade.

Antiques exhibition

Every October a large antiques exhibition is held in the old Stock Exchange (see A to Z).

Auction Rooms

See below

Old Danish dinner service in Royal Copenhagen porcelain

Auction Rooms

The following are some of the main Copenhagen auction houses:

Arne Brun Rasmussen
Bredgade 33
Tel. 33 13 69 11

Bukowskis
Kongens Nytorv 20–22
Tel. 33 33 01 05

Lauritz Christensen
Søtorvet 1–3
Tel. 33 15 55 12

P. Herholdt Jensen
Hammerichsgade 14
Tel. 33 11 40 14

Kunsthallen Art Auctions
Købmagergade 11
Tel. 33 13 85 69

Københavns Auktioner
Æbeløgade 4
Tel. 31 29 90 00

Antiques shop on the Gammel Strad

C. E. Fritzsche – glass dealer since 1788

Sagførernes Auktioner
Nørre Farimagsgade 43–45
Tel. 33 11 45 30

Babysitting

Studenternes Babysitters
Smållegade 52A
Tel. 31 22 96 96

Office hours: Mon.–Thur. 7am–9am and 3pm–6pm, Fri. 3pm–6pm, Sat. 3pm–5pm.
Multi-lingual babysitters will also look after children in hotels.

Banks

Opening times

Mon.–Wed., Fri. 9.30am–4pm, Thur. 9.30am–6pm

Exchange offices (Bureaux de change)

Money can be changed outside normal banking hours at the following places:

Central Station: Apr. 15th–Sept. 30th 6.45am–10pm; Oct. 1st–Apr. 14th 7am–9pm
Tivoli in the season: noon–11pm
Kastrup Airport, arrivals hall: 6.30am–10pm
Kastrup Airport, departure hall: 6.30am–8.30pm
American Express, H. A. Andersen Boulevard 12 and Amagertorv 18 (Strøget): Mon.–Fri. 9am–5pm, Sat. 9am–noon

Handelsbanken, Østergade 26 (Strøget): Mon.–Wed. 9am–5.30pm, Thur., Fri. 9am–6pm, Sat. 9am–2pm
Mercur bygningen, Nyropsgade: Mon.–Wed. 9am–5pm, Thur. 9am–6pm, Sat. 9am–noon

Currency

See entry

Beaches

Though few visitors presumably go to Copenhagen for bathing, there are nevertheless many suitable beaches on the Baltic. These are to be found particularly around Dragør on the island of Amager (see A to Z, Amager), and there are also half a dozen beaches in Køge Bay, south-west of Copenhagen, particularly in the Køge Bugt Beach Park.
Many fine beaches can also be found on the north and west coasts of Zealand, including the broad beaches at Hornbæk, Dronningmølle and Gilleleje, some 55km/34 miles north of Copenhagen, and Sejrø Bay near Holbœk, nearly 60km/37 miles west of the city. Perhaps the most beautiful stretches of all lie in northern Zealand near Tisvildeleje and Liseleje, about 60km/37 miles from Copenhagen, and near Nykøbing and Rorvig, 100km/62 miles away.
Rødvig (75km/47 miles) and Fakse Ladeplads and Karrebæksminde (95km/59 miles) in southern Zealand also boast some fine beaches.

Bicycle Rental

Copenhagen has a well laid-out network of cycle lanes, and this is a good way to get to know the city. Bicycles can be rented from a private firm or at

Bathing beach near Tisvildeleje

the railway station, where a visitor from abroad will be required to show a passport and leave a deposit.

Private firms

Cykeltanken, Godthåbsvej 247; tel. 31 87 14 23
Danwheel Rent-a-bike, Colbjørnsensgade 3; tel. 31 21 22 27
DSB Cykelcenter, Central Station, Reventlowsgade; tel. 33 14 07 17, 33 12 06 07 (open Mon.–Fri. 7am–7pm, Sat. 9am–3pm)

Bicycles can also be rented at the railway stations in Østerborg, Klampenborg, Lyngby, Hillerød and Helsingør.

Boat Excursions

Harbour and canal cruises

Harbour and canal cruises operate from April 26th to September 15th. Information: tel. 33 13 31 05.

Harbour and canal tours:
Departures from Gammel Strand and Kongens Nytorv at Nyhavn every half hour from 10am–6pm (with guide).

To the Little Mermaid:
Departures from Gammel Strand every hour from 10am (without guide).

"Under Twelve Bridges" canal tour:
Departures from Kongens Nytorv and Christianshavn every 30 minutes from 10.15am (without guide).

On the Øresund

Twice weekly between June and September the two-masted schooner "S/V Saga" operates sailing trips on the Øresund. Departures: Tues.

Boats for the "Little Mermaid" leave from Gammel Strand

10.30am from the quay near Amaliehavn Park; Sun. 11am from Dragør harbour.
Information and reservations: tel. 32 53 91 72.

The two-masted schooner "Isefjord" operates by arrangement. From May to October it can be hired for excursions on the Øresund.
Departure: from the quay by the Hotel Admiral, Toldbodgade.
Information and reservations: tel. 33 15 17 29.

Excursions by arrangement on the yacht "Anne Gitte" to the Swedish island of Hven and to Helsingør.
Information and reservations: tel. 42 22 24 60.

Trips from Havnegade by hydrofoil to Malmö in Sweden (journey time 40 minutes).
Information and seat reservations: Flyvebådene; tel. 33 12 80 88.

From Dragør to Limhamn in Sweden, about 20 services a day (journey time 55 minutes).
Information and seat reservations: Scandinavian Ferry Lines in Dragør; tel. 31 53 15 85.

From Tuborg Havn to Landskrona in Sweden (journey time 90 minutes).
Information and seat reservations: Scarlett Line; tel. 31 29 55 22.

Business Hours

See Opening Times

Cafés and Tea-rooms

After a walk around the city it is a good idea to visit one of Copenhagen's many cafés and tearooms to sample the delightful Danish cakes and pastries. Some also offer smørrebrød (see Food and Drink) and substantial sandwiches.

A selection of cafés and tea-rooms

Amalie, Amaliegade 11
Ambrosius, N. Hemmingsengade 32
Arkade Konditoriet, City Arkaden
Cafe Charlottenburg, Nyhavn 2
Cafeen i Nikolai, Nikolai Kirke
Cafe & Ølhalle "1892", Rømersgade 22
Cafe Smukke Marie, Knabrostræde 19
Conditori Hans Christian Andersen, Rådhus-Arkaden 22
Croissanten, Frederiksborggade 3
Gades Konditori, Vester Voldgade 7
Galathea Kroen, Rådhusstræde 9
*La Glace, Skouboegade 3–5 (fantastic ice-creams and old-fashioned Danish specialities)
Kanal-Kafeen, Frederiksholms Kanal 18
Konditoriet, Vesterbrogade 3
*Krasnapolsky, Vestergade 10 ("laid-back" atmosphere)
*Lille Lækkerbisken, Gammel Strand 34 (Italian-like espresso bar)
Marstrands Konditori, Købmagergade 19
Petersborg, Bredgade 76
*Royal Copenhagen, Amagertorv 6 (excellent coffee and cakes stylishly served using old china cups and plates)
Schønnemanns Cafe, Hauser Plads 16
Toldboden, Amaliegade 41

The Huset Gallery includes cafés and a video gallery

Tivolihallen, Vester Voldgade 91
Victor, Ny Østergade 8 (popular haunt of artists)

Calendar of Events

The following are some of the main events celebrated in Copenhagen.

January	New Year concert
April	April 16th is the Queen's Birthday, with a parade of the palace guard.
End of April to mid September	Bakken Amusement Park: special children's festival every Wednesday from the end of June to the beginning of August. Tivoli Amusement Park: open 10am–midnight; fireworks on Wed., Fri., Sat., Sun.; special children's festival every Tuesday from the end of June to the beginning of August.
May to end of August	Sophienholm (Lyngby): children's entertainment and promenade concert every Sunday.
Whitsun	Copenhagen Carnival In the early 1980s students and local groups formed the Whitsun Carnival, based on South American themes. The festival ends with a children's carnival.
June	June 23rd (Midsummer's Eve): bonfires north of Copenhagen to drive away witches. Roskilde Festival: pop festival (jazz, blues, rock and folk-music).

Copenhagen Summer Festival with many events held in squares, streets, pubs, parks and castle grounds.
Dancin' City Dance Festival. — June/July

Youth Festival, Blues Festival, Jazz Festival; International Rowing Regatta; organ concerts in many churches. — July

Amager:
Music Festival (church concerts). — September, October

Antiques exhibition in the Old Stock Exchange. — October

Christmas market.
Christmas concerts. — November, December

Camping

The Danish camping association, Campingrådet, carries out an annual check on camping sites and awards them one, two or three stars according to their standard. Three-star sites are subject to constant checks. A detailed list of sites can be obtained from Campingrådet, Olaf Palmes Gade 10, DK-2100, København Ø, tel. 31 42 32 22. A brochure listing the more important camping sites can be obtained from Tourist Offices (see Information).

Camping sites in and around Copenhagen

Absalon (2 stars)
Kordalsvej 132, DK-2610 Rødovre
Tel. 31 41 06 00
Open throughout the year. 1000 places

Bellahøj (2 stars)
Hvidkildevej, DK-2400 København NV
Tel. 31 10 11 50
Open: June–Sept. 670 places.
Buses: 2, 8, 63 and 68 from Town Hall Square.

Nærum (2 stars)
Ravnebakken, 2850 Nærum
Tel. (02) 42 80 19 57
Open: early Apr.–mid-Sept. 375 places.
15km/9 miles north of city centre, on the E 55/E 47.

Nivå
Campingvej, 2990 Nivå
Tel. 42 24 52 26
Open: early-Apr.–mid-Sept. 130 places.
About 25km/16 miles north of Copenhagen.

Strandmøllen (2 stars)
Strandmøllevej, 2942 Skodsborg
Tel. 42 80 38 83
Open: mid-May–end of Aug. 120 places.
About 14km/9 miles from city centre, via Strandvejen.

Car Rental

To rent a car in Denmark the visitor must be at least 20 years old (in the case of some firms 25) and produce a valid driving licence.

Car rental firms in Copenhagen:

Avis — Kampmannsgade 1; tel. 33 15 22 99
Kastrup Airport; tel. 31 51 22 99

Hertz — Ved Vesterport 3; tel. 33 12 77 00 and 33 13 40 11
Kastrup Airport; tel. 31 50 93 00

InterRent/Europcar — Gyldenløvsgade 17; tel. 33 11 62 00
Kastrup Airport; tel. 31 50 30 90 and 31 50 66 66

Pitzner — Trommesalen 4; tel. 33 11 12 34
Kastrup Airport; tel. 31 50 90 65

Sixt/Budget — Nyropsgade 6; tel. 33 13 39 00
Kastrup Airport; tel. 32 52 39 00

Casino

Since 1991 the Hotel Scandinavia, at Amager Boulevard 70, has had a licence to run a casino. French and American roulette, blackjack and baccarat are all played there.
Information: tel. 33 11 51 15. Open: daily 2pm–4am.

Chemists

Visitors who require special regular medication should take a supply with them. For occasional needs, however, Copenhagen is well supplied with chemists' shops, which are open Mon.–Fri. 9am–5.30pm and Sat. 9am–1pm.
EC citizens producing Form E111 pay only a small proportion of the cost of prescribed medicines (see Medical Assistance).

Open day and night

City centre:
Steno-Apotek
Vesterbrogade 6 C (opposite Central Station)
Tel. 33 14 82 66

On the island of Amager:
Sønderbro-Apotek
Amagerbrogade 158 (near the airport)
Tel. 31 58 01 40

Suburbs:
Glostrup-Apotek
Hovedvejen 101 (road leading west to Roskilde)
Tel. 42 96 00 20

Lyngby-Apotek
Hovedgaden 27
Tel. 42 87 00 96

Cinemas

The cinemas in Copenhagen show foreign films with Danish sub-titles – only the titles on the bill-boards are given in Danish. Monday performances are usually cheaper, and some cinemas offer reductions for matinées.

Palads – a luxury cinema in the Axeltorv

Cinemas
(A selection only)

Cinema 1–8, Rådhuspladsen/Vesterbrogade; tel. 33 11 06 06
Dagmar, Jernbanegade 2; tel. 33 14 32 22
Grand, Mikkel Bryggers Gade 8; tel. 33 15 16 11
Imperial Bio, Ved Vesterport; tel. 33 11 18 21
Palads, Axeltorv 9; tel. 33 13 14 00
Palladium, Vesterbrogade 1; tel. 33 11 18 18
Scala, Axeltorv 2; tel. 33 13 81 00

Reduced prices also apply for evening performances at the following cinemas:
Græshoppen, Huset, Rådhusstræde 13; tel. 33 12 53 53
Klaptræet, Kultorvet 11; tel. 33 13 00 09
Park Bio, Østerbrogade 79; tel. 31 38 33 62
Vester Vov Vov, Absalongsade 5; tel. 31 24 42 00

City Sightseeing and Organised Excursions

City tours and organised excursions

Copenhagen Excursions & Vikingbus operate daily coach tours with English-speaking guides. They leave from Town Hall Square, near the famous statue. Tickets can be purchased from the Tourist Office or from DANVISIT, at H. C. Andersens Boulevard 22, tel. 33 11 13 25.

Short City Tour
Mid-May–mid-Sept., daily, lasting 90 minutes.
A short tour taking in Copenhagen's main features.

Long Copenhagen Tour
Daily all the year round, lasting two and a half hours.
A coach trip to all the important sights in the city.

The most extensive view of Copenhagen is from the tower of the City Hall

Around the City and the Harbour
Early May–mid-Sept., daily, by bus and boat, lasting three hours.
Picking-up points at seven hotels.

Royal Copenhagen Tour
June–mid-Sept.: Thur. 10am, lasting three hours.
Takes in Christiansborg, Rosenborg and Amalienborg castles.

Romantic Historical Afternoon
Mid-June–mid-Aug.: Sat. 2pm, lasting four hours.
Tour to north Copenhagen through Lyngby, with its thatched houses, a boat trip on the Mølleå, then to see some old Danish farmhouses in the Frilandsmuseet, ending with a visit to the Dyrehaven deer-park.

The Castles of Northern Zealand
May–Oct.: Wed., Sat., Sun. from 10.15am, lasting seven hours.
A full day tour of the castles of Kronborg, Fredensborg and Frederiksborg, with a stop for lunch in Helsingør.

Hamlet Tour
May–Sept.: daily 1.30pm, lasting four and a half hours.
A half-day tour of the castles of Kronborg, Fredensborg and Frederiksborg.

To the Land of the Vikings
Mid-May–mid-Sept.: Tues., Sat. 9am, lasting six hours.
Tour of Roskilde, taking in the Cathedral and Viking Ship Museum.

Sweden Trip
End of May–mid-Sept.: Mon., Fri. 8.15am, lasting nine hours.
A full day excursion to the fishing village of Dragør, then by ferry across the Øresund to Malmö, then to the university city of Lund and a visit to the Cathedral, finally returning by ferry to Copenhagen.

On foot

Since distances within Copenhagen are not great, sightseeing walks have become popular as a means of getting to know the city, particularly the old town. There are English-speaking guides. The walks take place at weekends in the early and late season and daily in the high season.
Each walk lasts about two hours, and will be called off only in the event of heavy rain: no one worries about the occasional shower. They are arranged by Guide Ring, Helge S. Jacobsen, Kongelundsvej 91, 2300 Copenhagen S; tel. 31 51 25 90 and 42 73 00 66. Information about the programme, times and meeting place can be obtained from the Danish Tourist Office (see Information).

Themes of the walks:
The heart of the city.
The old canals.
The town of seamen, nobles and soldiers.
Christianshavn – Little Amsterdam
Flowers and art.
Rosenborg – Palace and Park.

Viewpoints

It is always a good idea to get a general view of a city from some suitable high viewpoint. The highest point in Copenhagen is the tower of the Town Hall (113m/370ft); the somewhat exhausting climb will be rewarded with a superb panoramic view. There are guided tours from June 1st–September 30th, Mondays to Fridays at 10am, noon, and 2pm. Saturdays at noon. The spire of the Church of Our Saviour (Vor Frelser Kirke) in Christianshavn is also of respectable height (87m/285ft). More modest eminences are the Round Tower (Rundetårn) and the outlook tower (43·5m/143ft) in the Zoological Gardens, which has the advantage of being the only one with a lift.

Sightseeing Programme

See entry

Boat Excursions

See entry

Rail trips

See entry

Copenhagen Card

See Public Transport

Currency

The Danish unit of currency is the crown (krone, kr.) of 100 øre. There are banknotes of 50, 100, 500 and 1000 crowns, and coins of 25 and 50 øre and 1, 5, 10 and 20 crowns.

Rates of exchange

Current rates of exchange can be obtained from banks, exchange offices and tourist bureaux, and are published in many national newspapers.

There are no restrictions on the import of currency into Denmark. Amounts in excess of 50,000 Danish crowns can be taken out only if at least an equal amount was declared on entry.

Travellers' cheques Eurocheques

Eurocheques and travellers' cheques are accepted by all banks, the larger hotels and shops.

Credit cards

Credit cards are accepted in almost all the larger shops, hotels and many restaurants.

Banks

See entry

Customs Regulations

Entering Denmark

Items for personal use – sports and photographic equipment, radios, jewellery, etc. – can be imported duty free into Denmark, and food for consumption during the journey is permitted. However, meat and meat products (other than canned goods) may not be brought in. A permit must also be obtained on arrival for a CB radio, and hunting-rifles and video equipment must be declared.
The following may be imported duty free from EC countries into Denmark; figures in brackets are the allowances for nationals of other countries: 5 litres (2 lt.) wine and 1·5 litres (0.75 lt.) spirits or 3 litres (2 lt.) fortified wine (below 22%), and 5 litres (3 lt.) of other wine; 75 gr. (50 gr.) coffee or 400 gr. (200 gr.) coffee extract; 200 gr. (100 gr.) tea or 80 gr. (40 gr.) tea extract; 300 (200) cigarettes or 150 (100) cigarillos or 75 (50) cigars or 400 gr. (250 gr.) tobacco; 75 gr. (50 gr.) perfume and ⅜ths litre (¼ lt.) toilet water or after shave. The duty free alowances on other goods and gifts is the equivalent of 4700 Danish crowns. The allowances are lower for goods purchased in duty-free shops.

Leaving Denmark

Similar limits apply on departure.

Diplomatic Representation

Embassies

United Kingdom

Kastelsvej 36–40, DK-2100 Copenhagen Ø; tel. 31 26 46 00

United States

Dag Hammarskjølds Allé 24, DK-2100 Copenhagen Ø; tel. 31 42 31 44

Canada

Kr. Bernikowsgade 1, DK-1264 Copenhagen K; tel. 33 12 22 99

Electricity

Current in Denmark is supplied at 220 volts AC, 50 cycles. Since British plugs will not fit Danish sockets an adaptor is necessary and can be obtained from a suitable dealer.

Emergencies

Emergency

Anywhere in Denmark dial 000 (no coins required)

Medical assistance

See entry

Breakdown service

See Motoring

Excursions

General

For those staying for some time in Copenhagen there are a number of interesting places to visit in the surrounding countryside. They are easily reached by public transport or on organised tours.

Rail trips

See entry

Organised excursions

See City Sightseeing and Organised Excursions

Charlottenlund

Ordrupgårdsamlingen: see Museums

Dronningmølle

Rudolf Tegners Museum: see Museums

Dyrehavn

See A to Z

Esrum Sø

Location: 47km/29 miles north of Copenhagen.
By Lake Esrum stands a monastery of the same name, built by Benedictine monks in the 14th c. Some buildings in the Romanesque style remain.

Farum Bastrup Nature Park

Location: 15km/9½ miles north-west of Copenhagen.
Between Lakes Farum Sø and Bure Sø lies the charming woodland and lakeside scenery of the Farum Bastrup Nature Park. The hills and lakes in this region were formed over 10,000 years ago when the ice-masses receded at the end of the Last Ice Age. Nature-lovers will be able to wander here to their hearts' content. A good setting-out point is the little town of Farum by the lake, from where paths lead through the forest to Bastrup Sø, where the ruins of the medieval Bastrup Tårn (tower) stand on a hill 40m/130ft high. From there the walk can be continued through the forests of Krogelund Slov and Ganløse Eged to Lake Bure.

Fredensborg Slot

See A to Z

Frederiksborg Slot

See A to Z

Frederikssund

Location: 41km/25½ miles north-east of Copenhagen.
During the Middle Ages the town of Frederikssund developed on the site of a ferry on the narrowest part of Roskilde fjord. It became famous for its annual "Viking Festival Plays". The yellow museum building at Jenriksvej 4 is dedicated to the Danish painter and sculptor J. F. Willumsen (1863–1958). The artist's paintings, drawings, prints, ceramics and scupltures are on display (see under Museums).

Fredericksborg Palace

Frederiksværk

Location: 57km/35 miles north-east of Copenhagen.
Frederiksværk, at the northern end of Roskilde fjord, developed here thanks to the completion in 1719 of the canal between the Arrsø – which covers an area of 41sq.km/16sq. miles and is Denmark's largest lake – and Roskilde fjord. However, the town was not actually established until the mid 18th c., with the opening of the cannon foundry and a gunpowder factory, part of which is now a museum. The large old foundry (giethuset) was made into an arts centre in 1988–90. A row of old houses have been preserved along the canal in the town centre.
It is also worth paying a visit to the Museum GeoArt at Frederiksvej 160, which was opened in 1991 and boasts an interesting collection of stones and minerals; it is open daily except Mondays 10am–5pm, and until 8pm on Thursdays. In July and August courses are run here on the polishing of stones and amber.

Frilandsmuseet

See A to Z

Furesøen, Lyngby Sø, Bagsvørd Sø, Mølleå

Location: 15km/9½ miles north of centre of Copenhagen.
The holiday areas near Copenhagen embrace the three lakes known as Furesøen, Lyngby Sø and Bagsvørd Sø, all linked by a canal. Surrounded by woodland, these lakes offer facilities for bathing, sailing, surfing, rowing and fishing, while long walks can be taken along the paths on their banks. The Fure and Lyngby lakes are watered by the Mølleå. In medieval times a number of water-mills were built along its banks to grind corn grown locally. Later copper and paper mills also used the water-power provided by the river. Only two of these old mills have survived.

Gilleleje

Location: 59km/37 miles north of Copenhagen.
Gilleleje, with its lively fishing port, lies at the northernmost tip of Zealand. Among the places worth a visit is the Gilleleje Museum (see Museums), with models of local boats. However, it is the charming countryside around which is the main attraction. A bird sanctuary has been established at Gilbjerg Hoved, and to the east of the town stand two lighthouses, the more easterly of which, built in 1772, was the first of its kind to be fired by coal.

Hellerup

Telephone Museum (Telefonmuseet): see Museums

Helsingør

Location; 45km/28 miles north of Copenhagen.
Helsingør is the site of the castle in "Hamlet" (see A to Z, Kronborg Slot). Also worth seeing are the many old half-timbered buildings along Stengade (a pedestrian zone), including some typical 18th c. houses which have been carefully restored and are now listed buildings. The church of St Olai, the building of which was begun in 1200 but not completed until 1559, is the country's largest church outside a city, and possesses beautiful altar-paintings, an artistic choir-screen and a fine baptistry. Just 200m/220yds further north on Sct. Annæ Gade stands the late medieval church of the Virgin Mary, with its magnificent organ. This church forms the south wing of the Carmelite monastery, built in 1430 and the best preserved one in Denmark. This is where Dyveke (d. 1517), the mistress of King Christian II, lies buried. Today the monastery houses the municipal museum, the Bymuseum (open: daily noon–4pm). Also worth a visit are the art exhibitions in the Marienlyst Slot (see Museums) and the natural history collections in the Museum of Technology (Danmarks Tekniske Museum; see Museums). From this old trading port there are ferries across the Øresund – which is only 4·5km/2¾ miles wide here – to Helsingborg in Sweden.

Hillerød

Location: 35km/22 miles north of Copenhagen.
Most of those who visit Hillerød come to see Frederiksborg Slot (see A to Z, Frederiksborg Castle). However, Helsingørgade and Slotsgade are also attractive pedestrian zones, ideal for window-shopping.

Holmegaard Glass Works

See Facts and Figures, Danish Design
See Museums

Holte

Søllerød Museum (Vedbæk Finds): see Museums

Hornbæk

Location: 50km/31 miles north of Copenhagen.
Hornbæk is the oldest fishing town on the north coast of Zealand. The resort, very picturesque with its red and yellow painted houses, boasts a large marina and a wide beach of fine sand. The blue interior of the 1737 village church symbolises the importance of the sea to the good folk of Hornbæk, which is further underlined by a row of model ships hanging from the roof. The reredos was the work of the Danish artist C. W. Eckersberg.
Early in the 19th c. trees were planted in the neighbouring "Hornbæk Plantage" nature park to provide protection from strong winds; today it is a popular spot for a day out.

Hornsherred, Jægerspris, Selsø

Location: 50km/31 miles west of Copenhagen.
A number of megalithic graves on Hornsherred show that this peninsula between Isefjord and Roskilde fjord was inhabited thousands of years ago. In 1987 archaeologists found the site of a house dating from the third millennium B.C., to date the oldest one known to have existed in Denmark. It is well worth paying a visit to "Jægerspris", the royal hunting-lodge in the north of the peninsula, built in the 16th c. and renovated in the 18th c. Its last inhabitants were Frederick VII and his third wife, the illegitimate daughter of a serving-maid, who became Countess Danner when she married the king. Following the death of the king the countess set up a trust to assist girls of little means who fell upon hard times. In the palace park are 54 columns erected in honour of famous Norwegian and Danish noblemen.
East of Skibby stands Selsø Palace, built in the 16th c. and redesigned in the 18th c., and noted for its rooms decorated with Versailles mirror glass dating from 1733, as well as for its paintings by H. Krock.

Hundested

Knud Rasmussens Hus: see Museums, Rasmussen House

Hørsholm

Museum of Hunting and Forestry: see Museums

K. Blixen Museet

See A to Z

Kronborg Slot

See A to Z, Kronborg Castle

Køge

Location: 32km/20 miles south of Copenhagen.
The little town of Køge is renowned for its picturesque old 16th and 17th c. half-timbered houses. The Køge Museum and Køge Skitsesamling (see Museums) are interesting for students of art and the history of art. For a pleasant change and a rest take a trip to the Koge Bugt, a beach-park some 7km/5 miles long.

Lejre Forøgscenter

See A to Z

Louisana

See A to Z

Lyngby

Sophienholm: see Museums
Frilandsmuseet: see A to Z

Nærum

Sommers Veteranbil Museum: see Museums

Roskilde

See A to Z
Craft Museum (Håndvårksmuseet), Palæsamlingerne, Roskilde Museum: see Museums.

Food and Drink

Although the cuisine of Copenhagen does not enjoy the reputation of that of France, it is possible to eat very well in the city. There is the usual variety of international dishes, but visitors should not miss the chance to sample Danish specialities.

Mealtimes

Breakfast (*morgenmad*) can be obtained in restaurants and hotels until about 11am. It usually consists of rolls, cheese, egg, marmalade and a variety of assorted cold meats. Lunch is taken between noon and 2pm, and the evening meal usually between 6pm and 9pm.

Frokost

Typically Danish are the varied cold and slightly warm buffets spread out in restaurants, which make lunch in Denmark such an important meal. The first course is always fish – usually marinated herring, followed by smoked or marinated salmon – and then a choice between rissoles, roast pork, liver paté or brisket of beef, finishing with cheese (*ost*) served with a topping of rum. Beer and aquavit are usually drunk with the meal.

The Copenhagen Menu

Smørrebrød

The legendary *smørrebrød* is an open sandwich topped with every conceivable variety of tempting delicacy, such as roast beef, salmon, filleted fish, smoked eel, liver paté or shrimps. Note that white bread is called *franksbrød* and brown bread *rugbrød*. Ready-made smørrebrød can be bought at lunch-time in most of the city's numerous restaurants and in some specialist shops, such as Centrum Smørrebrødsanretning, Vesterbrogade 6C (opposite Central Station).

Fish

Fish is prepared in many tasty ways in Copenhagen. Many courses include trout, small flat-fish or fried plaice. Delicacies which should not be missed include smoked salmon or *graved lachs*, salmon marinated in a mixture of sugar, salt, pepper and dill.

Meat

Also very popular are the tasty bacon and substantial meat dishes, such as roast pork with crispy crackling and red cabbage (*flæskesteg med røkål*),

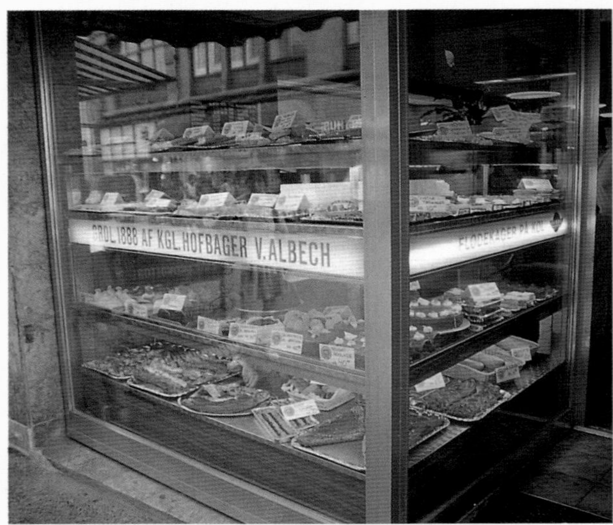

"Kransekager" and "Wienerbrød" delicacies

fried sausage (*pølser*) from roadside stalls, spicy rissoles of pork or beef, pea-soup with sausages and pork (*gule årter*), and roast venison with cranberries (*dyreryg*).

Sweets

Danish sweets are always good. Among particular favourites are *rødgrød med fløde* (red fruit pudding with cream), marzipan cakes such as *kopenhagener*, *wienerbrød* and *kransekager*, and of course *fløde-is* (cream ices).

Restaurants

See entry

Drinks

The national drinks of the Danes are coffee and beer. Wine, mainly imported from Germany, France and Italy, is relatively expensive, although prices have tended to fall in recent years.
A typical Danish *schnaps* (brandy), often drunk following a greasy meal, is *aquavit* (water of life), a brandy with the aroma of caraway seeds and other spices, with an alcohol content of at least 38%. The most popular brands are Rød Aalborg and Jubilæums-Akvavit. Gammel Dansk is recommended for those who like a bitter drink to settle the stomach. Fizzy drinks are known as *vand*, an abbreviation of *sodavand*; examples are *appelsinvand* (fizzy orange) and *citronvand* (fizzy lemonade). Mineral water is called *danskvand*. Meals usually end with coffee, which is served in all pubs and bars.

Beer

The usual drink is a light lager (*øl*), normally sold in small bottles. There is also a Danish keg beer, not dissimilar to British beer.
By far the biggest brewery chain in Denmark is United Breweries Carlsberg and Tuborg, which produces over fifteen different brands for domestic consumption. These include various beers such as the light Grøn Tuborg

"Apollo" – Denmark's smallest brewery, opposite the Tivoli

and Hof by Carlsberg, both with 3·7% alcohol content, and the darker Rød Tuborg and Gammel Carlsberg. Somewhat stronger are Carlsberg Guld Export (4%) and Guld Tuborg (4·6%). Stronger still, up to 6·2%, are the light-coloured Elefanten Beer, Tuborg F.F., and Tuborg Påskebryg, as well as the amber-coloured Carlsberg 47, known as C47 for short, the number referring to the year 1847, when the Carlsberg brewery was founded. Gammel Porter is a sweet stout similar in appearance to Guinness, with an alcohol content of 6·1%.

A Danish speciality is what is known as *kande*, much favoured by connoisseurs, a mixture of two kinds of beer (a sort of "black and tan"), plus aquavit, Pernod and lemonade.

Opposite Tivoli, in the "A Hereford Beefstouw" restaurant, Denmark's smallest brewery, the Apollo, brews its own keg beer. With the support of the Wiibroe Breweries this little brewery was set up in the middle of the restaurant.

Some Gastronomic Terms

English	Danish
restaurant	restaurant
cafeteria	cafetaria
breakfast	morgenmad
lunch	middagsmad
evening meal	aftensmad
food	spise
drink	drikke
much, many	meget, mange
a little	lidt
bill	regning
to pay	betale
at once	straks
menu	spisekort
soup	suppe
meat	kød
grilled	stegt på grill
roast	steg
roast mutton	fåresteg
veal	kalv
lamb	lam
reindeer	okse
ham	skinke
pork	svin
roast pork	flæskesteg
sausage	pølse
fish	fisk
fried	stegt
boiled	kogt
fish dumplings	fiskeboller
cod	torsk
trout	ørred
herring	sild
salmon	laks
smoked lobster	røget laks hummer
prawns	reje
crab	krebs
vegetables	grøn(t)sager
cauliflower	blomkål
beans	bønne

peas	ært
cucumber, gherkin	agurk
potatoes	kartoffel
cabbage	kål
green salad	grøn salat
red cabbage	rødkål
spinach	spinat
tomato	tomat
ice cream	is
stewed fruit, etc.	kompot
red fruit pudding	rødgrød
pudding	budding
whipped cream	flødeskum
fruit	frugt
apple	æble
orange	appelsin
pear	pære
strawberry	jordbær
bilberry, blueberry	blåbær
raspberry	hindbær
cherry	kirsebær
plum	blomme
drinks	drik
beer	øl
coffee	kaffe
milk	mælk
mineral	mineralvand
cream	fløde
tea	te
water	vand
wine	vin
white wine	hvidvin
red wine	rødvin
bread	brød
white bread	franksbrød
rolls	rundstykke
cake	kage

Getting to Copenhagen

By air

The quickest way to get from the United Kingdom to Copenhagen is by air. There are several flights daily from London and Copenhagen, and less frequent flights from Aberdeen, Birmingham, Dublin, Glasgow and Manchester. Direct flights operate from the United States and Canada to Copenhagen.

By rail

There is a through train from Esbjerg to Copenhagen; the journey lasts about five hours.

By road

There are car ferries to Esbjerg in Jutland from Harwich (approx. 21 hours) and Newcastle (approx. 21 hours). From Esbjerg the route to the capital runs eastwards via Kolding and crosses the bridge on to Funen (Fyn), continuing east via Odense to the ferry from Knudshoved (Nyborg) to Halsskov (Korsør) on Zealand; then north-east to Copenhagen. The road distance from Esbjerg to Copenhagen is about 180 miles.

Help for the Disabled

From the Danish Tourist Board (see Information) can be obtained free of charge a brochure on "Travel for the Disabled in Denmark".
Details of shops, etc., which provide easy access and facilities for the disabled may also be obtained from:
Bolig, Motor-og Hjælpemiddeludvalget
Landskronagade 66
DK-2100 København Ø
Tel. 31 18 26 66

Hospitals

Hospitals
Accident stations
(hospitalet)

In cases of acute illness or worsening of a chronic condition, tourists can be treated free in hospital, provided they have not come to Denmark specifically for this purpose and that returning home is not practicable.
The following hospitals have accident stations for emergency cases which are open day and night.

City centre

Rigshospitalet, Blegdamsvej 9
Kommunehospitalet, Øster Farimagsgade 5

South (Amager)

Sundby Hospital, Italiensvej 1

West

Frederiksberg Hospital, Nordre Fasanvej 57

North

Bispebjerg Hospital, Bispebjerg Bakke 23

Surroundings

Københavns Amts Sygehus (KAS), Nordre Ringvej, Glostrup
KAS, Niels Kildegårdsvej, Gentofte
Hvidovre Hospital, Kettegård Allé 30, Hvidovre
Herlev Sygehus, Herlev Ringvej 75

Medical Assistance

See entry

Emergency Services

See entry

Hotels

Booking

In the high season especially, Copenhagen has hardly enough beds for its many visitors, so it is advisable to book accommodation in plenty of time. Visitors arriving without accommodation should apply to:

Kiosk P in the arrival hall of Central Station
Opening hours:
Apr. 1st–Apr. 30th: Mon.–Sat. 9am–5pm
May 1st–Aug. 31st: daily 9am–midnight
Sept. 1st–Sept. 30th: daily 9am–10pm
Oct. 1st–Oct. 31st: daily 9am–5pm
Nov. 1st–Mar. 31st: Mon.–Fri. 9am–5pm, Sat. 9am–noon

Danvisit
H. C. Andersens Boulevard; tel. 33 32 77 73

Reservations

Reservations can be made through travel agents, motoring associations or direct to the hotel, as well as through:

EASY-BOOK
Nordre Frihavnsgade 23
DK-2100 København Ø
Tel. 31 38 00 37 (daily 9am–11pm)

Rooms can be reserved up to a year in advance by writing to:

Hotelbooking København
Hovedbanegården
DK-1570 Copenhagen V
Tel. 33 12 28 80 (Mon.–Fri. 9am–5pm)

Hotel prices

In Copenhagen a double room with bath will cost at least 600 crowns, rising to 750–1500 crowns for a middle-class hotel and to 1000–2200 crowns for one in the luxury bracket.

Hotel-Cheques

A number of hotels have joined the Hotel-Cheque system; one cheque, or voucher, is valid for a night's stay for one person in a double room. Further details of this discount system can be obtained from tourist information offices (see Information).

Conferences and conventions

A number of hotels offer excellent conference facilities. Further details can be obtained from the Danish Convention Bureau, Skindergade 27, DK-1159 København; tel. 33 32 86 01.

Hotel lists

The Danish Tourist Board (see Information) publishes annually an excellent list of hotels, pensions (guest-houses) and motels, with tariffs, which can be obtained from their branches and from tourist information offices. The rates shown include 15% service charge, 22% VAT and, usually, also breakfast. There is no official classification of hotels in categories according to quality and price.

A Selection of Hotels

City centre

*Absalon, Helgolandsgade 19; tel. 31 24 22 11; 478 beds.
*Altea Scala, Colbjørnsensgade 13; tel. 31 22 11 00; 291 b.
*D'Angleterre, Kongens Nytorv 34; tel. 33 12 00 95; 243 b.
*Christian IV, Dronningens Tværgade 45; tel. 33 32 10 44; 80 b.
*City, Peder Skramsgade 24; tel. 33 13 06 66; 145 b.
*Grand, Vesterbrogade 9A; tel. 31 31 36 00; 233 b.
*Imperial, Vester Farimagsgade 9; tel. 33 12 80 00; 321 b.
*Komfort, Løngangstræde 27; tel. 33 12 65 70; 323 b.
*Kong Arthur, Nørreøgade 11; tel. 33 11 12 12; 172 b.
*Kong Frederik, Vester Voldgade 25; tel. 33 12 59 02; 212 b.
*Mercur, Vester Farimagsgade 17; tel. 33 12 57 11; 208 b.
*Neptun, Sct. Annæ Plads 18–20; tel. 33 13 89 00; 228 b.
*Palace, Rådhuspladsen 57; tel. 33 14 40 50; 286 b.
*Phoenix, Bredgade 37; tel. 33 33 00 33; 324 b.
*Plaza, Bernstorffsgade 4; tel. 33 14 92 62; 165 b.
*Richmond, Vester Farimagsgade 33; tel. 33 12 33 66; 237 b.
*Romantikhotel 71 Nyhavn, Nyhavn 71; tel. 33 11 85 85; 82 b.
*SAS Royal, Hammerichsgade 1; tel. 33 14 14 12; 447 b.
*Sheraton, Vester Søgade 6; tel. 33 14 35 35; 731 b.
Admiral, Toldbodgade 24–28; tel. 33 11 82 82; 815 b.
Alexandra, H. C. Andersens Boulevard 8; tel. 33 14 22 00; 117 b.
Astoria, Banegårdspladsen 4; tel. 33 14 14 19; 163 b.
Carlton, Halmtorvet 14; tel. 31 21 25 51; 100 b.
Centrum, Helgolandsgade 14; tel. 31 31 31 11; 190 b.
Cosmopole, Colbjørnsensgade 5–11; tel. 31 21 33 33; 363 b.
Danmark, Vester Voldgade 89; tel. 33 11 48 06; 80 b.
Excelsior, Colbjørnsensgade 4; tel. 31 24 50 85; 100 b.
Opera, Tordenskjoldsgade 15; tel. 33 12 15 19; 135 b.
Park, Jarmers Plads 3; tel. 33 13 30 00; 108 b.

The traditional Hotel d'Angleterre in Kongens Nytorv

Savoy, Vesterbrogade 34; tel. 31 31 40 73; 133 b.
Selandia, Helgolandsgade 12; tel. 31 31 46 10; 166 b.
Sophie Amalie, Sct. Annæ Plads 21; tel. 33 13 34 00; 258 b.
Triton, Helgolandsgade 7–11; tel. 31 31 32 66; 208 b.
Viking, Bredgade 65; tel. 33 12 45 50; 153 b.
Webers Hotel, Vesterbrogade 11B; tel. 31 31 14 32; 175 b.

To the west

*Scandic, Kettevej 4; tel. 31 49 82 22; 450 b.
Avenue, Aboulevarden 29; tel. 31 37 31 11; 143 b.
Capriole, Frederiksberg Allé 7; tel. 31 21 64 64; 45 b.
Cab. Inn, Danasvej 32–34, 1910 Frederiksberg C; tel. 31 21 04 44; 276 b.
Josty, Pile Allé 14A, 2000 Frederiksberg; tel. 31 86 90 90; 14 b.

To the south

*Sara Hotel Dan, Kastruplundgade 15, 2770 Kastrup; tel. 31 51 14 00; 456 b.
*Scandinavia, Amager Boulevard 70; tel. 33 11 23 24; casino
Amager, Amagerbrogade 29; tel. 31 54 40 08; 52 b.
Bella Danica, Kongelundsvej 292, 2770 Kastrup; tel. 31 50 29 30; 30 b.
Dragør Færgegaard, Drogdensvej 43, 2791 Dragør; tel. 31 53 05 00; 46 b.
Flyverbo, Alleen 72, 2770 Kastrup; tel. 31 50 21 23; 65 b.
Scandic Airport, Løjtegårdsvej 99, 2770 Kastrup; tel. 31 51 30 33; 357 b.

To the north

*Marina, Vedbæk Strandvejen, 2950 Vedbæk; tel. 42 89 17 11; 235 b.
Eremitage, Lyngby Storcenter 62, 2800 Lyngby; tel. 42 88 77 00; 192 b.
Gentofte, Gentoftegade 29, 2820 Gentofte; tel. 31 68 09 11; 136 b.
Hellerup Parkhotel, Strandvejen 203, 2900 Hellerup; tel. 31 62 40 44; 132 b.
Schæffergørden, Ermelundsvej 105, 2820 Gentofte; tel. 31 65 60 65; 130 b.
Frederiksdal, Frederiksdalsvej 360, 2800 Lyngby; tel. 42 85 43 33; 117 b.
ISS Center, Kongevejen 195, 2840 Holte; tel. 42 42 24 55; 123 b.
Kollekolle, Frederiksborgvej 105, 3500 Værløse; tel. 42 98 42 22; 140 b.

Hotel Phoenix . . .

. . . and Palace Hotel

Information

In the United Kingdom

Danish Tourist Board
Sceptre House
169–173 Regent Street
London W1R 8PY
Tel. (071) 734 2637–8

Danish State Railways
c/o DFDS (UK) Ltd
Mariner House, Pepys Street
London EC3N 4BX

In the USA

Danish National Tourist Office
75 Rockefeller Plaza
New York, NY 10019
Tel. (212) 582 2802

In Canada

Danish National Tourist Office
151 Bloor Street West, 8th floor
Toronto M5S 1S4, Ontario
Tel. (416) 960 3305

In Copenhagen

Danmarks Turistråd (Danish Tourist Board)
H. C. Andersens Boulevard 22 (opposite Town Hall)
Tel. 33 11 13 25
Open: May 1st–May 31st: Mon.–Fri. 9am–5pm, Sat. 9am–2pm, Sun., public holidays 9am–1pm. June 1st–Sept. 15th: daily 9am–6pm Sept. 16th–Apr. 30th: Mon.–Fri. 9am–5pm, Sat. 9am–noon.

Information centre for young people

Student & Youth Information "Use it" (Huset)
(Advice for young people about cheap overnight accommodation and meals, hitch-hiking, daily events, etc.)
Rådhusstræde 13; tel. 33 15 65 18
Open: June 15th–Sept. 14th: daily 9am–7pm Sept. 15th–June 14th; daily 10am–4pm.

DIS
(Information on study facilities, holiday courses, student meetings, etc.)
Kattesundet 3; tel. 33 11 01 44

Accommodation — See Hotels

Tourist ticket — See Copenhagen Card

Embassies — See Diplomatic Representation

Insurance

General

Visitors are strongly advised to ensure that they have adequate holiday insurance including loss or damage to luggage, loss of currency and jewellery.

Medical Insurance

Under European Community regulations British visitors to Denmark are entitled to medical care under the Danish social insurance scheme on the same basis as Danish citizens. Before leaving home they should apply to their local social security office for form E 111 and the accompanying leaflet on "How to get medical treatment in other European Community countries".
These arrangements may not cover the full cost of medical treatment, and it is advisable, therefore, even for EC citizens, to take out short-term health insurance. Visitors from non-EC countries should certainly do so.

Vehicles

Visitors travelling by car should be ensure that their insurance is comprehensive and covers use of the vehicle in Europe.

See also Travel Documents.

Language

English is widely understood in Denmark, so that visitors are unlikely to have any difficulty in getting about even if they know no Danish. It is worthwhile, however, learning a few words of Danish – phrases of the "please" and "thank you" variety – and to carry a small dictionary or phrase-book.
Danish is a Germanic language, and is not difficult to read if you have some knowledge of German or Dutch; but spoken Danish is difficult, mainly because of the frequent use of a glottal stop and a tendency (shared with English) to "swallow" part of the word.
The pronunciation of some letters differs from English: d after a vowel is softened to the sound of th in "the", or may be mute; g is hard, as in "go", at

the beginning of a syllable, but at other times is like the ch in "loch" or is mute; j is like y in "yes"; r is a soft sound, not trilled; v before a consonant or at the end of a word becomes the vowel u; the vowel y is pronounced like the French u in "lune"; ej is like the vowel sound in "high"; æ is like a in "take"; ø is like eu in French "deux"; and å has the vowel sound of "awe". It should be remembered, when consulting a dictionary or telephone directory, for example, that the letters æ, ø and å come at the end of the alphabet.

Language schools

K.I.S.S., Nørregade 20; tel. 33 11 44 77
Studieskolen, Antonigade 6, tel. 33 14 40 22

Some important words and expressions

English	Danish
America	Amerika, de forenede Stater
an American	en Amerikaner
England	England
an Englishman	en Englaender
Denmark	Danmark
Danish	dansk
do you speak . . .	taler De . . .
I do not understand	jeg forstår ikke
yes	ja, jo
no	nej
please	værsågod
(yes) thank you	(ja) tak
thank you very much	mange tak
no thank you	nej tak
excuse me	undskyld mig
I beg your pardon	omforladelse
good morning	god morgen
good day	god dag
good evening	god aften
good night	god nat
good-bye	farvel
gentleman	herre
lady, woman	dame, kvinde
young lady, miss	frøken
where is . . .?	hvor er . . .?
road, street	gaden
the road to . . .	gaden vejen til . . .
square (in town, etc.)	plads
church	kirken
museum	museet
when?	hvornår?
open	åbnet
town hall	rådhuset
post office	posthuset
police station	politistation
bank	bank
railway station	banegården, stationen
hotel	hotel
overnight (stay)	overnatning
I would like a room	jeg vil gerne have et værelse
with one bed (single room	enkelt værelse
with two beds (double room)	dobbelt værelse
with bath	med bad
without bath	uden bad
the key	nøglen
toilet	toilettet
doctor	læge
(on/to the) right	til højre

	English	Danish
	(on/to the) left	til venstre
	straight ahead	lige ud
	above	oppe, ovenpå
	below	nede
	old	gammel
	new	ny
	how much is it?	hvad koster?
	dear (expensive)	dyr
Traffic signs	Stop!	Stop!
	Customs	Told
	Caution!	Pas på!
	Slow!	Langsom!
	One-way street	Ensrettet
	No thoroughfare! No through road!	Ingen indkørsel!
	Roadworks	Vejabejde
	mountain	bjerg
	peak	høj
	mountain ridge	ås
	hill	bakke
	valley	dal
	river	elv
	small river	å
	waterfall	foss
	waterway	sund
	inshore waters	vand
	beach, flat stretch of coast	strand
	steep rocky bank	klint
	island	ø
	wood, forest	skov
	moor	mose
	marsh, swamp	sump, kær
	town, city	by
	church	kirke
	tower	tårn
	castle, palace, mansion	slot
	garden, park	have
	country road	landevej
	road	vej
	(market) place	torv, plads
	bridge	bro
	railway	jernbane
	ferry	færge
Gastronomic expressions	See Food and Drink	

Libraries

National Library

Royal Library (Det kongelige Bibliothek)
Christians Brygge 8 (entrance from courtyard of Christiansborg Palace)
Tel. 33 93 01 11
Open: Reading and Catalogue rooms: Mon.–Fri. 9am–7pm, Sat. 10am–7pm
Issue: Mon.–Fri. 10am–4pm
This is not only the National Library, but also fulfils the function of a Danish Book Museum. The Old Reading Room is very interesting.

Royal Library

University Library (Universitetsbiblioteket), Fiolstræde 1
Amager branch: Njalsgade 80
Open: Mon.–Fri. 9am–6pm, Sat. 9am–4pm

University Library

Copenhagen Municipal Library (Københavns Kommunes Biblioteker) Kultorvet 2
Frederiksberg Municipal Library (Frederiksberg Kommunes Biblioteker), Solbergvej 21–25

Municipal libraries

There are specialised libraries and archives in some of Copenhagen's museums: e.g. there is a film library in the Film Museum (see A to Z) and an art library in the State Museum of Art (see A to Z).

Specialist libraries

Lost Property Offices

The lost property office for articles lost in the street is at Carl Jacobsensvej 20, 2500 Valby; tel. 31 16 14 06.
Open: Mon.–Wed., Fri. 10am–3pm, Thur. 10am–5pm.

Articles lost in the street

Losses in an aircraft should be reported to the appropriate airline or at Kastrup Airport; tel. 31 50 32 60.
Open: daily 8am–9pm
Loss of hand luggage: tel. 31 50 32 11
Open: Mon.–Fri. 10am–noon

In aircraft

Lyshøjgårdsvej 80, 2500 Valby; tel. 31 46 01 44
Open: Mon.–Fri. 10am–5pm

In buses

Lyshøjgårdsvej 80, 2500 Valby; tel. 36 44 20 10
Open: Mon.–Fri. 10am–5pm
Written enquiries: Depotet for fundne sager, Hovedbanegarden, DK-1557 København V.

In trains and trams

Markets

Fish market

The sole reminder of the old fish market at Gammel Strand is the "Fiskerkone", a stone memorial to the old fishwives (see A to Z, Gammel Strand).

Flea markets

Flea markets are held:
Every Sat. from May–Sept., 8am–2pm, behind the Frederiksberg Town Hall (buses 1, 14 from Town Hall Square), at Nørrebros Runddel and at Israel Plads.
Frelsens Hær (Salvation Army), Hørhusvej 5, Tues.–Thur. 1pm–5pm, Fri. 1pm–6pm, Sat. 9am–1pm (buses 30, 33, 34 or 35 from Town Hall Square to Brydes Allé and then on foot to Hørhusvej).

Medical Assistance

Emergency call

Anywhere in Denmark dial 000 (no coins required).

Medical Emergencies (Lægevagt)

In case of emergency apply to the Medical Emergency Service:
City centre; Mon.–Fri. 8am–4pm; tel. 33 93 63 00, 4pm–8am
Frederiksberg; tel. 31 10 00 41
Vesterbro, Valby, Sydhavn; tel. 31 22 00 41
Payment must be made in cash.

Dental Emergencies (Tandlægevagen)

Oslo Plads 14 (at Østerport Station, near the tram station)
Consulting hours: Mon.–Fri. 8pm–9.30pm; Sat., Sun., public holidays 10am–noon and 8pm–9.30pm.
Payment must be made in cash.

Hospitals

See entry

In the event of illness

A citizen of another EC country can receive treatment and obtain essential medicaments under the Danish National Health Service, provided that he or she has obtained Form E111 from the Department of Social Services before departure.
Medical and dentists' fees must be paid in cash (see above), but can subsequently be recovered in whole or in part – consult the Danish Tourist Board (see Information) for details.
Citizens of other countries are not entitled to free treatment under this scheme, but it is usually offered at hospitals and accident stations for acute illnesses, subject to certain conditions.
However, ALL travellers are strongly recommended to take out adequate insurance before they leave (see Insurance).

Motoring

Roads

Danish motorways (motorvej) and numbered main roads (A . . ., hovedvej) are well maintained and quiet compared with many other major European roads.

Rules of the road

Vehicles travel on the right, as in the rest of continental Europe.

Priority

Trams have priority, as have buses leaving a stop with their indicators flashing.
A line of white triangles painted across the road indicates that priority is given to traffic on the road ahead.

Seat belts

Seat belts must be worn by drivers and all passengers, front and rear. Motorcyclists must wear a crash-helmet.

Use of horn

The use of the horn must be kept to a minimum in built-up areas.

Warning triangle

A warning triangle must be carried.

Maximum speeds

100kph/62mph on motorways
70kph/43mph for cars with trailers
80kph/50mph for coaches
80kph/50mph on ordinary roads.
50kph/31mph in built up areas.

Even minor infringements of the speed limit can result in heavy fines; anyone unable to pay must surrender his vehicle to the police.

Lights

Cars and motor cycles must use dipped headlamps or fog-lights at all times. There are heavy fines for failing to obey this regulation.

Traffic signs

Traffic signs and road markings are in line with international standards.

Drinking and driving

The maximum permitted blood alcohol level is 8 milligrammes per millilitre.

Parking

See entry

Motoring organisation

Forenede Danske Motorejere (FDM)
Blegdamsvej 124, Copenhagen Ø
Tel. 35 43 02 00. Open: Mon.–Fri. 9am–5pm.
The above organisation will give technical, legal and tourist advice, but will not assist in the event of a breakdown.

Breakdown assistance

In Denmark breakdown and towing services are provided by the state FALCK organisation (tel. 33 14 22 22) and the DAHU (tel. 31 31 21 44).
Both organisations are on call day and night. A fee is charged for their services.

On motorways

On motorways emergency telephones are provided. English is understood.

Accidents

If a foreign driver is wholly or partly responsible for a traffic accident details should be reported to:
Dansk Forening for International Motorkøretøjsforsikring
Amaliengade 10
DK-1256 Copenhagen. Tel. 33 13 75 55

Emergency calls

Throughout Denmark dial 000.

Service garages

There are garages for the servicing and repair of most makes of car in Copenhagen. For their addresses, consult the classified telephone directory for Zealand (''Telefon-Fagbog-Sjælland'') under the heading ''Automobiler''.

Fuel

Lead-free (blyfri) petrol is now obtainable at all filling stations.
The following grades of fuel are normally available:
Lead-free normal (blyfri): 91 octane
Lead-free super: (blyfri): 95 octane
Low-lead content (medium): 96 octane
Super leaded (premium): 98 octane
Diesel

Museums

Copenhagen Card

Those who possess a Copenhagen Card (see Public Transport) are entitled to reduced or free entry to most of the museums in and around Copenhagen.

Museums in and around Copenhagen

Amager Museum
See A to Z, Amager

Aquarium
See A to Z, Akvarium

Architectural Centre
See A to Z, Christianshavn, Arkitekturcentret Gammel Dok

Arsenal Museum
See A to Z, Tøjhusmuseet

Bing & Grøndahl Museum
See A to Z, Bing & Grøndahl Museet

Brøste Collection (Brøste's Samling)
See A to Z, Christianshavn

Burmeister & Wain Museum
See A to Z, Christianshavn, B & W Museet

Carlsberg Museum
See A to Z, Carlsberg Brewery

Festal Hall in the Ny Carlsberg Glyptotek

Old dolls in the Legetøjsmuseet

Dinosaur outside Geological Museum

City Museum
See A to Z, Københavns Bymuseum & Søren Kierkegaard Samlingen

Craft Museum (Håndværksmuseet)
Ringstedgade 68, Roskilde
Train to Roskilde
Open: Mon.–Fri. 6.30am–4.30pm, Sun. 9am–noon
Traditional tools.

Customs Museum (Toldmuseum)
Amaliegade 44
Buses: 1, 6, 9
Open: May–Aug.: Tues.–Thur. noon–3pm; Sept.–Apr.: Wed. 1pm–3pm
The history of customs and excise.

David's Collection
See A to Z, C. L. Davids Samling (Museum of Art)

Dragør Museum
See A to Z, Amager

Dukke Theatrical Museum (Puppet Theatre Museum),
See A to Z Dukketeatermuseet, Priors Papirteater

Eksperimentarium
See A to Z

Film Museum
See A to Z, Christianshavn

Lightship XVII (Fyrskib XVII)
See A to Z, Nyhavn, Museum Harbour

Fredensborg Palace
See A to Z, Fredensborg Slot
Frederiksborg Museum
See Frederiksborg Slot (National Historical Museum)

Freedom Museum
See A to Z, Frihedsmuseet

Gammel Dok Architecture Centre
See A to Z, Christianshavn, Arkitekturcentret Gammel Dok

Geological Museum (Geologisk Museet)
Øster Voldgade 5–7
Buses: 10, 24, 43, 84, 384
S-Bane: Nørreport
Open: Tues.–Sun. 1pm–4pm
The museum illustrates the geology of Denmark and Greenland, with collections of minerals, fossils and meteorites.

Georg Jensen Silver Museum (Sølvmuseum)
Bredgade 11
Buses: 1, 6, 9
Open: Mon.–Fri. 10am–5.30pm, Sat. 10am–2pm.
Silver work from 1904.

Gilleleje Museum
Rostgårdsvej 2, Gilleleje, Hovedgaden 49
Train from Hillerd
Open: June 15th–Sept. 15th; Tues.–Sun. 2pm–5pm
Fishing and local museum (models of boats)

Glyptothek
See A to Z, Ny Carlsberg Glyptotek

Hall of Viking Ships
See A to Z, Roskilde, Vikingeskibshallen

Hirschsprung Art Collection
See A to Z, Hirschsprungske Samling

Holmegard Glass Works
Fensmark near Næstved, 80km/50 miles south-west of Copenhagen
Train: to Næstved, then bus to Fensmark
Glass factory open: Mon.–Thur. 9.30am–noon, 12.30–1.30pm, Fri. 9am–noon (from Mar. 23rd–Oct. 20th), Sat., Sun. 11am–3pm; closed for three weeks in July
Glass museum open: Mon.–Fri. 10am–4pm, Sat., Sun. 11am–4pm

Holography Museum
H. C. Andersens Boulevard 22
Buses: 13, 30, 33, 34
Open: Apr. 24th–Sept. 17th: daily 10am–midnight; Sept. 16th–Apr. 23rd: daily 10am–6pm

HT Museum
Islevdalvej 119, Rødovre
Buses: 12, 125, 148
Open: Wed., Sun. 10am–4pm
Old Copenhagen trams and buses.

Karen Blixen Museum
See A to Z, Karen Blixen Museet

Kastrupgård Collections
Kastrupvej 399, Kastrup
Buses: 9, 32
Open: Apr.–Dec.: Tues.–Sun. 2–5pm, Wed. also 7–9pm
Temporary exhibitions of modern Danish and foreign drawings.

Knud Rasmussens Hus
Knud Rasmussens Vej 9, Hundested
Train: Hundested
Open: Feb. 16th–Apr. 15th: Tues.–Sun. 11am–2.30pm; Apr. 16th–Oct. 21st: Tues.–Sun. 11am–4pm; Oct. 22nd–Dec. 14th: Mon.–Sun. 11am–2.30pm.

Kronborg Castle
See A to Z, Kronborg Slot

Køge Collection
Nørregade 29, Køge
S-bane
Open: Tues.–Sun. 11am–5pm
19th c. sketches, models and drawings.

Køge Museum
Nørregade 4, Køge
S-Bane
Open: June–Aug.: daily 10am–5pm; Sept.–May: Mon.–Fri. 2–5pm, Sat., Sun. 1–5pm.
Cultural history collection, including furniture and costumes.

W. Ø. Larsen's Pipe Museum
See A to Z, Amagertorv

Lejre Historical and Architectural Research Centre
See A to Z, Lejre Forsøgscenter

Lifeguards' Historical Collection (Livgårdens historiske Samling)
Gothersgade 100. Buses: 7, 14, 16, 17, 43
S-bane: Nørreport
Open: May–Sept: Tues., Sun. 11am–3pm; Oct.–Apr.: Sun. 11am–3pm
A collection of uniforms, weapons, pictures and documents from 1658 to the present day displayed in the 200-year-old barracks.

Literary Museum (Bakkehusmuseet)
Rahbeks Allé 23
Buses: 6, 18
Open: Wed., Thur. Sat., Sun. 11am–3pm
Collections from the "Golden Age" of Danish literature and culture, 1800 to 1850.

Louisiana Museum
See A to Z, Louisiana

Marienlyst Palace
Marienlyst Allé 32, Helsingør
Buses: 340, 801, 802
Open: daily 2–5pm
Temporary art exhibitions

Mindelunden (Memorial to Danish Resistance Fighters)
See A to Z, Mindelunden

Museum of Hunting and Forestry
Folehavevej 15–17, Hørsholm
Open: Feb.–Nov.: Tues.–Fri., Sun. 10am–4pm, Sat. noon–4pm
Hunting utensils from the Stone Age to the present day.

Museum of Industrial Art
See A to Z, Kunstindustrimuseet

Museum of Medical History (Medicinisk-historisk Museet)
Bredgade 62
Buses: 1, 6, 9
Open Tues., Thur. and Sun.; conducted tours in English at 11am, 12.30 and 2pm.

Museum of Musical History
See A to Z, Musikhistorisk Museum og Carl Claudius' Samling

Mølsted's Museum
See A to Z, Amager, Mølsteds Museet

National History Museum
See A to Z, Frederiksborg Slot (National Historical Museum)

National Museum
See A to Z, Nationalmuseet

Nivågård Collection (Nivågård Malerisamling)
Gammel Strandvej, Nivå
Train: Nivå
Open: Tues.–Fri. 1–4pm; Sat., Sun. noon–5pm
Italian and Dutch paintings of the Renaissance as well as the Danish "Golden Age" (1800 to 1850).

Nyboders Mindestuer
Sct. Pauls Gade 20
Buses: 1, 6, 9
Open: May–Aug.: Tues.–Fri. noon–2pm, Sun. noon–4pm;
Sept.–Apr.: Wed. noon–2pm, Sun. 1–4pm.

Ny Carlsberg Glyptotek. See A to Z

Ole Roemer's Museum
Kroppedals Allee 3, Taastrup
Bus: 133 from Taastrup
Open: Mon.–Thur. 9am–4pm, Fri. 9am–3pm, Sat., Sun. 2–5pm
Museum devoted to the Danish astronomer Ole Roemer (1644–1710).

Open-Air Museum. See A to Z, Frilandsmuseet

Ordrupgård Collections (Ordrupgårdsamlingen)
Vilvordevej 110, Charlottenlund
S-Bane: Klampenborg/Lyngby, then bus 388
Open: Tues.–Sun. 1–5pm
Mainly Danish and French Impressionists of the 19th and 20th c. Large park.

Palæ Collections
Stændertorvet, Roskilde
Train to Roskilde
Open: May 15th–Sept. 15th: daily 11am–4pm; Sept. 17th–May 14th: Sat., Sun. 1–3pm.
18th and 19th c. paintings and furniture

Pipe Museum
See A to Z, Amagertorv, W. Ø. Larsens Pipe Museum

Ordrupgårdsamlingen: a Matisse . . .

. . . Gauguin's "Mademoiselle Goupil"

Postal and Telegraph Museum (Post-og Telegrafmuseet)
Valkendorfsgade 9
Buses: 1, 2, 5, 7, 8, 24, 30, 32, 33, 43, 63, 84
S-bane: Nørreport
Open: May–Oct.: Tues.–Sun. 1–4pm; Nov.–Apr.: Tues., Thur., Sat., Sun. 1–4pm.

Rosenborg Palace
See A to Z Rosenborg Slot

Roskilde Museum
Sct. Olsgade 18, Roskilde
Train to Roskilde
Open: June–Aug.: daily 11am–5pm; Sept.–May: Mon.–Sat. 2–4pm, Sun. 2–5pm.

Royal Naval Museum
See A to Z, Christianshavn, Orlogsmuseet

Royal Stables and Coach Museum (Kongelige Stalde og Kareter)
Christiansborg Ridebane 12
Buses: 1, 2, 5, 6, 8, 9, 10, 31, 37, 43
Open: May–Oct.: Fri.–Sun. 2–4pm; Nov.–Apr.: Sat., Sun. 2–4pm.

Sommer's Veteran Car Museum
Nærum Hovedgade 1, Nærum
Bus: 195 from Holte
Open: Mon.–Fri. 9am–5pm, Sat. 9am–1pm, Sun. 11am–3pm.
38 veteran and old cars 1908–60), about 1000 model cars and models of ships and aircraft.

Sophienholm
Nybrovej 401, Lyngby
S-bane to Lyngby Sstation, then bus 191
Open: Tues.–Sun. 11am–6pm.
Temporary art exhibitions.

State Art Museum
See A to Z, Statens Museum for Kunst

Storm P.-Museum
See A to Z, Storm P.-Museet

Sweet factory
Nørregade 36
Open: Mon.–Thur. 9am–5.30pm, Fri. 9am–6.30pm.

Søllerud Museum (Vedbæk Finds)
Attemosevej 170, Holte
Bus: 195 from Holte
Open: Tues.–Fri. 2–4.30pm; Sat., Sun. 11am–4.30pm
Local prehistoric archaeological finds.

Søren Kierkegaard Collection
See A to Z, Københavns Bymuseum and Søren Kiekegaard Samlingen

Technical Museum (Danmarks Tekniske Museum)
Nordre Strandvej 23 and Øle Rømers Vej, Helsingør
S-bane: Klampenborg, then bus 188
Train: Helsingor, then bus 340
Open: daily 10am–5pm
Comprehensive natural history and technical collections. The motor vehicle and public transport section, on Øle Rømers Vej, includes an old car dating from 1886 and an aeroplane from 1906.

Trade and Seafaring Museum (Handels- og Søfartsmuseet)
See A to Z, Kronborg Slot

Rudolf Tegner's Museum
Museumsvej 19, Dronningmølle
S-bane: Hillerod, then bus 306
Open: Mar. 24th–Oct. 20th: Tues.–Sun. 9.30am–5pm
Park and museum on a heath-covered hill; works of the painter and sculptor Rudolf Tegner (1873–1950)

Telephone Museum (Telefonmuseet)
Svanemøllevej 112A, Hellerup
Bus: 1
Open: Tues.–Wed. 10am–4pm, Sun. 1–4pm
Telephones from 1876 to the present day.

Theatre Museum
See A to Z Teatermuseet

Thorvaldsen's Museum
See A to Z, Thorvaldsens Museum

Toy Museum
See A to Z, Legetøjsmuseet

L. Tussaud's Wax Museum
See A to Z

Willumsen Museum
Jenriksvej 4, Frederikssund
Train to Frederikssund
Open: Apr.–Sept.: daily 10am–4pm; Oct.–Mar.: Mon.–Sat. 1–4pm, Sun. 10am–4pm.
Paintings by J. F. Willumsen (1863–1958).

Zoological Museum
See A to Z, Zoologisk Museum

Music

Concerts

Danish radio has three permanent orchestras, the Radio Symphony Orchestra, the Radio Light Orchestra and the Radio Big Band.
The Radio Symphony Orchestra plays regularly on Thursdays in the Radio Concert Hall (Radiohusets Konzertsaal, Julius Thomsensgade 1), the Radio Light Orchestra gives weekend concerts and Saturday matinées. In addition concerts are held throughout the summer in the Tivoli Concert Hall (Tietensgade). The chamber music evenings in the Odd Fellow Palæet (Bredgade 28; tel. 33 11 27 22) also enjoy a large following. Student concerts are regularly held in the Royal Music Conservatoire at Niels Brocksgade 1, and others in the Louisiana Museum of Modern Art in Humlebæk.

Information

Information concerning concerts, festivals and other musical events can be obtained from the MIC (Dansk Music Informations Center), Vimmelskaftet 48; tel. 33 11 20 66.

Opera and ballet

Det Kongelige Teater
Kongens Nytorv 9
Buses: 1, 6, 7, 9, 10, 17, 28, 29, 31, 41

For tickets apply to: Postbox 2185, DK-1017 København K
Tickets can be booked for the same evening and for up to three weeks in advance on tel. 33 14 10 02 (between 1pm–8pm).
Programme details: tel. 33 15 22 20
Forthcoming events are published in the daily newpapers and in the brochure "Copenhagen this week", obtainable from the Danish Tourist Board (see Information).

Plays, opera and ballet performances are held on the old and new stages of the Royal Theatre. The best-known ballets include works by the legendary Danish dancer and choreographer Auguste Bournonville (1805–79), who for most of the time was Director of the Royal Danish Ballet from 1830 to 1877, and his interpretations are still performed abroad as well as in Denmark, including those of "Sylphide" (1836), "Napoli" (1842) and "Et Folkesagn" (1854). The latest production of the last named was performed in 1991 in front of Her Majesty Queen Margarethe II. The operatic repertoire extends from Mozart and Verdi through to Carl Nielsen and Kurt Weill. Overseas artistes are frequent guest performers. The theatrical season begins in September and ends in May.

Jazz, blues folk and rock

Copenhagen is well-known for its annual jazz and blues festivals, when local bands join larger international groups to play in the open outside one of the many pubs or on one of the city's squares. Traditional and modern jazz can also be heard live at all other times of the year in many music clubs and cafés.
For details of some of the main centres of the music scene see Night Life, Jazz, blues, folk and rock.

Theatres

See entry

Newspapers

The oldest Danish newspaper is the Conservative "Berlingske Tidende", founded in 1749; its circulation is about 130,000 (twice as much on Sundays).
The morning paper with the largest circulation of about 150,000 (186,000 on Sundays) is the Liberal "Politiken".
The paper with the highest circulation of all is the tabloid "Ekstrabladet" (240,000), followed by its competitor "B. T." with 172,000.

Night Life

Discothèques

Annabel's, Lille Kongensgade 16; tel. 33 11 20 20
Open: Mon.–Sun. 9pm–5am

Blue Heaven, Vestergade 10; tel. 33 32 88 00
Open: Mon.–Thur., Sun. 11pm–5am, Fri.–Sat. 11pm–7am

Fellini Night Club (SAS Royal Hotel), Hammerichsgade 1; tel. 33 14 14 12
Open: Mon.–Sat. 10pm–4.30am

IZIS, Ny Østergade 23; tel. 33 14 38 35
Open: Mon.–Sun. 11pm–5am

Le Mirage, Vesterbrogade 33; tel. 31 24 64 17
Open: Tues.–Sat. 10pm–5pm

Monte Christo, Studiestræde 31; tel. 33 11 06 20
Open: Mon.–Sun. 10pm–5am

New Daddy's, Axeltorv 5; tel. 33 11 46 79
Open: Fri. 10pm–7am; Sat. 10pm–8am

No. 1, Amagertorv 23; tel. 33 12 13 34
Open: Fri., Sat. 10pm–5am

On The Rox, Pilestræde 12–14; tel. 33 12 39 12
Open: Mon.–Sat. 10pm–5am

Privé, Ny Østergade 14; tel. 33 13 75 20
Open: Mon.–Sat. 10pm–5am

Students Club Discothèque, Købmagergade 26C; tel. 33 12 81 02
Open: Fri., Sat. 9pm–5am

Sweet Dreams, Allégade 8; tel. 31 21 20 42
Open: Mon.–Sat. 10pm–1am

Tordenskjold, Kongens Nytorv 19; tel. 33 12 43 56
Open: Mon.–Sun. 10pm–5am

Trocadero, Jernbanegade 6; tel. 33 11 00 10
Open: Mon.–Fri. 4pm–2am, Sat. 10pm–2am

U-Matic, Vestergade 10; tel. 33 32 88 00
Open: Tues.–Sat. 11am–5pm

Jazz, blues, folk and rock

Bananrepublikken A/S, Nørrebrogade 13; tel. 31 39 79 21
Open: Mon.–Sun. 11am–2am

Bar Blue, Rådhusstræde 13; tel. 33 11 29 32
Open: Mon.–Sun. 10pm–2am
(Fri., Sat. punk and disco)

Barcelona, Fælledvej 21; tel. 31 35 76 11
Open: Mon.–Sun. 11am–2am

Ben Webster, Vestergade 7; tel. 33 93 88 45
Open: Mon.–Sat. noon–3am; Sun. 5pm–1am

Ca 'Feen Funke, Sct. Hans Torv; tel. 31 35 17 41
Open: Mon.–Sun. 11am–1am

City Rock, Scala, Axeltorv; tel. 33 15 45 40
Open: Mon.–Sun. 11am–2pm

De Tre Musketerer, Nikolaj Plads 25; tel. 33 12 50 67
Open: Mon.–Sat. 10pm–2am
(mainly jazz)

Finn Zieglers Hjørne, Vodroffsvej 24; tel. 31 24 54 54
Open: Mon.–Sun. 8pm–1am

Hånd i Hanke, Griffenfeldtsgade 20; tel. 31 37 20 70
Open: Mon.–Sun. 9pm–1am
(mainly folk)

La Fontaine, Kompagnistræde 11; tel. 33 11 60 98
Open: Mon.–Sat. 11pm–8am

Jazzhus Montmartre, Nørregade 41; tel. 33 12 78 36
Open: Mon.–Thur., Sun. 8pm–1am; Fri., Sat. 8pm–5am

Jazzhus Tivorleans, Tivoli; tel. 33 14 30 74
Open: Thur., Fri., Sat. 9pm–2am

Musikcafeen, Rådhusstræde 13; tel. 33 11 29 32
Open: Mon.–Sun. 9pm–1am
(mainly rock)

Rådhuskroen, Løngangsstræde 21; tel. 33 11 64 53
Open: Mon.–Sat. noon–4am; Sun. 4pm–4am
(mainly folk)

Shamrock Inn, Scala, Axeltorv; tel. 33 14 06 02
Open: Mon.–Sun. 10pm–2am
(mainly rock)

Vognhjulet, Thorsgade 67; tel. 31 83 15 70
Open: Mon.–Sun. 8pm–2am
(mainly folk)

Woodstock, Vestergade 12; tel. 33 11 20 71
Open: Mon.–Wed., Sun. 9pm–2am; Thur. 9pm–3am; Fri., Sat. 9pm–5am

Dancing
(Danse-
restauranter)

Amphora Bar (Sheraton Copenhagen Hotel), Vester Søgade 6;
tel. 33 14 35 35
Open: Sun.–Thur. 9.30pm–2.30am; Fri., Sat. 8.30pm–2.30am

Annabel's, Lille Kongensgade 16; tel. 33 11 20 20
Open: Mon.–Sun. 9pm–5am

Cicero Bar, Skindergade 43; tel. 33 11 58 16
Open: Mon.–Sun. 10pm–8am

Club Exalon, Frederiksberggade 38; tel. 33 11 55 14
Open: Mon.–Sun. 9pm–2am or 5am

Fellini (SAS Royal Hotel, Night Club), Hammerichsgade 1; tel. 33 14 14 12
Open: Mon.–Sun. 10pm–4.30am

Hongkong, Nyhavn 7; tel. 33 12 92 72
Open: Mon.–Sun. 5pm–5am

Kakadu Bar, Colbjørnsensgade 6; tel. 31 21 78 19
Open: Mon.–Sun. 8pm–5am

Nezer's Bar, Århusgade 99; tel. 31 38 62 27
Open: Mon.–Sat. 11am–11pm

Den Røde Pimpernel, H. C. Andersens Boulevard 5–7; tel. 33 12 20 32
Open: Mon.–Sat. 8pm–2am or 3am

Søpavillonen, Gyldenløvsgade; tel. 33 15 12 24
Open: Mon.–Sun. 11.30am–2am

Vin & Ølgod, Skindergade 45; tel. 33 13 26 25
Open: Mon.–Sat. 8pm–2am

Xanadu Bar, Helgolandsgade 2; tel. 31 31 03 28
Open: Mon.–Sun. 8pm–4am

Pubs/bars (saloons)

Galathea Kroen, Rådhusstræde 9; tel. 33 11 66 27
Open: Mon.–Sun. 6pm–2am

Halvvejen, Krystalgade 11; tel. 33 11 91 12
Open: Mon.–Sun. noon–1am

Hviids Vinstue, Kongens Nytorv 19; tel. 33 15 10 64
Open: Mon.–Sun. 10am–1am

Peder Oxe's Vinkælder, Gråbvrødretorv; tel. 33 11 11 93
Open: Mon.–Sun. noon–1am

Universitetskaféen, Fiolstræde 2; tel. 33 14 72 18
Open: Mon.–Sat. 10am–5am; Sun. 5pm–5am

Wonder Bar, Studienstræde 69; tel. 33 11 17 66
Open: Mon.–Sun. 9pm–5am

Opening Times

Banks

See entry

Offices

Normal office hours, although there may be variations, are from 9 or 10am to 4 or 5pm. They are usually closed on Saturday.

Post

See entry

Shops

Normal opening times are 9am–5.30pm Monday to Thursday (some shops may stay open until 7pm), Fridays 9am–7pm (large department stores to 8pm). On Saturdays some close at 2pm, others at 5pm. Some shops close on Monday or Tuesday.
During the summer months a number of shops in the city centre also open in the afternoons on Saturdays and Sundays. Special opening times apply during the pre-Christmas period. Bakers' shops, those selling smørrebrød, flowers and souvenirs, together with stalls and kiosks, are usually open on Sundays.

There is a supermarket in the Central Station which remains open until midnight every night, including Sundays.

Parking

Car parks

The are various car parks in and around the city, but in the city centre itself, with its one-way streets and pedestrian precincts, it is easier to get about on foot.

Parking meters

Parking meters operate from 9am to 6pm Monday to Friday, 9am to 1pm on Saturdays. The time limit is three hours.
Charges vary from three to ten crowns an hour.

Parking discs

The sign "P-shive pådbudt" means that parking discs must be displayed. The discs should be set at the quarter-hour following the time of arrival. They can be obtained at police stations, post offices, banks and filling stations.

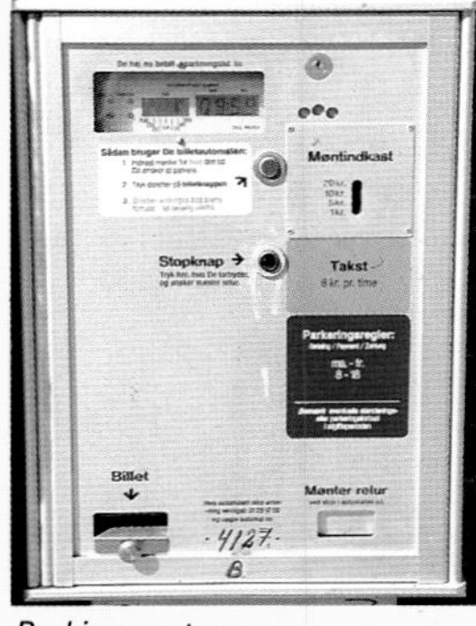

Parking meter

Parking ticket machines

Wherever there is a "P" sign at the side of the road together with the word "ZONE" parking is allowed for a fee. Vehicles loading and unloading need not pay.
Payment is made at the nearest ticket machine, which will be quite close to the "P" sign. After insertion of the required coin the digital display will show the parking time allowed, and this will also be entered on the ticket which it will then print. There are four different parking zones with varying periods of permitted parking: the red zone allows a maximum of three hours, the yellow, green and blue zones up to ten hours; charges vary between four and fifteen crowns per hour. Tickets must be displayed in all zones from Monday to Friday between 8am and 6pm, and in the yellow and blue zones on Saturdays and Sundays also between 8am and 2pm. The ticket must be clearly displayed, preferably on top of the dashboard of the car.

"Parkering forbudt"
"Stopforbudt"

These signs mean that parking and stopping respectively are forbidden.

Multi-storey car parks

Opening times

Multi-storey car parks in the central area of the city are usually open from 6am or 8am to 8pm, sometimes until midnight. Some are closed on Saturday afternoons and Sundays.

The following firms have parking facilities for customers:
Illum, Købmagergade
Magasin du Nord, Bremerholm
Den Danske Bank, Asylgade/Vingårdstræde

Other multi-storey garages are:
City Auto Parkering, Jernbanegade 1
Industriens Hus, H. C. Andersens Boulevard 18
Langebro Garage, Puggaardsgade 21
Q 8, Landgreven
Q 8 Service, Nyropsgade 8
Q 8, Nyropsgade 42
Statoil City Parkering, Israels Plads 1
Statoil Service Center, Dronningens Tværgade 4

Parks

Amalieparken
Between Amalienborg Palace and Langelinie.
Buses: 1, 6, 9, 10.
Copenhagen's newest park provides a pleasant walk along the harbour from Amalienborg Palace to Langelinie. It is decorated with tiles, granite, marble and bronze sculptures.

Botanisk Have:
See A to Z

Frederiksberg Have:
See A to Z

Kongens Have:
See Rosenborg Palace

Rosenhaven
Valbyparken, Hammelstrupvej
Bus: 3
Open: daily 9am–7pm
Between June and August 12,000 roses of many varieties are in bloom.

Police

Police headquarters	Polititorvet Tel. 33 14 14 48
Emergency	Dial 000 (no coins required)

Post

Postage rates	Postcards within the Scandinavian countries, EC countries and Austria, Liechenstein, Yugoslavia, Malta, Cyprus, Switzerland and Turkey cost 3·5 crowns. The same rate applies to letters up to 20gr. Rates for other countries are: postcards 3·75 crowns, letters up to 20gr 4·75 crowns.
Poste restante	Letters addressed "poste restante Copenhagen" go to the Head Post Office, Tietgensgade 37, which is open weekdays 9am–7pm, Sat. 9am–1pm.
Post Office at Central Station	Open: Mon.–Fri. 8am–10pm, Sat. 9am–4pm, Sun. 10am–5pm.
Telephone and Telegraph	See entry.

Programme of Events

Information	The Danish Tourist Board produces twice a year a calendar of events throughout Denmark, including Copenhagen. It is obtainable from tourist information offices (see Information), and is arranged under various headings – sport, music, opera and ballet, exhibitions, folk-festivals, markets, etc. – so that visitors can quickly find their own particular field of interest.
Trade Fairs and Conventions	Information regarding conventions and trade fairs can be obtained at any time of the year from:

Danish post-box

Danish Convention Bureau
Skindergade 27
DK-1159 København K
Tel. 33 32 86 01

"Copenhagen This Week"

A very useful monthly publication is "Copenhagen This Week", which combines a brief guide to the city with up-to-date information about cultural and sporting events (in English). It is available free of charge from tourist information offices (see Information), hotels, the larger banks, etc.

Events during the summer

Weekly leaflets are obtainable from tourist information offices (see Information).

Theatres, concerts, etc.

For information about theatres, concerts, etc. see the last page of the daily newspapers, under the heading "Forlystelser". See also Music.

Public Holidays

January 1st
Maundy Thursday
Good Friday
Easter Monday
Day of Repentance (beginning of May)
Ascension
Whit Monday
June 5th (Constitution Day: from noon)
December 25th and 26th.

Public Transport

Buses/S-bane

Copenhagen is served by an extensive network of bus services. Town Hall square alone is served by no fewer than 21 routes, Kongens Nytorv by eleven and Nørreport by ten.
The S-bane (suburban railway) links the city centre with outlying areas, trains run at intervals of 10–20 minutes.
Both buses and suburban trains run from 5am (Sundays 6am) until half an hour after midnight, with some additional night buses continuing until 4.30am.

Transport Association

In Copenhagen and Northern Zealand the S-bane and buses operate within a unified transport system and therefore have a common fare structure which is based on zones. A ticket is valid for both S-bane and buses, and is purchased in a bus or at a station. The price depends on the number of zones through which the journey passes. The ticket must be cancelled by the bus driver or in a yellow cancelling machine at the station from which the journey starts.

Copenhagen Card

Visitors who would like to get to know Copenhagen and its surroundings intimately by travelling on public transport are recommended to buy the Copenhagen Card. It is available for one, two or three days and allows unlimited transport on buses and trains in the whole of the capital region, reductions on crossings to and from Sweden as well as free admission to museums and sights of the city, the surroundings and Northern Zealand. The card can be obtained in hotels and travel agents or at the office of the Tourist Board (see Information) and at Central Station.

Other savings

Day tickets, valid for a whole day within the Greater Copenhagen district and Northern Zealand, are also worth considering. Special tickets covering eleven journeys within three tariff zones also provide a saving.

Children's tickets

Children under seven travel free, and those between seven and twelve pay half fare.

Radio and television

Danish radio and television are run by a public corporation, Danmarks Radio. Between May 1st and August 31st there is a news bulletin in English (8.10am), German and French on the first programme (90.8 MHz) and on medium wave (1062 kHz) at 8.35am Monday to Saturday.

Railway Station

Central Station

Copenhagen's Central Station (Hovedbanegården), lies west of Tivoli in the city centre. Trains leave every hour for all the larger towns in Denmark. Local trains run twice every hour to Helsingør, and four to six times every hour to Roskilde. Between 6am and 9pm InterCity and expresses (Lyntog) run every hour on the hour to Fünen and Jutland. Seat reservations are necessary for all connections beyond the "Great Belt" (Store Bælt).

Information: tel. 33 14 17 01
Reservations: tel. 33 14 88 00.

Interrail Center

Between June and September Interrail Center – which also provides recreation rooms, canteens, wash-rooms and left luggage facilities – offers a free multi-lingual information pack on Copenhagen to all young people holding an Interrail ticket, a Eurail Youthpass or a BIGE ticket.

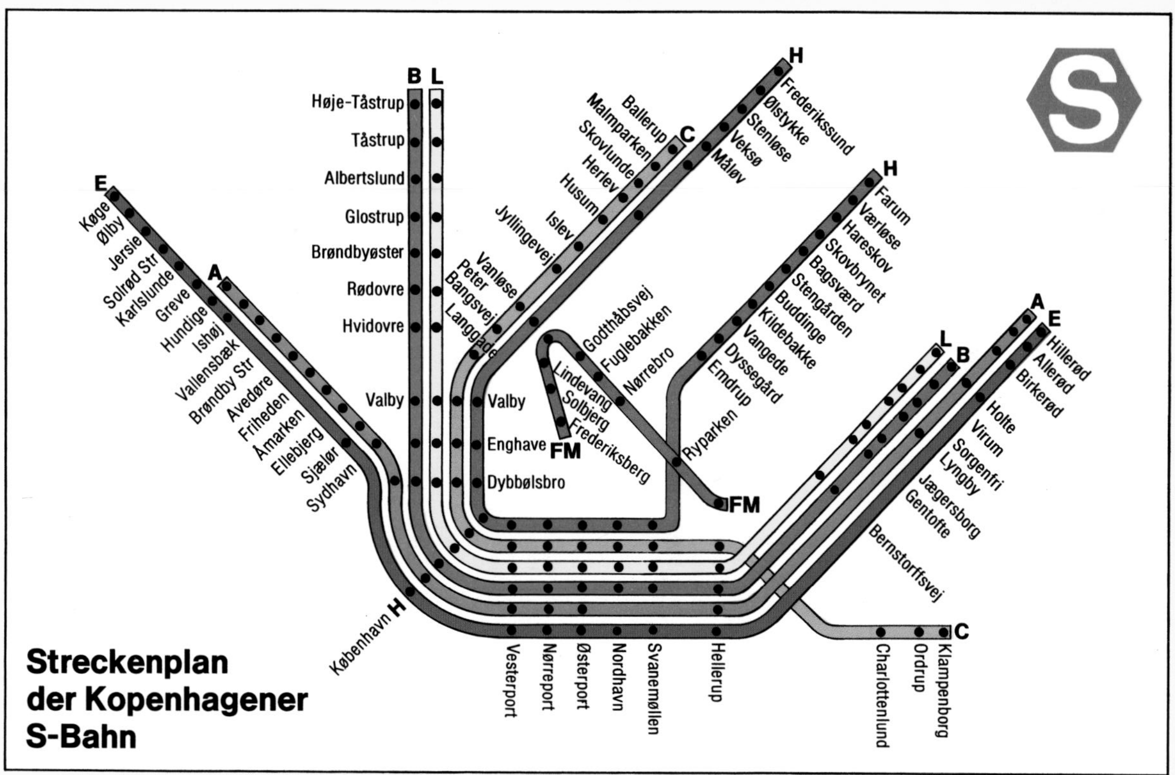
Streckenplan
der Kopenhagener
S-Bahn
B
L
Høje-Tåstrup
Tåstrup
Albertslund
Glostrup
Brøndbyøster
Rødovre
Hvidovre
Valby
E
Køge
Ølby
Jersie
Solrød Str
Karlslunde
Greve
Hundige
Ishøj
Vallensbæk
Brøndby Str
Avedøre
Friheden
Åmarken
Ellebjerg
Sjælør
Sydhavn
A
København H
C
Ballerup
Malmparken
Skovlunde
Herlev
Husum
Islev
Jyllingevej
Vanløse
Peter
Bangsvej
Langgade
H
Frederikssund
Ølstykke
Stenløse
Veksø
Måløv
H
Farum
Værløse
Hareskov
Skovbrynet
Bagsværd
Stengården
Buddinge
Kildebakke
Vangede
Dyssegård
Emdrup
Ryparken
FM
Godthåbsvej
Fuglebakken
Nørrebro
Lindevang
Solbjerg
Frederiksberg
FM
Valby
Enghave
Dybbølsbro
A
E
Hillerød
Allerød
Birkerød
Holte
Virum
Sorgenfri
Lyngby
Jægersborg
Gentofte
Bernstorffsvej
L
B
Vesterport
Nørreport
Østerport
Nordhavn
Svanemøllen
Hellerup
C
Charlottenlund
Ordrup
Klampenborg

TeleCom Centre

Business travellers can find telephone, telex and fax facilities at the Statens Teletjeneste (State Telephone Service); offices, conference rooms, personal computers and secretaries can also be hired here. Tel. 33 14 20 00, fax 33 93 98 55; open Mon.–Fri. 8am–10pm, Sat. 9am–4pm, Sun. 10am–5pm.

Rail Trips

Special excursions

Danish State Railways (DSB) run the following cheap excursions from the Central Station from June to mid September.
For information tel. 33 14 17 01.

Ørseund Tour
By train to Helsingør, then by ferry to Helsingborg in Sweden, followed by a train journey through southern Sweden to Malmö, and finally returning to Copenhagen by hydrofoil. The tour can also be made in the reverse direction.

Louisiana Modern Art Centre (see A to Z)
Every half-hour by train from Copenhagen (return trip, including visit to museum)

Hans Christian Andersen
To Odense to see Hans Christian Andersen's house, and the zoo, railway museum, art museum and museum of the FALCK Rescue Service.
Entry ticket obtainable at Odense railway station on production of rail ticket.

Roskilde
Return trip, including tickets for the cathedral, art collection and Viking Ship Museum.

Holmegard Glass Works
Rail trip to Næstved, then by bus no. 75 to Fensmark.
Tours of the factory all the year round, Mon.–Thur. 9.30–noon, 12.30pm–1pm, Fri. 9am–noon. For information tel. 53 74 62 00.

Restaurants

General

Copenhagen offers an immense choice of restaurants – over 2000, including cafés and snack bars. Almost all offer fine fare, ranging from good plain cooking to luxury dishes for the gourmet. Many provide a variety of foreign cuisines.
Prices in many restaurants may seem high, but it should be remembered that they include a service charge of 15% and the Danish Value Added Tax (MOMS) of 22%.

Frokost-kælder

For a typically Danish meal try one of the numerous basement cafés known as frokost-kælder, where substantial and usually very tasty and genuine Danish dishes can be obtained. Examples of such cafés can be found at Kompagnistræde 20, Gammel Torv 20 and at Gilleleje in Nyhavn (no. 10), which is fitted out with old ship's furniture.

Smørrebrød

Famous for its smørrebrød (see Food and Drink) is the Ida Davidsen restaurant at Store Kongensgade 70. The length of its smørrebrød menu earned its owners a place in the Guiness Book of Records in the 1960s. The Slotskælderen Gitte at Fortunstrde 4 also offers a wide selection of smørrebrøder.

Kolttbord (cold table)

A cheaper alternative offered by some restaurants at lunchtime – the most reasonably priced being the DSB restaurant in Central Station – is the cold table which many visitors will first encounter on the North Sea ferries. This is an assortment of dishes (hot as well as cold) of which you can take as much as you like.

Dan Menu

In restaurants displaying the "Dan Menu" sign a very reasonably priced Danish two-course menu is served at lunchtime and in the evening.

Diabetics

A number of restaurants in Copenhagen offer special menus for diabetics. A list of such restaurants can be obtained from the Danish Tourist Board (see Information).

Restaurants (a selection)

Gourmet restaurants

*Alsace, Pistolstræde; tel. 33 14 57 43
Baghuset, Gothersgade 13; tel. 33 12 32 61
Bodille Steak House, Krægtorvsgade 5; tel. 31 24 00 85
*Els, Store Strandstræde 3; tel. 33 14 13 41
Era Ora, Torvegade 62; tel. 31 54 06 93
*Kommandenten, Ny Adelgade 7; tel. 33 12 09 90
*Kong Hans, Vingårdsstræde 6; tel. 33 11 68 68
Leonore Christine, Nyhavn 9; tel. 33 13 50 40
*Nouvelle, Gammelstrand 34; tel. 33 13 50 18
Philippe, Gråbrødretorv 2; tel. 33 32 92 92
*Pinafore, Toldbodgade 24; tel. 33 11 82 82
Søpavillon, Gyldenløvergade 24; tel. 33 15 12 24

Fish restaurants

Byblos, Lavendelstræde 6; tel. 33 13 55 08
Den gyldne Fortun, Fiskekælderen, Ved Stranden 18; tel. 33 12 20 11
Fyrskib 71, Nyhavn 71; tel. 33 11 85 85
Havfruen, Nyhavn 39; tel. 33 11 11 38
*Krogs Fiskerestaurant, Gammelstrand 38; tel. 33 15 89 15
La Mer, Scala, Axeltorv; tel. 33 15 90 20
*Nyhavns Fiskerestaurant, Nyhavn 29; tel. 33 11 18 27
*Skipperkroen, Nyhavn 27; tel. 33 11 99 06

Vegetarian restaurants

Beerola, Scala, Axeltorv; tel. 33 14 10 73
Dins Grønne Café, Lille Kannikerstræde 21; tel. 33 93 87 87
Green World, Blågårdsgade 4; tel. 31 35 36 11
Greens, Grønnegade 12–14; tel. 33 15 16 90

Afghan cuisine

Bolan, Eskildsgade 13–15; tel. 31 24 94 91

Arab cuisine

Det Gamle Køkken, Linnésgade 16A; tel. 33 11 14 22 (belly-dancing)
The Pyramids, Gothersgade 15; tel. 33 91 25 91 (belly-dancing)

Balkan cuisine

Adriatic, Sct. Pederstræde 34–36; tel. 33 14 20 34
Hercegovina, Bernstorffsgade 3; tel. 33 15 63 63

Chinese cuisine

Bamboo, Rådhuspladsen 77; tel. 33 14 40 77
Cathay, Kultorvet 14; tel. 33 12 92 82
Chinese Palace, Jernbanegade 4; tel. 33 13 85 86
Dahua, Gammel Torv 8; tel. 33 15 78 75
Lotus House, Nørrebrogade 1; tel. 31 39 69 37
Mei Chiang, Gothersgade 129; tel. 33 11 84 60
*Shanghai, Nygade 6/Strøget; tel. 33 12 10 01

Greek cuisine

El Greco, Skindergade 20; tel. 33 32 93 44
Kreta, Nørregade 22; tel. 33 32 14 19
Zorbas, Fiolstræde 21; tel. 33 14 05 00

Indian cuisine

Bombay, Linnésgade 14; tel. 33 93 99 77
*India Palace, Hans Christian Andersens Boulevard 13; tel. 33 91 04 08

Kashmir, Nørrebrogade 35; tel. 35 37 54 71
Maharadja Indian, Studiestræde 12; tel. 33 32 70 38

Indonesian cuisine
Bali, Lille Kongensgade 4; tel. 33 11 08 08

Italian cuisine
Napoli, Købmagergade 63; tel. 33 12 19 62
Pasta Basta, Valkendorfsgade 22; tel. 33 11 21 31
Ristorante Firenze, Vimmelskaftet 29; tel. 33 12 50 85

Japanese cuisine
EDO, Dr. Tværgade 30; tel. 3 15 16 07
Ginza, Gl. Kongevej 9; tel. 31 23 17 46
Hana Kyoto, Vimmelskaftet 39; tel. 33 32 22 96
Sapporo, Larsbjørnstræde 9; tel. 33 14 90 94

Korean cuisine
O Mo Nim, Gasværksvej 21; tel. 31 31 52 20
Seoul House, Bagerstræde 9; tel. 31 31 96 15

Mexican cuisine
Chico's Cantina, Borgergade 2; tel. 33 11 41 08
El Gusto, Havnegade 47; tel. 33 11 32 16
Mexicali, Åboulevarden 12; tel. 31 39 47 04

Mongolian cuisine
Djengis Khan, Nørregade 45; tel. 33 32 41 43
Mongolian Barbecue, Stormgade 35; tel. 33 14 63 20

Pakistan cuisine
Koh-I-Noor, Vesterbrogade 33; tel. 31 24 64 17
Shezan, Viktoriagade 22; tel. 31 24 78 88

Thai cuisine
*Bangkok, Vesterbrogade 107; tel. 31 23 03 50
Rama, Bredgade 29; tel. 33 11 51 27

Tunisian cuisine
*La Rose de Tunis, Vesterbrogade 120; tel. 31 24 06 51

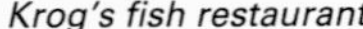
Krog's fish restaurant

Restaurant Shanghai

Marmaris, Viktoriagade 11; tel. 31 23 82 18
Merhaba, Abel Katrinesgade 7; tel. 31 22 77 21

Turkish cuisine

Tan Viet, Landemærket 27; tel. 33 13 08 47

Vietnamese cuisine

Shopping

The Danes have reached a very high standard in the sphere of design, with much attention to detail. As well as furniture, the simple lines suited to the material used even in everyday items and craft products give them a modern and yet timeless charm (see Facts and Figures, Danish Design). Shopping, therefore, can be one of the greatest pleasures to be derived from a stay in Copenhagen, even though – largely as a result of the 18·03% rate of VAT – goods may sometimes seem expensive.

An extensive range of high quality goods will be found in the large department stores of Illum and Magasin du Nord, while Illums Bolighus, Amagertorv 10, is the place to go for furniture and furnishings. A wide range of goods, with many specialist dealers, can be found in the shops around the pedestrian precincts of Strøget (see A to Z) and Købmagergade (see A to Z). The Skala on Axeltorv (see A to Z) is one of the city's newest shopping centres. Particularly popular are the products of the Royal Porcelain Factory (see A to Z, Amagertorv) which can also be seen and admired in their true surroundings during a visit to the factory, porcelain by Bing & Grøndhal (see A to Z, Amagertorv) or from the Rosenthal studio, as well as jewellery (including silver and amber items), some from the famous Georg Jensen workshop (see A to Z, Amagertorv), and hand-blown glass, including that from the old-established Holmegaard Glass Works (see Museums). Antiques, textiles (especially material, sweaters and jackets), furs, toys, lamps and handmade pipes all find a ready market.
Smoked salmon, liver pâté, bacon, cheese, the sweet kransekager and wienerbrød are examples of the fine food on offer. Speciality spirits such as aquavit are relatively expensive.

Tax-free shopping

When making large purchases it is worthwhile considering whether a saving can be made by electing to have the goods despatched net of VAT, which will then almost certainly be added back at the rate pertaining in the visitor's own country. Shops which offer this facility and display a notice to that effect can offer advice. Information can also be obtained by telephoning 32 52 55 66.

Department stores

Daells Varehus, Nørregade 12
*Illum, Østergade 52
*Magasin du Nord, Kongens Nytorv 13
Magasin, Kongens Nytorv

Specialist shops (a selection)

Amber

Rav-Specialisten, Frederiksberggade 2

Antiquarian books

Branner Bibliofile Antikvariat, Bredgade 10
Busck Antikvariat, Fiolstræde 24
Frederiksberg Antikvariat, Gammel Kongevej 120
Harcks Einar Antikvariat, Fiolstræde 34

Antique Dealers

See entry

Audio and video equipment

*Bang & Olufsen, Østergade 3

Books

Boghallen, Politikens Hus, Rådhuspladsen 37
G. E. C. GAd, Vimmelskaftet 32
Nordisk Boghandel, Østergade 16

Camping and sports equipment
Forst & Jagthuset, Gammel Kongevej 119
Lerche Sport, Nørregade 36
Spejder Sport, Nr. Farimagsgade 39

Cheese
J. Chr. Andersen's EFTF. Ost en gros, Købmagergade 32

Craftwork
*Bjørn Winblads Hus, Ny Østergade 11
Butik Amagertorv, Amagertorv 8
Kaj Bojesen, Bredgade 47
Sahva, Esplanaden 32 (work from Greenland)

Delicatessen
Osatehjørnet, St. Kongensgade 56

Fashion boutiques
Along Strøget (see A to Z) can be found a string of fashion boutiques, offering everything from an individual designer collection to crazy avant-garde designs and current fashion hits. Best value for money is to be found in the boutiques situated in the side streets off Strøget and Købmagergade. For young fashion in old buildings look in the "Latin quarter" around the university, in Fiolstræde, Krystalgade and Rosengården. Cheaper fashion shops lie on Vesterbrogade west of Central Station.
Some of the shops offering clothes which have gone out of fashion are:
*Maria Sander, Ny Adelgade 6: elegant evening dress.
*Rie Christiansen, Rosengården 12: exclusive ladies' designer models.
*Mads Nørgaard, Amagertorv 1: ready-made clothes for the younger man.

Furs
A. C. Bang, Østergade 27
Birger Christensen, Østergade 38
Karsten Philip Pelse, Vimmelskaftet 43

Handmade articles
Clara Wæver, Østergade 42
CUM Garnmarked, Rømersgade 5–7
Håndarbejdets Fremme, Vimmelskaftet 38

The Magasin department store

Mads Nøgaard – gentlemen's outfitter!

Illums Bolighus

Jewellery and silverware

Art Deco, Sct. Strandstræde 19
H. Danielsens, Læderstræde 11
English Silver House, Pilestræde 4
* Georg Jensen Sølv, Amagertorv 4 and Østergade 40
Griegst, Pistolstræde 6
Labon, Sværtegade 7
Museums-Kopi Smykker, Grønnegade 6
Peter Krog, Bredgade 10

Knitted goods

Royal Hand-Knits, Hammerichsgade 1
Strikkeboden, Fiolstræde 20
Sweater Market, Frederiksberggade 15

Pipes

Anne Julie's Pipemagerier, Vester Voldgade 8
* W. Ø. Larsen, Amagertorv 9
Pibe Dan, Vestergade 13
Remo Sørensen Danish Pipes, Nygade 4

Posters

Monkey Tricky, Larsbjørnstræde 22

Porcelain, glass and ceramics

Artium, Vesterbrogade 1
* Bing & Grøndahl, Amagertorv 4
* Royal Copenhagen, Amagertorv 6
* Holmegards Glass, Østergade 15
Match Design, Vimmelskaftet 42
* Rosenthal Studio House, Frederiksberggade 21

Shoes

Billing Sko-Bally Sko, Østergade 53
* Bruno & Joel, Ny Østergade 3
Earth Shoe, Bredgade 10

Stamps

Robert Bechsgaard, Julius Thomsensgade 7
Postens Filateli, Rådhuspladsen 59 (Danish stamps)
Jørgen Rasmussen, Skinnergade 22 (world stamps)

Tea — A. C. Perch's Thehandel EFTF. Aps., Kronprinsensgade 5

Tin goods — Tin Centret, Ny Østergade 2

Toys — Bojesen & Wengler, Læderstræde 9

Wines and spirits — *Kjær & Sommerfeldt AS, Gl. Mønt 4 (wine dealers founded in 1875)

Sightseeing Programme

The following recommendations should enable anyone visiting Copenhagen for the first time and staying for only a limited period to make the best use of the time available.

Flying visit

Visitors who are staying only a few hours in the city are recommended to join one of the organised tours (see City Sightseeing and Organised Excursions).

Note

In the following description places which have main headings in the A to Z section are printed in **bold** type.

One day

Visitors with only one day to spend in Copenhagen should limit themselves to a longish walk, taking in the most important sights.

A good starting point is the Town Hall (**Rådhus and Rådhuspladsen**), from the tower of which the best panoramic view of the city can be enjoyed. The northern end of Town Hall Square is where **Strøget** pedestrian precinct begins. This is Denmark's most famous shopping street, with its fashion boutiques, souvenir shops, department stores, delicatessens, restaurants and cafés. It leads into **Kongens Nytorv**, which is only a stone's throw from **Nyhavn** and its museum ships. In New Harbour boats lie ready to take visitors on harbour and canal trips, including Hans Christian Andersen's fairy-tale figure of the Little Mermaid (**Den lille Havfrue**) and the **Christianshavn** part of the city.

From the Kongens Nytorv follow Bredgade as far as Frederiksgade. On the left can be seen the massive dome of the **Marble Church**, and on the right **Amalienborg Palace**). The changing of the guard takes place in front of the palace every day at noon.

Some 450m/500yds further north, having passed the **Alexander Newski Kirke** and the **Kunstindustrimuseet**, we reach **Kastellet**. On the southern edge of its park stands the **Frihedsmuseet**, which documents the history of Denmark between 1940 and 1945, and nearby is the massive **Gefion Springvandet** fountain on the Langelinie bank.

Having returned to Kongens Nytorv walk through Kongensgade and past **Nikolaj Plads** to **Højbro Plads**, where stands a memorial to the founder of the city, Bishop Absalon (see Famous People).

Anyone interested in antiques can make a detour here to the west down Læderstræde and Kompagnistræde and visit at least one of the many antique shops to be found there.

Along Højbro Plads runs **Gammel Strand**, with its Fiskerkone monument. At the foot of the stone statue to the fisherwomen more boats leave on tours of the harbour and canals, out to the Little Mermaid and **Christianshavn**.

From **Højbro Plads** it is only a stone's throw to the island of Slotsholmen with its palace (**Christiansborg**), which has been the seat of the Danish Parliament (Folketing) since 1918, to the former Stock Exchange, the **Børsen** and to **Thorvaldsens Museum**, which is dedicated to the great Danish sculptor Bertel Thorvaldsen (see Famous People).

To the north-west, opposite the palace, stands **Holmens Kirke**, in which Queen Margarethe II and Prince Henrik were married in 1967.

Passing over the **Marble Bridge** and along the southern side of the **Nationalmuseet** we come to Dantes Plads, where a relaxing few minutes can be spent in the Mediterranean-like atmosphere of the Winter Garden of the **Ny Carlsberg Glyptotek**.
The evening should be reserved for a visit to **Tivoli**, a veritable sea of light at that time of day. Its unique mix of fair-grounds, side-shows and centres of culture make it a beautiful and unforgettable experience.

Two days

With two days to spend in Copenhagen the itinerary should include a visit to **Rosenborg Slot**, as well as to one or more museums (see Museums). As an example we would suggest the exhibitions of 13th–18th c. art in the **Statens Museum for Kunst** (State Museum of Art). Danish applied art and design is displayed in the **Kunstindustrimuseet** (Museum of Industrial Art), and wax figures of famous stars and politicians can be found in **L. Tussaud's Wax Museum** in the Hans Christian Andersen Palace. Another popular spot is the **Legetøjsmuseet** (Toy Museum) with its collection of toys from bygone days. Anyone who is particularly interested in the wonders of the universe should not miss seeing the **Tycho Brahe Planetarium**, while a visitor who enjoys trying out new technology and experimenting with the laws of nature should visit the **Eksperimentarium** in the old bottling plant of the **Tuborg Brewery**. Those interested in brewing can have a guided tour through the neighbouring works or watch beer being made in the **Carlsberg Brewery**. If a stroll through narrow old streets is preferred the Latin quarter near the **Universitet** would be a good choice, possibly combined with shopping in the side streets off **Strøget** and **Købmagergade**.
Great fun for young and old can be had with a visit to the animal enclosures at the **Zoologisk Have** or to the excellent permament Benneweis Circus (**Cirkus Bygningen**).
After a pleasant meal of typically Danish or foreign cuisine (see Restaurants), the evening can be rounded off with a visit to the ballet at the Royal Theatre (see Music) at **Kongens Nytorv** or to one of Copenhagen's many jazz-clubs and bars (see Night Life).

Three days

Staying for three days will mean that, after enjoying the sights of Copenhagen itself, there is still time to visit others around the city and further afield in Zealand.
Such excursions should include those to the island of **Amager**, together with the **Christianshavn** district and **Frederiksberg Have**. It is also interesting to walk around **Assistens Kirkegård**, where so many famous Danes have found their last resting place.
About 10km/6 miles north of the city, on the edge of **Dyrehaven**, lies the **Bakken** amusement park, the popular equivalent of Tivoli, with hundreds of attractions for all the family.
Lovers of modern art will enjoy a trip to Humlebæk, 35km/22 miles north of Copenhagen, with its **Louisiana Museum**, a centre of art and culture. One of the latest museums to be opened, in 1991, is the **Karen Blixen Museet** in Rungstedlund, on the parental estate of the Danish authoress whose name it bears.
The highlight of any trip to Zealand must be **Frederiksborg Slot**, near Hillerød, the most beautiful Renaissance palace in all Denmark, and "Hamlet's Castle", **Kronborg Slot**, near Helsingør.
The **Frilandsmuseet**, an open-air museum near Lyngby gives a comprehensive insight into traditional country life and working conditions in Denmark between the 17th and 19th c., while prehistoric dwellings have been reconstructed in the **Lejre Forsøgcenter**.
Finally, some 30km/19 miles west of Copenhagen lies **Roskilde**, with its cathedral church and Viking Ship Museum, to which a whole afternoon should be devoted.

Souvenirs

See Shopping

Sport

There are abundant facilities for various sports in and around Copenhagen.

Bowling

Brygenns Bowling Centre
Islands Brygge 83; tel. 31 54 00 50
Bus: 40
Open: Mon.–Fri. 4pm–11pm, Sat. 1pm–6pm

Grøndal Centret
Hvidkildevej 64; tel. 38 34 11 09
Bus: 2
Open: Mon., Wed., Fri. noon–11pm, Tues., Thur. 10am–11pm, Sat., Sun. 10am–5pm (closed in July).

Rødovre Bowling
Rødovre Centrum, Rødovre; tel. 31 41 12 47
Open: Mon.–Fri. 11am–11pm, Sat., Sun. 9am–9pm.

Fishing

From boats on the Øresund (5–7 hours; warm clothing)

M/S Arresø
Kalkbrænderihavnen; tel. 30 22 36 30
S-bane: to Nordhavn
Bus: 20

M/S Skipper
Kalkbrænderihavnen; tel. 47 38 26 63

M/S Kastrup
Kastrup Industrihavn; tel. 31 50 54 38

No licence is required for sea and coastal fishing, but one is needed for freshwater fishing.
Further information from Danmarks Sportfiskerforbund, Worsåesgade 1, DK-7100 Vejle.

Football

League matches, and occasionally internationals, are played each week-end at Idrætsparken, Østerbro.

Golf

Københavns Golfclub
Eremitagen, Klampenborg
Tel. 31 63 04 83
S-bane: Klampenborg

Riding

Fortunens Ponyudlejning
Grethe Carstensen
Ved Fortunen 3, DK-2800 Lyngby
Tel. 42 87 60 58
S-bane: Lyngby

Sports Riding Club
Maltegårdsvej, Gentofte
Tel. 31 65 17 02
S-bane: Bernstorffsvej and bus no. 27

Surfing

Bellevue Surfskole
Hornemansgade 28, 3 t.h.
DK-2100 København Ø

Swimming

See Beaches and Swimming Pools

Tennis

Grøndal Centret
Hvidkildevej 64; tel. 38 34 11 09
Bus: 2

Københavns Boldklub
Pile Allé 14; tel. 31 30 23 00
Buses: 28, 41

Swimming Pools

Open-air pools

Amager-Helgoland Søbadeanstalt, Øresundsvej (June 1st–Aug. 31st)
Bavnehøj Friluftsbad, Enghavbevej 90 (May 15th–Aug. 31st)
Bellahøj Friluftsbad, Bellahøjvej 1–3 (May 15th–Aug. 31st)
Emdrup svømmebad, Bredelandsvej (May 15th–Aug. 31st, covered at other times of the year)
Sundby svømmebad, Sundbyvestervej (May 15th–Aug. 31st, covered at other times of the year)
Vestbad, Nykær 26, Rødovre

Indoor pools

Frankrigsgades svømmehal, Frankrigsgade 35
Frederiksberg svømmehal, Helgesvej 29

Opening times

Information about opening times can be obtained from the Tourist Board (see Information).

Beaches

See entry

Taxis

"Fri"

A taxi which is available for hire displays a green sign "Fri"
Most drivers understand English.

Telephone

To call a taxi tel. 31 35 35 35 or 31 35 14 20.
To call a minibus tel. 31 39 35 35

Telephone

Public telephones

These accept 1, 5 and 10 crown coins. Coin telephones do not return any money, even when the number is engaged. However, coins not used can be utilised for another call.

Long-distance calls

Long-distance calls can be made from telephone kiosks and post offices.

International dialling codes

From Great Britain to Copenhagen 010 46, followed by subscriber's number.
From the United States or Canada to Copenhagen 011 46, followed by subscriber's number. There are no area codes in Denmark.

From Copenhagen to Great Britain 009 44, followed by area code (less the initial 0) and subscriber's number.
From Copenhagen to the United States or Canada 009 1, followed by area code (less the initial 0) and subscriber's number.

Help and information — If trouble is experienced in getting a number, dial 0030 for calls within Denmark and 0039 for overseas calls.

Head Telegraph Office — Hovedtelegrafkontor
Købmagersgade 37
Open: Mon.–Fri. 9am–6pm, Sun. 9am–1pm

Telecom Centre — See Railway Station

Theatres

The programmes of the Copenhagen theatres are attractive, but for visitors there is, of course, the language difficulty. The Mermaid Theatre, Sct. Pederstræde 27, tel. 33 11 43 03, puts on performances in English.

Ticket agencies — See Advance Booking Offices

Royal Theatre (Det Kongelige Teater) — See Music

Opera and ballet — See Music

Time

Denmark observes Central European Time, i.e. one hour ahead of Greenwich Mean Time (six hours ahead of New York time). Danish Summer Time, between the end of March or early April and the end of September, is two hours ahead of GMT, seven hours ahead of New York time.

Tipping

There is relatively little tipping in Copenhagen, and visitors need not fear any unpleasantness if a tip is not offered.

Hotels, restaurants, taxis — Service charges are usually included in hotel and restaurant prices and in taxi fares, so a tip is expected only if some special service has been given.

Porters — Porters are paid according to a fixed tariff.

Toilets — For the use of a wash-basin in a public lavatory the attendant should be given a small sum, perhaps a crown.

Tourist Card (Copenhagen Card)

See Public Transport

Tourist Information

See Information

Traffic Regulations

See Motoring

Travel Agencies

The following is a selection of the travel agencies to be found in Copenhagen:

American Express, Amagertorv 18; tel. 33 12 23 01
Bennett, Rådhuspladsen 45; tel. 33 12 78 78
DSB (Danish State Railways), Vesterbrogade 5; tel. 33 14 11 26
DFDS Seaways, Vesterbrogade 4A; tel. 33 15 63 41
EAC-WB Travel, Vermundsgade 38; tel. 39 27 27 00
FDM, Blegdamsvej 124; tel. 35 43 02 00
HHK Travel, Gl. Kongevej 95; tel. 31 23 35 11
Rejsecentret/Dansk Rejsebureau, Bredgade 28; tel. 33 12 66 11
United Tours, Rådhusstræde 5; tel. 33 13 55 22

Travel Documents

Passport

Visitors to Denmark from the United Kingdom, Commonwealth countries, the United States, Canada and many other countries require only a valid passport, without visa, for a stay of up to three months.
Children not entered on a parent's passport must have a passport of their own.

Driving licence, car registration document

Motorists must carry their national driving licence and car registration document, which are recognised in Denmark.

Green Card

It is not now a legal requirement for motorists from EC countries, including the United Kingdom, to carry an international insurance certificate (Green Card), but it is very desirable to have this additional protection. Visitors from non-EC countries must have a Green Card.

Nationality plate

Foreign cars in Denmark must carry the oval nationality plate.

When to go

Climate

Copenhagen's climate displays all the characteristics of an island surrounded by the Baltic, that is, the winters are not too cold, the summers seldom hot, autumns long and mild and spring somewhat late. Rain is fairly common, so visitors should be prepared for that, but long periods of rain are comparatively rare. The evenings are frequently cool, even in summer.

Clothing

In view of the above it is always best to pack some warm clothing. Generally speaking, the Danes are fairly easy-going where clothes are concerned, but in the better hotels jackets and ties should be worn, especially in the dining-room.

High season

Copenhagen is at its brilliant best in summer, but of course a visit at this time carries with it the disadvantages associated with the main holiday season – crowded hotels and restaurants, heavy traffic in the streets. Those who can do so should avoid the height of the season and visit Copenhagen in May or June or at the beginning of September. It is significant that Tivoli is open only from May 1st to mid September. Copenhagen has a particular charm in the weeks before Christmas, when Strøget (see A to Z) is festooned with seasonal decorations.

Youth Hostels

Information centre

"Use It" (see Information), an information centre for young people, can provide details of cheap places to stay. Booking ahead is essential at all youth hostels between September 1st and May 15th.

List of youth hostels

The Danish Tourist Board (see Information) produces a free and informative brochure. There is also an official list of youth hostels available from booksellers and also from Danmarks Vandrerhjem, Vesterbrogade 39, DK-1620 København V; tel. 31 31 36 12.

Youth hostel card

There is no age limit in Danish youth hostels. A valid youth-hostel card is necessary; those not in possession of this can obtain, in Denmark, an annual international visitor's card, or alternatively a visitor's card for one night's accommodation.

Youth hostels in Copenhagen

Copenhagen has the following hostels:

Københavns Vandrerhjem Bellahøj
Herbergsvejen 8, 2700 Brønshøj; tel. 31 28 97 15
Bus: 2 from Town Hall Square
33 rooms, 324 beds
Open: Dec. 20th–Nov.

Størkøbenhavns Vandrerhjem
Sjællandsbroen 55, København S (on the island of Amager)
Tel. 32 52 29 08
Bus: 13 from Central Station to Sundbyvester Plads, then bus 37
144 rooms, 448 beds
Open: Jan..–Dec. 20th
Facilities for the disabled.

Lyngby-Tårbæk Vandrerhjem
Rådvad 1, 2800 Lyngby; tel. 42 80 30 74
S-bane: Lyngby, then bus 187 to Rådvad
10 rooms, 94 beds
Open: Jan.–Christmas

Dormitories

Vesterbro Ungdomsgaard
Absalonsgade 8, København V; tel. 31 31 20 70
Buses: 6, 28, 41
10 rooms, 160 beds
Open: May–Aug.
Membership card not required.

Baedeker's

COPENHAGEN

Imprint

145 illustrations, 15 plans, 3 drawings, 1 general map, 1 large map at end of book

Original German text: Madeleine Cabos, Dr Gerhard Eckert and Isolde Maier

Editorial work: Baedeker, Stuttgart
English language edition: Alec Court

General direction: Dr. Peter Baumgarten, Baedeker Stuttgart

Cartography: Gert Oberländer, Munich; Hallwag AG Bern (large map)

Source of Illustrations: Baedeker-Archiv (3); Madeleine Cabos (142); Karen Blixen Museet, Copenhagen (1); Historia-Photo, Hamburg (5); Ullstein Bilderdienst, Berlin (4)

English translation: Bruce Clark, David Cocking, Crispin Warren

Following the tradition established by Karl Baedeker in 1844, sights of particular interest and hotels and restaurants of particular quality are distinguished by either one or two asterisks.
To make it easier to locate the various places listed in the "A to Z" section of the Guide, their co-ordinates on the large city map are shown at the head of each entry.
Only a selection of hotels, restaurants and shops can be given; no reflection is implied therefore on establishments not included.
In a time of rapid change it is difficult to ensure that all the information given is entirely accurate and up-to-date, and the possibility of error can never be entirely eliminated. Although the publishers can accept no responsibility for inaccuracies and omissions, they are always grateful for corrections and suggestions for improvement.

3rd English edition 1992

US and Canadian edition
Prentice Hall Press

Distributed in the United Kingdom by the Publishing Division of the Automobile Association, Fanum House, Basingstoke, Hampshire RG21 2EA

Licensed user:
Mairs Geographischer Verlag GmbH & Co., Ostfildern-Kemnat bei Stuttgart

The name *Baedeker* is a registered trade mark
A CIP catalogue record of this book is available from the British Library

Printed in Italy by G. Canale & C.S.p.A – Borgaro T.se –Turin

ISBN UK 0 7495 0573 7
US and Canada 0–13–059569–1